# Reaching Beyond

The Mountains and Voyages of

## Denise Evans

An Autobiography

Published by Delfryn Publications, 2024

Edited by Kelly Davis
Maps by Don Sargeant
Book design by Bryan Maloney
Copyright © The Estate of Denise Evans, 2024

ISBN: 978-1-9163674-3-2

Printed on material from responsibly managed, Forest Stewardship Council (FSC) certified forests.

*Watercolour of the Snowdon Horseshoe by the author*

# *Contents*

*Maps*

# *Preface*

## CELIA BULL

Denise Evans was the first person I ever got on a boat with. She was an extraordinary bold climber and an audacious adventure sailor. To say my head was turned by her example is an understatement. I was lucky to hear some of her tales of derring-do and personal challenge recounted to me in person, as well as by her friends and family members. She marked a way forward for me, crossing the bridge between climbing and sailing. This fierce, delightful, quirky and formidable woman showed me such kindness and generosity at a time when I was reeling in my own life. I gravitated towards Denise and spent quite a few afternoons at Dickie's boatyard in Bangor, hopefully doing helpful maintenance on her yacht, *Dunlin of Wessex*, which was being prepared for a voyage to Greenland. Noticing my green-eyed envy, she invited me to join her voyage once she had arrived at Nuuk. I accepted in a flash.

While Denise and crew were sailing northwest through gales to Greenland in the summer of '98, I was overseeing the BMC's International Women's Climbing Symposium at Plas y Brenin. In front of a panel of magazine editors, the assembled climbers queried why more female voices were not heard reverberating through the pages of the climbing press. Their answer was simply that women were not submitting articles; there remained a reluctance to write that pervaded the female climbing psyche at that time.

Denise was more than reluctant; she had an aversion to writing publicly about her exploits. She was certainly nervous of my intentions when I asked to photocopy the pages of the ship's log at the end of my weeks aboard in Greenland. We had a few passionate discussions on the subject. She could pull an interesting face dismissing modern-day writers as adventurers motivated by self-publicity! Contrarily she was also a lover of the written word, the age-old tradition of storytelling; the sharing of tales to inspire, to delight, to arouse fear, to entertain, to make readers laugh and learn.

I'm not sure she realised what an inspirational person she was or how important it is to be inspired. It can feel like you are the only woman out there sometimes. I've rocked up in remote ports alone or with an all-female crew only to be gawped at and considered unusual, rather than another competent sailor or boatload of sailors. The 1990s was a time when more women were gaining access to adventurous sports, in climbing mainly due to the advent of climbing walls. I don't know about sailing. But literature certainly played an important part in disseminating information about those who had gone before. My friends and I devoured the written word.

I left Wales for distant seas, and almost two decades passed before our paths crossed again. In Arisaig, on the west coast of Scotland, I passed a delightful evening with Denise and her brother Ian, talking of adventures we had undertaken in the intervening years. Denise still twinkled with verve and amusement, and her thirst for life's great adventures had not diminished. The year she died, she finished writing her life story and copies were printed for family and friends. I saw a copy sent to my godmother, Sally Westmacott, a dear friend. It was a happy surprise when I was contacted by Cathy Woodhead to say that an editor had been engaged to craft Denise's words for publication. It has been a great honour to write this Preface.

There are no other women I know of in her league as both climber and sailor. That Denise was at the top of her game in each is something to be celebrated. Her story fills a gap and what she achieved across the oceans and mountains of our world is astounding and deserves recognition. The woman was mighty.

*Lady Denise Evans* PHOTO JOHN CLEARE

# Introduction

PETER EVANS

This is a book by Denise Nea Evans, my mother and companion for 58 years. I asked her why she was writing it because I thought she should have an idea of what she was starting – it took several years to complete. 'I want there to be a record,' she replied, 'for the family...' she paused, '...and anyone else who might be interested in my life and adventures.'

In my early teens Mum took me climbing, first as my leader and then as my second as I improved enough to go first on the rope. Very early memories include the two of us climbing *Lockwood's Chimney,* a notorious struggle in the Nant Gwynant Valley in North Wales. It was heavy rain and she, typically, wore a blue balaclava on her head and woollen socks over her rock boots to give more grip in the wet.

An early trip to Idwal Slabs in Ogwen saw us traversing off into the descent gully after climbing, where we were caught in a small rockfall, probably dislodged by sheep higher up the gully. Mum shouted 'Take cover!' but I just stood there stupidly as small rocks and mud and earth shot past, with some hitting me. It was over almost immediately and, when I looked round, Mum was nowhere to be seen. Then I spotted her, crouched below a small wall of rock, out of the line of fire – Alpine experience!

We climbed a lot on the east face of Tryfan, always in good weather. We would leave our sacks at the bottom of *Grooved Arête* or North Buttress, scrambling back after climbing and down the Heather Terrace to drink orange squash and look back up our route. On a damp day we failed to get up *Munich Climb* (now graded HVS 5a) and as we retreated from below the crux pitch, our abseil rope almost cut through on a sharp edge.

I recall struggling on *Sabre Cut* (VS) on Dinas Cromlech, in the Llanberis Pass, with little protection and some way above Mum, who was apparently thinking, 'He's either got it or he hasn't'. A fall would have been disastrous but this acceptance of risk was one of the characteristics that pervaded her climbing and sailing life. It was born out of her experiences and the whole style of climbing in those earlier years. I think also that the loss of her father Jean, whom she adored, 'set' something within her at an early age that never altered.

For her whole life all she knew was that Jean had simply disappeared on his way back from Gibraltar to the UK in March 1943. After Mum's death I read some of my grandmother Nea's letters from the time and I was able to identify the plane that Jean was travelling in – a Liberator AL587. Luftwaffe records on the Internet showed it was shot down by Ulrich Hansen in a Junkers 88. Hansen himself went missing two years later, over the Channel, at the age of 27. Mum would have liked to know, to have had that certainty about Jean's death. Occasionally when sailing, I would catch her staring out to sea and ask her what she was thinking about. Sometimes she would say '…of my father'.

Jean was an accomplished Alpinist with numerous first ascents, both in the Mont Blanc range and in the Dauphiné, between 1913 and 1939. These included routes on mountains including the Écrins, the Pelvoux and the Meije, as well as on the Charmoz, the Aiguille de Roc, the Requin, the Charmoz and the Aiguille Noire de Peuterey.

In 1926, at the Requin Hut above the Mer de Glace in Chamonix, he met Nea Barnard who offered to share her supplies with him and they spent the evening doing boulder problems outside the hut. The next evening, they met again with friends at the Montenvers Hotel further down the valley for dinner. They were married the next year. At that time, Nea was becoming an independent Alpinist in her own right and her record of climbs includes numerous first female ascents or first all-female parties on mountains including the Requin, the Aiguille de Blaitière, the Grépon, the Meije and many others throughout the Alps. In later post-war years many of these ascents were undertaken with Jean's sister Micheline Morin and Denise. Nea wrote about her life in her mountaineering memoirs *A Woman's Reach*.

Denise loved driving – the faster, the better. Her pride and joy was a gleaming white Mercedes 250 SE. We went to France in it one year that she describes. Robin and I would run up and down the back seat shouting out to other Brits abroad 'we're GBers too' when we saw their GB stickers. Later in life she would remind me, if I criticised her driving, that she had never had an accident, whilst I seemed to be having them on a regular basis. This wasn't quite true. She had a couple of smashes in the snow on the A5 and would once have had a speeding ticket in Bethesda, if it hadn't been for a friendly police officer exercising discretion.

She took me to Black Rock Sands one stormy winter day when I was about 12 years old. I sat on a cushion to look over the dashboard and under the top of the steering wheel as we hurtled up and down the beach. At 70 miles per hour, she said I was going fast enough. We stopped and she jumped out with a spade she'd brought and made little piles of sand all down the beach. Then we got back in the car and she had me swerving round them in a slalom.

We had a glorious summer when I was 17, ticking off harder and harder routes. By then I was driving furiously and Mum would sit in the back with her climbing helmet on as we shot down to Tremadog. An early attempt at the test piece climb *Vector* saw Mum swinging out into space above the trees. To have another go, she pulled slack through on one rope as she hung suspended 10 feet out and used it to lasso a chap belayed lower down and then pull herself back in. Another attempt at the crux and she was off again, flying out into space.

As well as climbing, Mum was now sailing. Her many adventures on the sea started in Scotland on her honeymoon, on a small wooden ketch owned by a friend of my father. Later my parents bought *Triune of Troy* – a 38-foot Laurent Giles cutter – fast and sleek but very wet with low freeboard. In her they sailed to Norway and Spain.

When Dad got ill they had to sell her, but Mum had caught the sailing bug and borrowed yachts from friends until, in 1983, they bought *Dunlin of Wessex*, a sturdy fibreglass 33-foot Tradewind designed by John Rock. In this boat she had her greatest sailing adventures over the next three and a half decades. These included trips to the Azores, a circumnavigation of South America, two trips to Greenland, a couple of circumnavigations of Iceland and trips to Norway and a voyage to Spitsbergen.

She also sailed extensively off the northwest coast of Britain. Even in a summer without an extended voyage, she would typically be in the Orkneys or Shetlands or cruising the Outer Hebrides. She was always the skipper and dealt with crews firmly but fairly, saying, 'there is no place for democracy on a small yacht!' She had much help on all these voyages from her crew but the vital element throughout was her determination to set out and persevere.

I once joined her in the Canaries to sail back to the UK. On the way to Madeira, we had some unpleasant weather and we needed to know our position. Mum was seasick but the sunsight had to be worked out to be sure that our position was safe. She struggled at the chart table doing the calculations, with a pencil in one hand and a bucket in the other. She'd throw up for a bit, then do a line of calculation, then back to the bucket. She was tough.

One year just the two of us came back from Greenland in the boat. No sat phone, just running downwind, southwest force 7. A week from anywhere, right in the middle of the North Atlantic. Mum didn't feel too good. She was sick and threw up a bit of blood. She came to the hatch and showed me the bucket. I ditched it. We looked at each other. Nothing to be done. She went back to bed.

She didn't go on about hardship, just took it for granted in any enterprise worth doing. Sometimes she was a little intolerant of others. In one famous family story she accused Bertie Bulmer, when he turned back from St Kilda, of not being a man 'for an enterprise of great pith and moment'. There were times when I too failed to live up to her requirements, as when I retreated from the Meije in the Dauphiné Alps in my teens. Her disappointment as we walked back to the valley was painful to bear. Happily, she returned to traverse the Meije in later years with a young man who had been in the Forces. 'Be careful when you wake me,' he told her, 'in case I kill you'!! She chuckled at that.

She was resilient in the face of adversity, with no off switch; she simply got on with things and wouldn't give up. In 1989 we sailed to South America. We had a rough time getting into the Magellan Straits and on one occasion as we were blown out of the entrance, surfing in big breaking seas whilst towing warps, I could hear her singing all alone in the cockpit. I shouted up to her 'You all right?' and she laughed slightly hysterically and shouted back 'You haven't really lived until you've been blown out of the Magellan Straits streaming warps!!'

Another great and typical utterance was reported to me by Jessica Abbott, who sailed round Spitsbergen with Mum. In bleak weather at change of watch, as Mum stuck her head out of the cabin and surveyed the scene, she would remark, 'Doom! Endless doom!'

She gained a bit of a reputation, which was reinforced by a story from John Whitley who sailed to the Azores and back on an early trip. John was chatting to Mr Zealot from Beaumaris who maintained the Menai Strait moorings. John asked him, 'Do you know Denise Evans? I think she has a mooring here?' and Mr Zealot replied, 'Oh yes, Denise Evans, hell of a man that woman, hell of a man'!

When she was little, she tucked her skirt into her pants and wore a Mowgli knife around her neck. She wanted to be a boy. 'Men get a better deal,' she said. She believed absolutely in the independence of women but chose not to dwell on feminism. 'If you want to do something then just do it… give it a go,' she would say. With her later financial position and my father's support and encouragement, this was possible, but reading back over the years I think of her as a fatherless 18-year-old, living unsupervised in Cwm Dyli, walking for hours to climb unprotected on big cliffs. After Mum died, Gwen Moffat wrote and reminded me of that sense of personal skill, independence and great ability of physique and mind that these young women had.

She could have apocalyptic rages. She'd say nothing, and still continue saying nothing, and then she'd explode and give full vent to her feelings. Once in Argentière, in the Chamonix Valley at the

Lognan ski lift, the staff had adopted a large German Shepherd that bit me. Mum went ballistic in fluent French in a shouted tirade that collected quite a crowd of onlookers. A Frenchman tried to intervene to calm her down as she reached the peak, with smashing of skis on the floor and threats to call the Mayor. 'Madame,' he said, 'I am the Mayor.'

On another occasion in the Pacific we started having a ding-dong that became more and more vitriolic. Just the two of us on a bright sunny day in the cockpit. Jack – our crew – had hidden in the fo'c'sle. I ran out of steam, but Mum went through the whole gamut of education, personal responsibility and my other failings using language that made my hair curl. And then it was over – like a squall blowing over. We sailed on. For a few years, when I was a troublesome teen, our relationship was a bit bumpy. I was struck once on the back of the head by a sleeping bag as I left the house with the words '…and don't come back any time soon.'

Mum met my dad, Charles Evans, at Plas y Brenin – an outdoor pursuits centre in Capel Curig – in 1957. He had been deputy leader of the 1953 Everest Expedition, and in 1955 had led the successful and very happy expedition that made the first ascent of Kanchenjunga. He had also climbed extensively in the Alps. He was working as a surgeon in Liverpool at the time and enjoyed driving over to Wales to take groups climbing. They loved each other without reservation. They shared a love of mountains and sea and art. They liked the same music and poetry and enjoyed reading together. They never argued that I recall.

There were three boys, Chuck, Robin and myself. There was so much to her life within the family that wasn't adventure but was equally challenging and rewarding. My father's illness (he developed multiple sclerosis in the early 1960s) was the biggest burden, as it impacted everything. For me it was the norm; but for Mum it was hard, as she had seen my father's physical decline and had to live through all the uncertainty about his illness and how fast it would progress. She was very bitter about it. Not that it was somehow unfair. It was just a miserable reality that blighted my parents' lives. Despite that, or because of it, we were a happy family. I think that was their greatest achievement.

She had no time for religion, perhaps influenced by its prevalence in her schooling. She couldn't fathom how an intelligent person could choose to believe in God.

Her favourite lines of poetry, often uttered apropos of nothing, between tea and toast at breakfast, were:

*Crooked eclipses 'gainst his glory fight…*
– SHAKESPEARE, *SONNET 60*

*O what can ail thee, knight-at-arms,*
*Alone and palely loitering…*
– KEATS, *LA BELLE DAME SANS MERCI*

*Night's black agents to their preys do rouse…*
– SHAKESPEARE, *MACBETH*, ACT 3, SCENE 2

When I was very little, I was sitting on the stairs in the dark in the house in Bangor. I had a moment's clarity as to the nature of our lives, of the bleakness and finality of dying, the loss of loved ones. It was so strong that it stopped me in my tracks and Mum found me there crying and asked me what was wrong. I explained somehow how utterly bereft I felt. She didn't try to rally me with false cheer. 'That's how it is,' she said and gave me a cuddle, 'but we're here and we love you, come on' and we went downstairs.

I am very pleased that the amazing woman who was my mother made time to write her autobiography, to bring her life and adventures to 'anyone who might be interested'.

Capel Curig, 2024

# *Note from the Editor*

## Kelly Davis

Copies of the first (very long and detailed) version of Denise's autobiography were printed in 2023, intended mainly for family and friends. However, it was felt that Denise's life and adventures were of wider interest and an edited version was needed to reach a more general audience. I was delighted when Cathy Woodhead and Julie Carter asked me to carry out this challenging but immensely enjoyable task.

In the editing, I have taken care to retain Denise's unique voice, while cutting and rearranging the text to create a clear and absorbing account of her life. There are some passages (such as the chapter on the Jagdula Expedition) which reveal attitudes that are very much 'of their time'. I would ask readers to bear in mind that, in the words of L.P. Hartley, 'The past is a foreign country: they do things differently there.'

I have included some text taken from transcriptions of audio interviews with Denise posted on the Pinnacle Club website, and a couple of quotations from Nea Morin's book *A Woman's Reach*. These extracts have been cut to adapt them for the book.

Editors usually aim for consistency, as far as possible. However, as this book spans a period when imperial measurements were used, and later replaced by metric, I have largely left them as they were in Denise's original text. I have also added chapter titles a glossary, a list of further reading and an Afterword to complete the narrative.

# *Acknowledgements*

This book was made possible by the generous donations from the Pinnacle Club and the Alpine Club and from the following individuals: Bernadette Anderson, John Barnard, Sheila Crispin, Hugh Clay, Stephanie Connor, Robin Evans, Peter Evans, Harriet Flew, Martin Fuller, Noelle Godfrey, Jo Hawkins, Dave Hillebrandt, Sue Hodginson, Teresa Hughes, Fi and Chris Jones of the Ocean Cruising Club, Linda Lane Thornton, David Mather, Joanne Miles, Milena von und zur Mühlen, Laurence Ormerod, Diana Proudfoot, Cliff Renshaw and Rosemary Scott.

Thanks are due to Kelly Davis for her excellent editorial work, Bryan Maloney for his skilled design and Don Sargeant for producing the beautiful maps.

The project was conceived and managed by Cathy Woodhead of the Pinnacle Club and the Alpine Club and by Julie Carter of the Pinnacle Club.

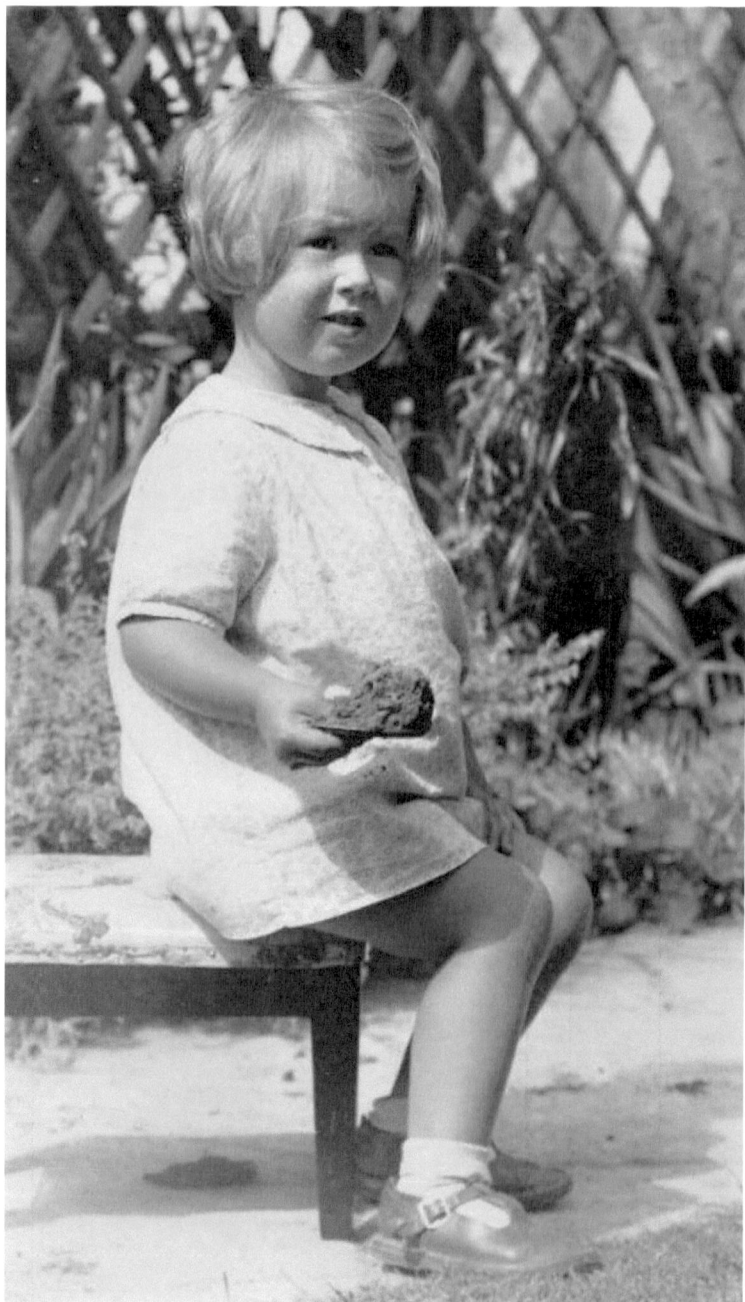

*L'enfant Denise*

## CHAPTER 1

# *Early Years*

I was born in Paris on 23rd August 1931, at no. 5, rue André-Colledeboeuf, in the 16th arrondissement, close to the Bois de Boulogne and the Longchamp Racecourse, where my parents rented an airy, sunny flat. We were not to be there for long. These were hard times and my father's difficulties in finding work soon obliged us to move into the Morin family flat at 137, rue du Ranelagh, where my paternal grandmother had lived with her daughter Micheline ever since the death of her husband, Rear-Admiral Michel Morin, some twelve years earlier. This was to be our home for the next seven years and my earliest memories are centred round it.

Built in the late 1880s, this once fashionable block of flats, with its wrought-iron balconies, had an air of faded grandeur. A wide entrance hall gave access to an elegant, polished wooden stairway, which led up to our fifth-floor apartment. There was also a hydraulic lift which must once have been considered the height of modern engineering, but it became wheezy with age and was apt to leave one stranded between floors.

The Morin flat was L-shaped, with one side overlooking the rue du Ranelagh and the other facing an inner courtyard, which was always filled with a rich medley of domestic sounds. My French grandmother, known locally as Madame l'Amirale, but to us as Bonne Maman, had furnished the flat in what the French called *le style empire* and had embellished it with trophies brought back from Michel's involvement in France's Algerian and Moroccan campaigns. A frieze of large brass trays adorned the walls of the dining room but more exciting was the weaponry hanging in the *salon*, where a number of fiendish-looking daggers and knives were displayed.

Technically speaking, English was my mother tongue, since my mother Nea was English and often spoke to me in English, but I did not have much trouble learning both languages at the same time. I do remember being told, when I was about three, that if only I would speak a bit more French they would take me to the circus. I don't remember if I complied but I certainly went to the circus, which was a fabulous affair in the heart of Paris. Not only were there acrobats performing amazing feats but at one point the arena floor was lowered and flooded and in came a hippopotamus with a man standing between its open jaws.

Most of our afternoons were more prosaic, with walks through the Ranelagh Gardens. With its merry-go-round and specially designated area for children on cycles and roller skates, it was very popular with all the local nannies and their charges.

Nearby lay the Bois de Boulogne. My mother would prepare a picnic, consisting always of brown bread marmalade sandwiches. It has occurred to me since that she might have been a bit homesick for England. Sometimes we would walk as far as the artificial lake, where there were some rather special black swans. One day as I gazed down through the shallow water I spotted a green fountain pen lying in the mud. Nea, with her long arms, was able to reach down for it.

On another occasion as we walked down the street I spotted a silver chain-mail purse lying on the ground. We took it to the local police station but I don't remember going back to claim it a year later, as was the custom in those days. I was quick to notice other things too, and it did not take me long to realise I was living in a man's world and to regret that I had not been born a boy. I even nursed the hope that I might turn into one. Everything masculine seemed so desirable, everything feminine much less so. That feeling has never quite left me, even after a lifetime.

Back then I was too young to understand how hard it was for my father, whom I adored, to find work in pre-war Paris, in spite of his remarkable and wide-ranging abilities, not to mention his army record in the First World War, during which he was gassed in the trenches. As a child I was mostly shielded from my family's financial worries. Although originally of Huguenot descent, Bonne Maman was a self-converted and devout Roman Catholic, as was her daughter, my Aunt Micheline who, until her marriage, lived with us in rue du Ranelagh. Perhaps this was how I came to be baptised. By the time my brother Ian was born, in November 1935, Nea and my father Jean (neither of them conventional believers) must have decided to dispense with the ceremony.

While Bonne Maman ran the household with the help of a couple of servants who cleaned and cooked, other helpers were brought in to look after me and my brother so that Nea could get away from time to time, to go climbing with Jean or to visit her mother Granny Barnard, who lived in Tunbridge Wells. Ian's birth livened up the flat considerably. Looking back, it seemed no time at all before my sturdy little brother was chasing 'Bib', his football, down the long corridor outside my bedroom. This passage used to frighten me at night as the creaking of the parquet flooring (probably due to changes in temperature) sounded like footsteps, and I imagined that wild animals were coming to gobble me up. I was already reading all sorts of stories by now and it was not long before my father, 'Daddy Jean', introduced me to the writings of Jules Verne which fired my imagination and my own longing to explore.

It must have been at about this time too that I first went to school, a small private primary school on the rue du Ranelagh. It was on the same side of the street as our flat, so I was able to walk there and back every day, unaccompanied. Our teacher taught us everything, including French grammar, and arithmetic. I was very much in awe of her. My arithmetic can't have been up to scratch, as I was made to do endless sums on little scraps of paper. Most of us sat together at a long table, but later on I was allowed to watch an elite pupil, a rather chubby fair-haired boy, sitting at a separate desk, writing in ink! This was obviously the high point of education. I also had special English reading sessions, to preserve my knowledge of the language. These took place in a curtained cubby-hole under the stairs where I was required to read out English texts, possibly by Dickens, to a lady who never said anything, either in English or in French, which was odd. I wondered even then if she knew any English.

Times may have been hard but there were compensations, and music was probably the most important for my father, who had composed from his earliest years and had hoped to make music his career, and also for Micheline, who became a piano teacher. We had two pianos in the flat, one in the *salon*, and another in what we called the *petit salon*, an adjoining room with removable panels. This meant that Jean and Micheline could play orchestral arrangements and pieces for two pianos together. Micheline soon began to give me music lessons and to motivate me she paid me a couple of sous for each lesson. The money was put into a small brass bowl and eventually, when I had amassed enough, I was able to buy a blue gauze aeroplane I had long coveted. It had a wind-up rubber motor and I could fly it in the park: marvellous!

*Above: Denise with her bike.*
*Opposite: Denise with her sledge and on skis.*

Another important compensation was the proximity of Fontainebleau forest to Paris. An hour's train ride from the Gare de Lyon took one to Bois-le-Roi, at the edge of the forest, through which one could walk to a number of sandstone outcrops, a favourite training ground for the city's mountaineers. Wild boar were reputed to live in the forest and, although we never actually saw any, I was always a bit nervous and very keen to ride on my father's shoulders, where I felt safe. I was of course too small to do any climbing but quite content to play in the sand below the rocks, along with the children of climbing friends, and enjoy a day-long picnic in the open air.

I don't remember feeling ill but some time in autumn 1935 the doctors diagnosed 'a spot on the lung', which meant I had tuberculosis (TB). I was sent to the Alps for a few months, to convalesce in a small family-run pension in Villard-de-Lans in the Vercors, an area of France later made famous during the war by the heroism of the *maquis* as they harassed the German occupying forces. I had a winter trousseau, a bespoke double-breasted navy ski suit, ski boots and thick woollen socks, hand-knitted by Bonne Maman, who decorated them with coloured star shapes, and to complete my outfit I was given a small felt hat with a feather. It was all very thrilling but more exciting still were my new skis, which I would soon learn to use. The long train journey through France felt more like the prelude to an adventure than the start of a period of convalescence.

The *pension* was probably chosen by Bonne Maman, as the ladies who ran it were also devout Catholics and no doubt keen to bring up their young charges in that faith. To this end I was given a colourfully illustrated children's catechism with pictures of the early life of the infant Jesus. I was particularly taken with scenes of Jesus and another saintly infant playing in the mud and making clay models of birds. Whereas the friend's bird was just a clay model, Jesus' bird miraculously flew away. The idea appealed to my imagination but not to my brain, which was already hard-wired to reality.

In those days Lans was not a resort; there were no ski lifts but less than half a mile away across the meadows was a snowy hillside, ideal for sledging and skiing. There were no instructors either and I had to find out for myself how to manage my skis, so my performance was sadly lacking in technique, but I loved the snow and I loved sledging.

On one occasion I was sledging with two adults when we ran into a hole and were all pitched forward. The two adults fell on top of me and I felt a sharp pain in my shoulder and was unable to lift my arm. Back at the *pension*, the good ladies wondered if I had broken my collarbone and decided to take me to the local *poseur d'os* (bone-setter). All the way there I was encouraged to wave my arm around, which I found excruciating. I was also very frightened of what the poseur d'os might do, as I felt sure it would be unbearably painful. But after examining my shoulder she said, to my great relief: 'Do nothing: it will get better by itself', and it did, though to this day my collarbone has always looked a bit odd.

The last important event at Lans that I can remember was

a visit from my father, Jean. We went into the woods above the ski slopes and built an improvised den with the fallen branches. This remains one of my happiest memories of him. But for my father this was a very difficult time as the various enterprises in which he was involved fell through. Eventually he went back into the army as an engineer, with the rank of captain, specialising in munitions. I still have postcards from him complaining about the ever-increasing quantity of bombs he had to order.

*Nea and Denise*

CHAPTER 2

## *School Days*

During the summer months in the late 1930s my mother used to take my brother and me over to England on the Dieppe–Newhaven Ferry to stay with Granny Barnard (my maternal grandmother) at 17 Church Road in Tunbridge Wells. We also spent time by the sea in places like Pevensey and Kingsgate on the south and southeast English coast. Ian and I both loved the seaside, where I was happy to float in my rubber ring quite far out from the shore. These were good times for us children.

In summer 1939, however, it was decided that we should stay in England instead of going back to Paris. For the next few months after war was declared, I was sent to a small day school in Tunbridge Wells, which was much more relaxed than my French school and my horizons began to expand. But my father was worried that we might be bombed by German planes on their way to strafe London. Jean thought we should move to the Lake District or North Wales, out of harm's way. Nea was familiar with both areas, having walked and climbed there, and chose North Wales. Rooms were booked for us at no. 16 Marine Terrace in Criccieth, on the south side of the Llŷn Peninsula, and Granny Barnard took Ian and me there by train. Meanwhile Nea went to France briefly to be with Jean, while it was still possible to travel there and back. There were other evacuee families on Marine Terrace and Granny Barnard fitted well into this 'expatriate' community. Always a keen gardener, she was soon growing vegetables in a nearby allotment, as fresh vegetables were hard to come by.

After the fall of France, my father managed to escape to England on a British destroyer and joined de Gaulle's Free French outfit in London, and Nea joined him there as often as she could. Meanwhile Ian and I enjoyed playing with our new friends on the beach, where we could dive or jump into the sea from a convenient breakwater. I taught myself to swim by getting out of bed very early in the morning and slipping down to the beach to practise my breast-stroke. Afterwards I would sneak back to bed until breakfast time.

At the end of August I was sent to a small private school at the west end of Marine Terrace, run by Miss Ennals. I remember my initial enthusiasm when Miss Jackson introduced the rudiments of algebra, but when we had to work out ever more complex equations my enthusiasm quickly vanished. Although Criccieth was spared the bombing that was going on in the cities, we were all very aware of it and our Marine Terrace gang decided to do something for the war effort. We would watch out for suspicious activities in our neighbourhood and record them in special notebooks. It was clear to us that we needed our own headquarters. At the west end of Marine Terrace stood an empty hotel building with a turret room at the top, commanding a fine view of the bay: the very place! I found a way in by forcing a basement window. It was a bit dark and spooky inside but we quickly made our way up to the turret room. We decided it needed refurbishing and repainted the walls in a pleasing shade of magnolia. Of course it wasn't long before we were discovered and it turned out that the building belonged to Miss Ennals, our headmistress!

On another occasion a detachment of commandos from a nearby army base arrived on our beach for a simulated attack on the castle, which they took by swarming up the steep rocky bastion on which it stood. We could have shown them a much easier way – climbing over the rocks at the sea's edge, followed by a grassy scramble up to the castle walls. My mother and grandmother must have decided it was time to send me away to boarding school, for I was soon summoned to meet the headmistress of St Winifred's, who had taken rooms on Marine Terrace for a few days. It was a meeting for which I was unprepared and under-dressed, as I went barefoot, wearing only a pair of swimming trunks. I might even have had my Mowgli knife round my neck as Kipling's *Mowgli Stories* were my favourite reading matter at the time. Nevertheless, all went well and the upshot was that I would be sent to St Winifred's School for Girls at Llanfairfechan in the autumn. I little realised what a big change it would be.

St Winifred's was one of several schools founded by Nathaniel Woodard, a man with strong Anglo-Catholic sympathies. It was very High Church Anglican. Like the other Woodard Foundation schools, St Winifred's had its own chapel and its own chaplain. We all went to chapel twice a day, and those taking Holy Communion had to go three times on Sundays. Whenever Easter fell within term-time, many extra hours were spent in chapel, where prolonged standing sometimes caused girls to faint.

I soon began to wonder why I had been sent to this kind of school, particularly as none of our family members ever went to church. Granny Barnard did tell me that she had been to a similar kind of school long ago. I also knew that, before he lost his faith, Gaffer, my English grandfather, had been in the Church and I wondered if this might explain why I was at St Winifred's. I was never explicitly told, but I was old enough to understand the difficulties my parents faced now that we were at war, I understood that we all had to accept a great many changes. Nevertheless, I began to think long and hard about the implications of Christianity and soon decided that, laudable as its precepts might be, it was obviously quite impractical, particularly in wartime, when everything was geared to fighting the enemy and not 'turning the other cheek'.

My headmistress wrote on my report that I was subversive – and I was, because I questioned everything and I didn't like being bullied into religion. They used to slap me down rather, because there were mistresses at the head of each table, and they overheard our conversations and I was the sort of person who would say, 'Well, really, is there such a thing as God?' I can remember mulling it over at playtime, in the garden, and thinking, 'Christianity is hopeless.' I still went to confirmation classes and got confirmed but it was all a ruse. After a bit, I turned against it all. And then, of course, they were very cross.

The school grounds, and indeed the whole village, nestled close beneath the great mass of Penmaenmawr, a northern outpost of the Carneddau mountain range, which we called 'the Hump'. Its summit was crowned by a conspicuous block of granite, which was still being quarried. A few years later, when I was about 15, I managed to get away from the school buildings for long enough one afternoon to make a solo ascent of the Hump in my gym slip. I managed to frighten myself thoroughly as I scrambled over the dangerously unstable granite slabs at the top. It was my first introduction to loose rock, I was quite alone and no-one knew where I was. I counted myself lucky to get back to school unobserved, unscathed and a lot wiser.

I boarded at St Cybi's, down at Plas Gwyn. With my untidy ways, I was obviously destined to fall foul of the Plas Gwyn matron, Miss Whitton, who declared in her inimitable Scottish brogue that my hair was like a crow's nest and that I looked like something from the back streets of Edinburgh. When I 'decorated' my wooden wash-stand by bevelling the corners with a small hacksaw I had purchased from Woolworths, she told Miss Archer that I had turned into a 'furniture maniac'. Otherwise I got on pretty well with the teaching staff, including Miss Sadd, who was our French teacher and pleased, I think, to have a French speaker in her class. I was grateful to her later when she coached me through the classical French Literature syllabus for the Higher School Certificate. Apart from maths, which never seemed to get any easier, I enjoyed school work; but I later regretted that I had been taught no science apart from maths and biology.

I very much enjoyed my twice-weekly piano lessons with Miss Roberts. Music was a life-saver which did much to reconcile me with religion. Because I could read music and sing, I soon found myself in the choir, which meant spending even more time in chapel. I found psalms rather boring but quite enjoyed hymns which often lent themselves to experimentation with an additional line of melody that would blend in with the main theme. I was careful not to be too noticeable. I loved practising the piano in the music wing down at Plas Gwyn. It was here too that I discovered Chopin, whose piano music delighted me ever after.

Apart from a week when my parents took Ian and me to

Beddgelert for a brief holiday, we hardly ever saw Jean, who was very busy in London working for General de Gaulle in the Free French Forces. Of this period, Nea wrote:

*From Moel y Gest, our nearest 'mountain', we could see the lovely outlines of the Moelwyns, Cnicht and Snowdon. I think those early years among the hills gave my children the same deep love of mountains that both their father and I had – and that in the same way it largely shaped their lives. Early in the war, during one of Jean's rare and brief leaves, we all four spent a happy week at Beddgelert. We made an ascent of Snowdon and Ian, who was nearly five, completed it almost entirely under his own steam; Denise, her feet hardened by the pebbly beach at Criccieth, made a barefooted ascent, which she enjoyed far more than wearing heavy boots.*

Nea and Jean, wedding

Jean having a cigarette

Jean did come to see me one weekend, when he and Nea spent a night or two in a Llanfairfechan pub. I was immensely proud to see him in his French lieutenant colonel's army uniform. There was a battered old piano upstairs in the pub, badly out of tune, on which I was able to play him a little piece I had composed. Jean then sat down at the piano and transformed my piece into a set of wonderful variations through some musical magic by which I was quite transported. I have forgotten my tune but not the emotions I felt.

I did not realise it but this was the last time I would ever see my father. Coming back to Criccieth after the Easter term in 1943, I was met at the station by Granny instead of Nea, which was unusual. Granny told me that Jean had been killed. I learned later that the plane on which he and some other French officers had been travelling back to Britain from Gibraltar had been shot down, off the French coast. Neither Nea nor I ever got over the tragic enormity of his death.

Nevertheless, school life went on and I threw myself enthusiastically into all forms of physical activity and was soon playing in netball and hockey teams, and tennis in the summer term. I was also keen on running and jumping and had hopes of becoming *victrix ludorum* that summer, but unfortunately went down with a bad dose of measles at Whitsun and was sent to the school sanatorium for a few weeks.

As the years passed, I became a house prefect, then a school prefect and then house captain for St Cybi's. My only contribution to St Cybi's so far had been to think up a tune for the house song, which included our motto *Nil desperandum*. It seemed to me that more could be done for the image of the house and I decided to put on Shakespeare's *Macbeth*, as a house play. We went to it with a will, rehearsing as often as we could in spare moments. It was ambitious and exciting and the final performance was well received.

I didn't get many opportunities to climb at this point. But my mother knew Evelyn Leech, who lived locally, and she must have said, 'Oh, do go and look up Denise sometime, would you? And take her out for something.' And so one Sunday afternoon, when I was all got up in the 'going out to tea' style of dress for girls, along came Evelyn, and she whisked me up to the Idwal Slabs. She brought some old clothes of her own, which were pretty ghastly, and said, 'Change into these and we'll go up.' And she took me up. I enjoyed it, but of course I had to get back into the posh afternoon outfit, and she had to get me back in time for chapel.

Preparing for the Oxford School Certificate was the next academic hurdle. Like most of the girls, I was nervous but in the event I gained 'matriculation exemption' in all subjects including maths, my particular bugbear. My last objective was the Higher School Certificate, for which I was studying English and French as main subjects with German and Music at subsidiary level. Now that we were in the upper fifth and sixth forms, Miss Archer coached us herself once a week upstairs in her study. She was also no doubt assessing our academic potential and was clearly angered later when I declared that I had no wish to go to university. What I really meant was that I did not want to spend another year at school. Not long after this exchange she summoned me again to tell me that she could not make me head girl as I was not religious enough! I left in 1946, at the end of the summer term.

*Above left: Denise and her brother Ian. Above right: Acting at school. Opposite: Denise as a young girl*

*Teenage Denise:
already addicted to
this peculiar sport…*

CHAPTER 3

# Early Climbing Experiences

At the end of the summer we all moved back to Granny Barnard's house in Tunbridge Wells. It was very different from the freedom of our Criccieth days. Tennis clubs, town swimming pools, sandstone outcrops and the nearby Ashdown Forest were no substitute for the hills and beaches of Wales.

Now that the war was finally over, we were keen to renew contact with our French relatives. My Aunt Micheline was in Austria, serving with French occupation forces and running holiday camps for disadvantaged French children. She arranged for us to join her at the rather classy Golf Hotel at Igls, near Innsbruck. This was a real eye-opener, a glimpse of life for the well-heeled, as it had been before the war. From about 4pm onwards, a lively band would strike up and play far into the night. My desire to learn German led to what I considered a very demeaning situation: the price of a lesson was apparently a hotel breakfast for my teacher. This post-war poverty upset me but did not stop me enjoying a fifteenth birthday party. There was also the opportunity to do some climbing, when Nea took me to the Kaisergebirge, where I had my first experience of dolomitic rock, and enjoyed it hugely.

I don't remember when the idea of spending a year in Paris was first mooted but I was understandably enthusiastic and some time in September I boarded the Newhaven–Dieppe ferry and took a train to Paris. Micheline and Bonne Maman were still living in the family flat at 137 rue du Ranelagh, but in somewhat reduced circumstances. It all looked much as I remembered it but it felt very different. I did not realise at the time the financial sacrifices they must have made to make my stay possible. There had always been a piano in the *salon*, for example; and there was one there now, but it was one they had hired especially so that I could practise.

17

As well as putting me down for various courses at the Sorbonne and the École du Louvre, Micheline also asked a Mr Neltner to give me private lessons on how to write an essay in French on a literary subject. Although I was eager to learn, I never quite got the hang of Mr Neltner's special investigative approach, which consisted first and foremost of unearthing what he thought was the 'real subject' of the essay. I had more success at the Sorbonne with the *Cours de français pratique* and at the Institut de Phonétique, where I learned to make my ps, bs, ds and ts less plosive by speaking close to a lighted candle without putting it out. More educative than any course, however, was the company of family and friends. Also staying in the Ranelagh flat at this time was a cousin of Bonne Maman called Adrien Bernelle, a philologist specialising in Slavonic languages, who was always ready with an opinion on any subject.

Exploring Paris on foot, and by bus or metro, was an endless source of pleasure. French buses in those days had an open-air platform at the back, where you could stand and savour the passing scene, an experience that was particularly enjoyable in the city's leafy avenues in spring. In the autumn, I would take the metro most days to reach the Sorbonne, which was in the *Quartier Latin* on the other side of the Seine, for my French courses.

The nearby Boulevard Saint-Germain and the Boulevard Saint-Michel were always very busy with streams of students and tourists. There were innumerable small cafés, some of them made famous by celebrities such as Jean-Paul Sartre, one of France's foremost philosophers and an exponent of 'existentialism', which was all the rage just then. I preferred a quiet sandwich in the nearby Arènes de Lutèce, the site of a Roman arena. It was extraordinary to think of those gory forms of entertainment taking place there centuries earlier. I became familiar with cathedrals, monuments and art galleries; and as well as attending lectures at the École du Louvre I spent hours exploring the museum's many treasures.

Now and then, my Aunt Micheline would take me to concerts and plays. I remember a stunning performance by Louis Jouvet, a famous French actor, in the title role of Don Juan in the seventeenth-century play by Molière which I had studied at St Winifred's. I felt a pang of regret that I had not been more grateful to Miss Sadd at the time. One day Micheline and I took a train to Versailles, where we explored the faded glories of the 'Sun King', walking through the once sumptuously appointed halls, and wondering how the ladies managed to get about the palace in their elegant but voluminous gowns. We wondered too, and not without a giggle, about the apparent absence of sanitation.

Bonne Maman and Micheline thought a girl of my age ought to have dancing lessons and I reluctantly complied. This meant wearing a dress, stockings and heeled shoes, only to have my toes mercilessly trampled by large, undiscerning male feet; but we did learn how to do the tango, which I enjoyed, and the rumba. More to my liking were riding lessons at a riding school near the Luxembourg Gardens. Our mounts were large cavalry horses and our instructor was an ex-cavalry officer who took exception to my doing the 'rising trot', a wayward British style, which he deplored. He was impatient too at the number of times I took a toss when negotiating jumps, for I had never learned to jump back in Criccieth.

Micheline had given me my first piano lessons and was glad to see that I was still practising. Now she introduced me to *solfège*, a system of singing along to a tune and naming the notes. We were able to play piano duets together and this was an opportunity for me to explore a whole new world of piano music beyond the range of the British Associated Board, under which I had passed Grade VII. I could now play Chopin's 'Minute Waltz' with some verve and expression and Micheline decided to take me for an audition, where a professional musician asked me if I really wanted to devote my life to the piano. I realised, of course, that I did not, though I was sorry that I might have disappointed my aunt.

One of the things I enjoyed most about living in Paris was getting out to Fontainebleau at weekends and climbing with family and friends, just as we had done before the war. The main difference was that I was now tall and strong enough to reach up and take my weight on the smallest of small holds so characteristic of Fontainebleau sandstone. Another difference was our footwear. Everyone was now wearing special close-fitting rubber-soled bootees marketed by Pierre Allain, which came to be known by the British as PAs. With toes painfully squeezed into these, and a small bag of powdered resin (known as 'poff-poff') at the ready, one had more chance of getting up some of these climbs. I became addicted to this peculiar sport which I learned by watching others, many of whom were already accomplished mountaineers. Later I went on to climb with some of them in the Alps and Dolomites.

One of these climbers was Jacques Monod, a noted biochemist and future Nobel Prize winner. Jacques was married to Odette, by whom he had twin sons. Half American and half French, Jacques had a bad leg, having contracted polio as a child. In spite of this, he was a remarkably good climber. He was also very musical, played the cello and ran a choir. He was fun and I was always glad to find myself in his company. I did a number of climbs with him during the next few years, some of which my mother described in her book, *A Woman's Reach*. For instance:

> From Les Contamines we walked and scrambled on Mont Joly and the other hills around. With Micheline, who had joined us, we went up to the Tré-la-Tête Hut for a night and the next morning Denise and I climbed Mont Tondu, her first 3,000m peak.

Nea also described our family party on the Aiguille de l'M, which I was allowed to lead and which I found quite easy. My chief recollection of Les Contamines, to which Granny Barnard had taken Ian and me earlier that summer, was of exploring the hillsides above the village, and being pursued by a large and seemingly fierce Alsatian dog as we fled at high speed all the way back to the main street. We were terrified – but not by the mountains.

From now on, our summer and winter holidays were largely based at Micheline's small house in the upper part of Briançon, a fortified town designed by Vauban. There were a number of forts on the hilltops around the town and we had fun exploring the *chemin de ronde*, a tunnelled passage beneath the nearest fort.

The ski resort of Serre Chevalier, a few miles away, was a major attraction in winter and Ian and I both learned to ski there. In the summer the mountains of the Dauphiné were all easily accessible by car, and these were the peaks where Ian and I first climbed.

I remember my mother Nea taking us climbing in Wales early on, and she used to climb in nailed boots. I was a little frightened when her boots made a scrabbly noise on the rock. She never fell off but nailed boots didn't appeal to me as climbing footwear! I later climbed with her in the Alps. I think I did my first 4,000-metre peak, the Écrins, with her on my eighteenth birthday. Later on, we did much more fiendish things together but I knew she was pretty safe and she always seemed at ease.

There was one climb, at which I was present, which Nea never wrote about. This was an early family party to the Aiguille de Sialouze, in the Dauphiné, a well-known and rightly famed climb. Six of us spent the night at the Lemercier Hut on the south side of the massif. Nea was leading me, my Aunt Micheline was leading my Uncle Ossie (Nea's brother), and lastly there were two young British climbers, Michael and James, whom I knew after climbing with them at Harrison's Rocks (in East Sussex); indeed, I was the one who suggested they join us. The weather was brilliantly fine and the rock dry. The climb started close to the hut, up the right-hand side of a steep rocky gully. We had barely got going before we were overtaken by a pair of French climbers, who climbed quickly past and vanished. Nea had soon reached the top of one of the first long pitches on the right of the gully and I was climbing up towards her when suddenly there was a tremendous commotion and it became clear that James had fallen and had passed out with a head injury, possibly a fractured skull.

None of us were strong enough to move him, so all we could do was make him secure where he lay. We whistled and shouted, in the hope that the French climbers might hear us, which they eventually did, and a few hours later they returned. We were incredibly lucky to have these two Frenchmen to help us. One of them, Serge, must have been very strong, as he managed to carry the injured man all the way back down to the valley below, where

an ambulance took him to hospital in Briançon. He eventually
made a good recovery and got back to Britain. I, meanwhile,
realised that I was largely responsible for this misadventure, and
that my judgment had been at fault in assuming that if you could
climb on sandstone at Harrison's Rocks you could automatically
climb in the Alps, on very different terrain. Nea repeated the climb
later with her own friends, and some years later, I too was able to
second Jacques Monod on this first-class rock climb.

*Above: Teenage Denise with her
climbing rope.
Above right: Working in London.
Right: A young Denise.*

CHAPTER 4

# *London, Dublin and Bavaria*

Back in England, after our first French Alpine holiday since the war, it was time for me to look for a job. For some months I worked for my uncles, Mordo and Osbert Barnard, who sold etchings and engravings at Craddock & Barnard, 32 Museum Street, in London. There was in fact no Craddock and the name may have been added to lend gravitas to the firm, which had been started by my grandmother, Alice Barnard. She was in the habit of touring France every year. Whenever she came across etchings or engravings she liked, she would buy them and bring them home in her suitcase, with a view to selling them on.

In the course of her travels she came across a doctor who had known the nineteenth-century French painter Corot, and had been given a number of prints by the artist. They had not been through the Corot *vente*, a sale at which works by Corot were certified as genuine, but my grandmother was sure they were by him and bought them. Back in Britain, her view was supported by Mr Campbell Johnson, Keeper of Prints and Drawings at the British Museum. My uncles, on the other hand, believed them to be fakes and they remained unsold.

I commuted every weekday by train from Tunbridge Wells to Cannon Street Station. It took me a little while to adjust to the noise, grime and commotion of London, but I soon found my way around. In those days you could get a cheap meal at a Lyons Corner House but before long I was exploring nearby Greek Street, where you could have a steak and salad for two shillings and sixpence. Meanwhile Uncle Ossie would step across the road to the pub directly opposite our shop for his beer.

In the office I was on hand to show visitors any prints they might want to examine, but my main tasks were secretarial, though I had no qualifications and was learning on the job. Ossie would pace about the office floor, dictating letters and requests to the Board of Trade for bulk export licences, for we exported prints to customers all over the world. Meanwhile Mordo, who had some chemical expertise, would be working from the brothers' shared house in Highbury, soaking and cleaning the prints in specially prepared solutions.

Roger Higgins, a nephew of Mordo's second wife Dorothy, also worked for the firm for a time. He and I would occasionally be sent off to bid for prints that came up for auction elsewhere, which I really enjoyed. One day I learned that Granny Barnard had acquired an etching by Rembrandt entitled *Flight into Egypt, Night Piece*, which depicted Joseph and Mary with the infant Jesus, fleeing from Herod's clutches. My uncles were keen to acquire this etching. I cannot recall what happened but I became uneasy about their relationship with their mother. It made me sad and I decided to find work elsewhere.

After my year in France, my spoken French was good enough for me to pass myself off as a 'Mamselle' and I was soon working in a small girls' boarding school, St Michael's, Limpsfield, which wasn't far from Tunbridge Wells by train. Before long, I found myself coaching a bright girl in the sixth form, who was aiming to read French at Oxford, while at the same time preparing to get into Lady Margaret Hall myself.

While I was working at St Michael's, I met John Sims, an RAF pilot and a climber with a massive motorbike. He persuaded me to try riding it, but it was far too heavy, though I was happy enough as a pillion passenger. Johnny became a very good family friend and would have liked to be closer still but I soon realised that I could not possibly marry him and found it hard to have to tell him so. Johnny introduced me to night climbing on some of the Oxford college buildings before I went up to LMH, which was exciting. One night, with the help of a friendly creeper, we climbed up a wall to the window of a first-floor room said to have once belonged to a Paymaster General. The occupant at the time, who did not seem surprised to see us, kindly opened the window and let us in.

A few years later, when I was a student at LMH, I arranged

to meet an undergraduate from one of the men's colleges with a view to climbing the Radcliffe Camera, a conspicuous Oxford landmark, by the lightning conductor, which runs from the top of the building down to the ground. When we met, however, we heard that another young man had fallen to his death there the night before, and our climb was called off. From then on, I contented myself with the flat areas of LMH's leaded roof, which was just the place to sunbathe while revising for exams. It was accessible through an attic full of old white china chamber pots, reminding me again, as at Versailles, of the advantages of modern plumbing.

Towards the end of 1950, my French godfather, Stanislas Ostrorog, a man of Polish origin who was in the French Diplomatic Service, invited me to visit him in Dublin, where he had been appointed minister plenipotentiary (virtually ambassador). He had fought in the First World War alongside my father, and they had been close friends, and shared a deep love of classical music. Stas, as he was known to us, was particularly fond of J.S. Bach, and while I was with him in Dublin he would often play some of the preludes and fugues himself, expecting me to do likewise. When, I played a Schubert impromptu I had been learning instead, he seemed disappointed in my musical taste. I have met others who are disparaging about Schubert but I think they are mistaken. Many years later, my brother Ian introduced me to his late quartets, and I realised that Schubert was unsurpassed at the musical expression of compassion.

It was so cold in early December that the waters of the Liffey were in danger of freezing over. I really loved Dublin. Stas's niece Anne, daughter of his brother Jean, was also staying with him and we used to go shopping for clothes together in the city, a novel experience for me. There were plays and concerts and outings and Stas gave us both a very good time. Most of all, I was grateful that he approved of my plan to go to Oxford. He confided that he too would have liked to study there but it had not been possible. Stas seemed to have friends and relatives all over Europe, and he introduced me to Elimar von Fürstenberg, a professor of philosophy at Bonn University, whose sister, Countess von Dehm, lived at Schloss Arnstorf in Lower Bavaria. I was invited to stay with them in the summer. I had to forgo the classic route up the Matterhorn, which Nea climbed with my brother, but my stay in the Schloss was also a unique experience.

Schloss Arnstorf lay in the middle of pleasant pastureland. You could drive over the moat and through a gateway into an inner courtyard. The family were all Roman Catholic and they had a resident priest. Upstairs there was a warren of rooms, large and small, and we were moved around according to who was coming to stay. I arrived not long after the Countess had given birth to her eighth son. (She had no daughters.) She employed a housekeeper to oversee the household and to keep an eye on the mischievous boys, who ran about the place barefoot, dressed in lederhosen. One day when we all sat down for lunch with some home-brewed beer, the resident priest, who was sitting beside me, opened the lid of his beer mug to see a drunken crayfish trying to crawl out. The boys must have found it in the river where we used to swim in the afternoons. I can't say I learned much German, as they all spoke French. I learned enough, however, to understand the preacher at the local Catholic church who used to drone on about the evil ways of those who lived *im fernen London.*

When it was time for me to leave, Elimar drove me to Munich in his big Mercedes. Somewhere along the way, a motorcyclist with a pillion passenger overturned on the road in front of us. The driver landed face down and skidded along the road, while the passenger, a small boy, was thrown clear. Elimar was able to lift the driver bodily from the tarmac and lay him down in the back of his roomy car. I got in the back as well with the small boy, who was crying uncontrollably. I cradled the man's head in my lap and kept it raised to prevent the blood, which was welling up, interfering with his breathing. Every now and then, Elimar would ask if the man was dying. 'No,' I would reply. So we drove on till we came to a town with a hospital, where the rider and the small boy were taken in. I never found out what happened to them but assumed they both recovered. I was presented with some flowers and we drove on to Munich. Elimar saw me onto my train for Paris and got me some eau de cologne. We said goodbye and I never saw him again.

CHAPTER 5

# *Going Up to Oxford*

I eventually passed the Girton and Lady Margaret Hall entrance examinations in 1952 and was offered a place at both. I decided to go to LMH, as originally planned. My English godfather, who we called Uncle Charles, drove me and my belongings, complete with bicycle, to Oxford in his battered old Rolls at the start of the academic year in October. I was given a room on the first floor of LMH's Deneke Building. My neighbour was a first-year English student called Gaie, who became a very good friend.

Rationing was still in operation in 1952 and each student was allowed only a couple of ounces of butter a week. Gaie and I soon had recourse to the Oxford market, where additional supplies of all kinds could be found. All our rooms had fireplaces and coal boxes, but coal was rationed too. In her coalbox Gaie kept a couple of pet mice, also bought at the Oxford market. Their incessant scrabbling at night was apt to keep one awake. We explored the Deneke Building from top to bottom. The college library was in the basement and here, tucked away in a side room, were a number of items, including furniture, from the Churchilliana collection. Gaie found a carved oak scroll bearing the inscription *dum spiro spero*, which she borrowed as an ornament to hang over the fireplace in her college room. Meanwhile I hung some of Granny Barnard's Corot sketches on the walls of my little room, which made it look pleasingly civilised.

The university offered so many possibilities that it was hard to choose which interests to pursue. I decided to join the Oxford Bach Choir and the Sculpture Club, and arranged to have organ lessons with the organist at nearby St Giles' Church. I also decided to re-invigorate the Oxford University Women's Mountaineering Club. For this last endeavour I painted five posters, one for each of the women's colleges, of mountain scenes, with the words 'Come

Climbing!' Unfortunately I fell foul of the proctors (the university police) because my posters exceeded the regulation size. But they attracted attention and I got a number of takers. A few Oxford women joined me for weekends in North Wales, where we stayed at Cwm Dyli in the Gwynant Valley, in a hut belonging to the Pinnacle Club (for women climbers), to which I already belonged.

LMH had its own chapel, with an organ on which I was allowed to practise. In return I offered to play for some of the chapel services. I enjoyed extemporising, just as I had on the piano. By slowing down the tunes of bawdy but little-known French and Italian songs to a funereal dirge, I found I could produce an atmosphere of quiet, religious devotion as the congregation filed in and out. Back in my room I would strum away on Pepita, my Aunt Micheline's guitar, but it wasn't until Segovia gave a concert in the Sheldonian Building one evening that I learned what could really be done with the instrument. Inexplicably, for I had not sought this job, I was asked to organise the allocation of the college punts and canoes to undergraduates for the following year, but it was a happy accident as I loved punting and canoeing. The boats were kept down by the River Isis, which flows past the lowest point of the college gardens. Here you could sometimes put a lighted match to the marsh gas, as it drifted up from the boggy depths, and produce a flame.

My most memorable punting expedition took place on 1st May, at the beginning of the summer term. Gaie and I got up very early and took a punt through Parson's Pleasure, down the river to Magdalen Bridge to hear the traditional May Day singing. Pausing on the way back for a snack in the meadows, we became aware of a crowd gathered round a large red flag on a pole, singing lustily. Although I had always thought of myself as apolitical, something suddenly prompted me to leave the punt, dart through the singers, snatch up the flag, and dash headlong across the fields, with some of the crowd in hot pursuit, until I reached Tom Tower (on St Aldates, at the entrance to Christ Church), where I climbed to the top and left the flag. By then I was feeling rather sheepish.

It would be wrong, however, to suggest that most of our time was spent in extracurricular activity. There were lectures to attend and tutorials, for which we were expected to write two essays a week. We also had to furnish French and German translations every week, and produce an essay in the main language we had chosen: in my case French. To acquire these skills we were sent to Madame Hibon, a Frenchwoman who lived nearby and was something of a martinet. The prospect of Preliminary Examinations at the beginning of the next term only added to the pressure.

Although I studied German as a subsidiary subject, I was still required to master a particularly rebarbative piece of German literary analysis entitled *Über naïve und sentimentalische Dichtung*. Help was at hand, however, in the shape of the two elderly Deneke sisters, who still lived in their family house next door, at the bottom of Norham Gardens. We were first invited to a hearty breakfast, followed by a German tutorial. They provided a delightfully civilised approach to learning.

Once Prelims were behind us, we first-year students were able to spend more time on subjects of our own choosing. I had already discovered a volume of Montaigne's *Essays* in my school library but had found them difficult to read, because of the sixteenth-century French. Now I could read them quite fluently, and understood their universal popularity. I was surprised, however, to find that André Gide, some of whose writings I had come across in Paris, should claim Montaigne as his mentor. This prompted me to write an essay on the influence of Montaigne on Gide's thought, for which I won a prize of £10. However, these glimmerings, I knew, would not lead me to a life of scholarship. I was too fond of the 'here and now' and the experiences it might bring.

Gaie and I began to gather round us a disparate little coterie of LMH friends, who brought other friends in their train. In this way I met Klaus, a Danish student, who was reading English, and spent time in a library where he wrote me copious letters on the backs of forms used for ordering books. He introduced me to his friend Maximilian Habsburg, scion of that noble house, who was reading French. Max's idea of study was to sit under a tree with a book. Like Klaus, he was convinced that being in 'the right ambiance' was the key to learning.

Max and Klaus were a jolly pair. Klaus had an ancient little Morris Minor with a canvas hood in which he occasionally used to drive me over to Woodstock and other places of interest. One day he invited me to join him in London for a concert by a well-known singer which included Schumann's *Frauenliebe und Leben*, a song cycle which I particularly liked. In those days it was impossible to get permission to spend a night away from hall in term time, but I decided to break the rules. We very much enjoyed the concert and spent the night in town, a misdemeanour for which I was 'gated'. This meant signing in every evening at 9pm for a fortnight, but it was a price worth paying.

Nea and I used to climb together in the Dolomites. She was a wonderfully good climber. I just followed her, and sometimes I followed easily and sometimes not so easily. She was a good leader – she inspired confidence. (Nea and Denise recorded first all-female ascents together in the Dolomites in 1953, traversing Winkler, Stabeler and Delago in the Vajolet Towers and climbing the north face of the Cima Piccola di Lavaredo. Later, in 1955, in the Alps, they became the first female party to climb the Mer de Glace Face on the Grépon in the Mont Blanc Range.)

*From left to right: Nea, Rie Leggett, Denise Shortall (later Wilson) and Denise at the 1957 Pinnacle Club Annual Dinner at the Pen y Gwyrd*

Back at Oxford, in my second year, Finals still seemed mercifully far away. At this stage, we could solicit particular dons to take us on for specific tutorials. We might have attended their lectures and would certainly have read their books, but their physical presence and conversation brought a new dimension to our studies. I was lucky enough to have Dr Enid Starkie as my tutor for the French symbolist poets, Mallarmé and Verlaine, but our conversations covered a much wider range of French literature. I was interested to learn that Dr Starkie had also lived in the rue du Ranelagh, but at the bottom end of the street, down by the Seine. For the German poets, Rainer Maria Rilke and Stefan George, I went to Dr Stahl. Because I was less advanced in my German studies I felt somewhat inadequate, conscious that I did not come up to my tutor's expectations, but I was nonetheless drawn to explore Rilke's extraordinary inner world.

In my third year, my brother Ian came up to Oxford to read Zoology at St Edmund Hall, known as Teddy Hall, and he soon got to know my little group of friends. One evening, he, Gaie and I repaired to the Mitre Inn, a favourite Oxford pub, and we were standing near the bar getting drinks when a young man came up and flipped Ian's tie from his shirt, presumably intending to start a fight. To my surprise and admiration, Ian did not respond and after a minute or two the young man moved away. We wondered if he might belong to the notorious Bullingdon Club.

After our early years of skiing down the pistes of Serre Chevalier, Ian had become a really good skier and was soon part of an Oxford ski team, with plans to go out to Zürs in the Easter vacation. I was allowed to tag along. Zürs is situated on a high and windy col in the Arlberg, but I enjoyed those pistes so much that I resolved to go back there at the earliest opportunity.

The last few months before Finals passed in a whirl. Like most others, I felt nervous about the exams but much less than I did when leading a hard climb, where my life was visibly at stake. My mind had already moved on to the question 'What next?'

CHAPTER 6

# An Expedition to West Greenland

For me that question resolved itself into getting a job with the BBC in London, translating corny little English sit-coms into French. It seemed rather infra dig, after years studying the best French writers, but it gave me a measure of independence. At the same time, I was following in my mother's footsteps as a translator of mountaineering literature, by translating Jean Franco's *Makalu*, an account of the first successful ascent of that Himalayan peak by a French expedition. It was well-written and a pleasure to work on.

At this time I was living in North London with Gaie and Toby, who were now a married couple, and for whose hospitality I was very grateful. Working for the BBC had become increasingly distasteful but miraculously, as if in answer to my prayers, came an opportunity for Ian and I to join an expedition to West Greenland in 1956, led by Michael Holland, an Oxford graduate and glaciologist. He planned to take a party out to Evighedsfjord on the west coast of Greenland to climb Mount Atter, the highest unclimbed mountain on that coast, to take samples of ice from the Taterat Glacier and to collect rock and plant specimens from the area. The expedition included two others: Ian Bennett, a dentist; and Gill Sutton, a medical student with whom my brother was already acquainted.

We first had to sail to Copenhagen with a mountain of tents, climbing and skiing gear, as well as enough food to last us about eight weeks in the wild. We had no eyes for the sights of Copenhagen but watched attentively from the Greenland wharf as our gear was loaded into the hold of the *Disko*, one of the ships that regularly supplied the colony with everything it might conceivably need. I came to realise in the following weeks what good colonists the Danes were, and to be grateful for their great hospitality. Early in the morning on our tenth day out we were woken by cries of 'Cape Farewell!' From the deck we could see a jagged black mountainous coastline stretching ahead. We reached Godthåb, now known as Nuuk, a couple of days later.

After putting us up and entertaining us most royally, Mr Hesselbjerg and his associates organised a police boat, the *Eli Knudsen*, to take us on the last part of our journey to Evighedsfjord, 150 miles further north on the west coast. We had a Greenlandic captain and crew who spoke neither English nor Danish but who looked and behaved rather like marine sherpas. In a few days we reached Kangaamiut, a little fishing settlement perched on glacier-worn rock at the edge of Evighedsfjord. Here we were made welcome by the Outpost Manager, who also managed the radio and the local store. From him we bought ammunition and a few 'tupilak' – soapstone or narwhal tusk carvings of grotesque monsters.

Looking up to the Taterat Glacier at the inner end of Evighedsfjord, we could see where it flowed down from the Sukkertoppen ice cap to end in a 200-foot ice cliff that calved into the fjord at frequent intervals. We were still a good 30 miles away from our anchorage, which lay off a spit on the north shore, about a mile from the calving edge of the glacier. As soon as we reached the anchorage, the crew ferried our loads ashore, before leaving us to pitch our Base Camp at the edge of the fjord about 12 feet above the high-tide level.

We grounded our dinghy on the west side of a rocky promontory which protected it from the calving waves. The mosquitoes were bad and we hurried to assemble our 10-foot by 10-foot Dexion Hut, which had an aluminium frame-work covered with a thick tarpaulin. We not only cooked our supplies in it but later also slept, ate and lived in it. Lined with guns, ammunition and all our climbing and skiing paraphernalia, it looked like a brigand's hideout. We spent a happy week here, ferrying equipment and food up to the snout of the glacier during the day; in the long, light evenings the men would shoot seabirds for the pot while Gill and I fished for a species of cod.

We used our dinghy all the time, to fish and to fetch water, as the sides of the fjord were too steep and smooth to allow us to reach our fresh water supply on foot, and to ferry loads. The journey up to the glacier snout only took ten minutes under engine, but we were soon to be deprived of its use and very nearly lost our boat as well. We had completely forgotten about the tides – and we suddenly noticed our dinghy drifting down the fjord. Ian Bennett nobly plunged into the icy water and swam about 60 yards to retrieve it. We were so preoccupied that we also forgot the outboard engine, which had been left lying against a rock. It was swamped by the tide and no amount of coaxing would bring it back to life. What idiots!

We were now obliged to row everything up to the glacier snout and then to carry it all onto the glacier, including the Nansen sledge, which weighed 80 pounds. Once on the glacier, it was worth its weight, however, as we were then able to manhaul our loads over the bare ice for 3 miles up to Advanced Base. This camp was pitched on a tongue of moraine at the western end of a range of mountains about 20 miles long, the highest of which is Mount Atter (7,300 feet). The range is bounded to the north by a deep valley containing the upper section of the Taterat Glacier, which separates the north faces from the Sukkertoppen ice cap, and to the south by a steep tributary glacier named Survey Glacier.

The 1938 Oxford University Greenland Expedition, led by Peter Mott, made an unsuccessful attempt to reach Mount Atter from the north, realising too late that the correct route lay on the south side. The ascent of Mount Atter was the first item on our agenda, and we therefore planned to find a way up Survey Glacier, which is about 3 miles long and rises in three icefalls to a snowy basin on the south side of the range. Michael and I flagged out a circuitous route through a maze of huge crevasses. The peaks on either side were incredibly steep, those on the north crowned with hanging glaciers and great cornices of ice. We reached the snow basin at 8pm. It extended for several miles in an easterly direction and was ringed round by snow and ice peaks.

To get enough food and equipment up to the snow basin for our third camp, we had to make a number of five-hour carries. It wasn't practical to take the unwieldy Nansen sledge up the heavily crevassed icefall, but it was well worth taking our skis, which were much safer both on the neighbouring snow-covered icefall and in the snow basin itself. (The vast accumulation of snow was not always reliable here, as we would later discover.) I worried at first that our camp might be pitched over a crevasse, but the pit we dug nearby revealed good, solid snow-ice. Dug for the purpose of taking density measurements, this pit was Michael's pride and joy.

The ascent of Atter by the west ridge proved both quicker and easier than expected. We set off in two parties on 12th August, planning to prospect for a route from a higher plateau on the south side of the Atter massif. When we converged there, we found that Atter's rocky west ridge was easily accessible. By now it was already 4pm but in view of a possible change in the weather we decided to press on as far as we could. Coming to a verglas-covered break in the ridge, we circumvented it by posting ourselves through a rocky letter-box, which my brother had spotted. The only awkward pitch occurred where the ridge abuts against the summit mass. Above this we were separated from the top, which we reached at 7pm, by steep but easy snow and ice. To the west we looked straight down the fjord and out to sea. Atter's ice-hung north face fell away beneath us to the main branch of the Taterat Glacier, from which Mott had first thought of climbing the mountain. North of the Taterat Glacier lay the Sukkertoppen ice cap, which we hoped to reach later with the sledge. Far away to the northeast, beyond the jagged mountains of the coastal strip, stretched the grey-white waste of inland ice.

During the fortnight we spent in the snow basin, the weather was on the whole very fine, and it was irksome to have to toil in the pit or go stone-bashing (collecting geological specimens) when there were new mountains waiting to be climbed. Between us, however, we managed to climb eight other peaks between 6,000 and 7,000 feet high. The first of these we named 'The Beautiful Mountain', its Greenlandic name being unpronounceable. All of us except Mike, who spent the day doing survey work near camp, set off on skis as our peak was a few miles away.

Once again, we were on the summit at sunset, and it was growing dark as we reached camp. Here we found a very shaken leader. Not long after we left, he told us, he had stopped a little way beneath camp to take off his skis and had barely taken a step, with the plane table under his arm, when he fell through a few feet of snow into an enormous bell-shaped crevasse, which widened out beneath him. By some miracle the legs of the plane table caught on the edge of the schrund, and he was able to extricate himself by doing a mantelshelf movement.

One of the best climbs from the snow basin by all five of us was a first ascent of Survey peak, the second highest in the region, by its rocky east ridge, which rose in four great steps and was, in places, knife-edged. On the left and south side of the mountain, sheer gneiss cliffs dropped away to the Survey Glacier, which looked dead flat. It was hard to believe it had cost us so much time and effort. To the north, precipitous snow slopes, scarred by nasty-looking crevasses, plunged towards the icefalls overlooking the main Taterat Glacier. Once again, as on Mount Atter, there was a choice of route. While my brother and I tended to follow the rock ridge, the others cut across the snow slopes in a diagonal line, to reach the summit, which was flat and rocky. Despite our attempts to revert to a more Alpine timetable, the sun was already setting and we hurried back down to our tents.

We left the snow basin regretfully on 26th August and went down to Base Camp for a few days' rest. It was good to smell saltwater again, to hear the noisy seabirds on Kittiwake cliff, the rumble of the Taterat, and to watch icebergs sailing idly up and down the fjord. Some looked like great white swans; others were blue or bottle-green or as transparent as glass. It was pleasant also to have fried fish for supper again and to be able to wash. But now, with the end of the month, came a deterioration in the weather. Mike spoke of cold fronts and it rained heavily. We wondered if we would have time for much more before winter set in. Ian and I wanted to spend ten days at Advanced Base, collecting bugs and flowers and climbing one of the lower but much steeper rock peaks that overlooked the north side of the fjord. We had named this peak

'Tupilak' on account of its resemblance to the Eskimo carvings we had bought in Kangaamiut, and we had already reconnoitred the first pitch, from which we had been obliged to retreat.

Mike, Ian Bennett and Gill went ahead with their plan to make a ten-day sledge trip up to the Sukkertoppen ice cap with a view to digging another pit. They left on 2nd September and disappeared up the main branch of the Taterat Glacier, harnessed to the Nansen sledge, which was stacked with 300 pounds of food and equipment. The next day the weather broke. Dark clouds rolled in from the sea, bringing first rain, then sleet and snow. Soon everything was plastered with fresh snow and rock climbing was out of the question. Bugs and flowers were dying off and, apart from a rather hairy descent by Ian down a moulin (or mill-hole) into the depths of the glacier, there was little we could do except wait for the weather to improve.

At night the big Niger tent flapped like an old coat and we were obliged to thread skis through the loops and weigh them down with stones. We wondered how the others were faring. At least our tent was partly protected from the wind by the big boulder under which it was pitched. The boulder itself, however, was more of a menace than a comfort, as it lay on a bed of rubble-covered ice which sloped steeply towards us. One very wet night, there was a sudden thunderous rumble and Ian and I, both still half asleep, flung ourselves bodily out of the tent. We came to on the sharp rocks outside, still in our sleeping bags! A close inspection by torchlight revealed that the boulder could only have shifted a fraction of an inch.

In a few days the weather cleared a little and on 10th September Ian and I decided it was time to find out what was happening to our friends, who were due back on the 12th. We planned to head for the Sukkertoppen ice cap via the Igloo Glacier, the route our sledge party had intended to take. We set off on skis, as the bare ice of the main Taterat Glacier was now under 2 or 3 feet of fresh snow. It took an age to reach the Igloo Glacier which, from the broad highway of the Taterat, looked relatively gentle and short, and we negotiated the first part of the icefall easily enough. To cross some of the crevasses, however, acrobatic techniques were needed, either on skis or on foot carrying our skis. We realised the others couldn't possibly have come this way with their sledge. Eventually we reached the flat part of the glacier and saw that the place where the Igloo Glacier ran into the ice cap was still some miles distant. After shouting for a while, we decided to retreat and got back to Advanced Base by 4am.

On 12th September, it snowed again and it was impossible to leave the tent. The next day, we put on our skis once more and went back up the main Taterat Glacier. After a while we saw strange markings in the snow – arrows, zigzags and footprints – and soon we saw our friends coming down towards us. They told us they had reached the head of the Taterat. They had apparently been obliged to build a rampart round the tent during the blizzard, and their only misadventure was the loss of a frying pan and the lid of the pressure cooker. We all moved down to Base Camp on 14th September, and we were able to ski right down to the glacier snout. The next morning Mike remarked from his sleeping bag that there were two icebergs moving rapidly up the fjord. They turned out to be the *Inger* from the marine biological station, and the *Tornak*, one of the fishery inspection vessels, come to take us back to Godthåb. So ended a memorable expedition.

*Above: Denise's painting of Evighedsfjord from the 1956 Base Camp, looking west towards the sea.*
*Left: One of the tupilaks brought back by Denise.*

## CHAPTER 7

# North Wales and Meeting Charles

For some years since I'd joined the Pinnacle Club in 1949, I had been making my way up to North Wales for holidays and weekends and staying in the club hut in Cwm Dyli. I used to go up there for quite long periods, and Gwen Moffat was there at much the same time. I went climbing on Lliwedd, not with Gwen, but with another girl, and the two of us would have great fun, climbing everything we could. Some of the climbs were really quite serious, but we were careful. I wore boots that were a bit like hockey boots, but with rubber soles, and we cut down the treads, to make them a bit smoother.

One day as I walked past Plas y Brenin on my way back to the Pen y Gwryd Hotel and the Gwynant Valley, I saw John Disley, the Chief Instructor at the new National Outdoor Centre, busy lighting a garden bonfire. I asked if he needed any voluntary instructors, and to my surprise he said 'yes'. There was no salary but bed and board were provided in return for taking students out climbing, canoeing or hill walking. It was an excellent arrangement in the Centre's early years, before the management went in for certification, and it generated great enthusiasm for climbing as a sport. Nea also spent time at Plas y Brenin but she was mainly focused on giving girls a start. My main aim was to spend a day climbing in the hills with anyone who had signed up to go climbing.

John Disley was already known as a very good rock climber, and when he invited me to join him on a new climb on Clogwyn y Bustach in the Gwynant Valley, not far from *Lockwood's Chimney*, I accepted with alacrity. In the evenings, after a day's work at the Centre, we would spend a few hours reconnoitring this steep, vegetated cliff, topped by a conspicuous overhang. Access could be achieved by a possible traverse line that ran right across the cliff face from west to east. By the end of the second evening, we had managed to traverse across to a stance and belay below the overhang. We were looking forward to completing the climb the next day; but when we got there, we found that another party had muscled in, using our belays, and were engaged in tackling the overhang. We were dismayed and disgusted but all we could do was continue our traverse of the cliff, which we named *Gallop Step*. Later on, John also led me up *Mur y Niwl*, a relatively new climb in those days, on north-facing Craig yr Ysfa, which Nea described in some detail.

Another volunteer, with whom I was soon to become much better acquainted, was Charles Evans, who was then a surgeon at one of the Liverpool hospitals. One day we found ourselves on the Gribin Facet, each with a party of beginners. After that, we began climbing together and Charles asked if I would join him for a climb up the Western Gully on Ysgolion Duon, the Black Ladders. To reach this north-facing cliff, we made our way down the main road towards Bethesda, on the east side of the valley, to a point where a small sheep track led off north, up steep grassy slopes, before winding east round into Cwm Pen Llafar. We soon came to Llech Ddu. Thinking this was the cliff Charles meant to climb, I put down my sack. 'No, no,' he said, 'that's much too hard,' and we moved further into the cwm for the start to Western Gully.

The prospects looked none too good to me. It wasn't actually raining but the black cliffs were gleaming, sheathed in water. Charles led off up the first pitch in his vibram boots, seemingly undismayed. When it came to my turn to climb, I winced, as every time I put my hand on the rock, water coursed down my sleeves with a horrid chilling effect, to which Charles seemed impervious. I soon began to see that Charles was different from my other fair-weather climbing friends, and that more would be required of me than simply the ability to climb.

After spending time at Plas y Brenin, I applied for a post as French mistress at St Margaret's at Yeaton Peverey, a village not far from Shrewsbury, thinking it was ideally situated for getting back to Wales at weekends. In other respects, sadly, it was far from

*Charles and Denise above Clogwyn Du'r Arddu*

ideal. It was desperately antiquated – almost Dickensian in fact. The school seemed to have no French textbooks at all and I don't remember a library either. Pupils and staff alike had to wear blue overalls, which were quite practical; but I was still young enough to look like one of the older girls, which was embarrassing. Miss Hainsselin and her assistant ran the school very frugally; there were days when we few teachers who 'lived in' went really hungry, and I began to wonder whether the children were also short of food. I had a small bedroom upstairs, next to one of the dormitories. On my first night, there was a small coal fire burning in the grate but this proved to be a unique event.

Charles had already introduced me to Patrick Childs, his old housemaster at Shrewsbury School, where he was still living with his wife Maud, and their younger daughter, Patricia. The latter, in her early teens, was recovering in bed from a viral infection and

I sometimes took a bus into Shrewsbury to sit with her for an hour or so. Before joining the school, I had been asked by Miss Hainsselin whether I was engaged to be married, and had been able to reassure her that I was not. But a few months later Charles came to see me at Yeaton Peverey, and as we were sitting on a gate in the grounds he asked if I would marry him. I said 'Yes' and soon afterwards I went back to see Miss Hainsselin to hand in my notice.

We planned to get married in the summer, after Charles and his friend Dennis returned from their spring expedition to Annapurna II. Their departure day, 7th March, came all too quickly. I was picked up from the school by our good friends Chris and Jo Briggs, who ran the hotel at Pen y Gwryd. They drove us first to Severn Hill to raise a glass with Patrick and Maud to celebrate our union, and then down to London Airport. Chris, Jo and Charles' old friend, Edwin Ker, sat in front, with Charles and I together on the back seat.

*A young Charles Evans*

CHAPTER 8

# *Getting Married and Sailing in Scotland*

Not long after Charles and Dennis had left for Nepal, I had a letter from Edwin, inviting me to spend a week with him at the Pen y Gwryd to do some climbing and get to know each other. I accepted readily enough, though I realised this was going to be a kind of vetting process.

For a man in his seventies, Edwin was remarkably fit and had no trouble walking up over the Glyders, for example, to climb on the east face of Tryfan and then walk back to the Pen y Gwryd. I chose classic climbs of moderate difficulty with which I was already familiar and where there were good stances and good belays. We had few problems with the climbing, the weather was fine and altogether these were very pleasant outings. In the evening, over a good meal and a bottle of wine, I told him about my family background and my early years in France. He told me about his friendship with Charles and how it had started when his friend Patrick Childs had brought Charles up to Scotland with him to crew on Edwin's first yacht. Now Edwin expressed his hope that Charles would soon take me up to Scotland to sail on his little yawl *Crystal II*.

As the weeks passed, letters filtered through from Charles and Dennis, and I began to take in the nature of the problems they were encountering, and to worry. With Dawa Tenzing as sirdar (lead mountain guide) and his well-tried Kumjung Sherpas, they had the best possible support, but the projected approach route to Annapurna II left much to be desired. It entailed a 2-mile traverse across a vast mountain face at a height of about 20,000 feet which, in modern terms was 'a big ask', and needed protracted porterage, so I wasn't surprised when we eventually heard that they had decided to retreat from this route. However, they did manage a repeat ascent of Annapurna IV which Charles was able to film, before making their way back to Pokhara, Kathmandu and home.

I drove over to Heathrow in my mother's little Renault on 15th June to welcome Charles and take him back to Tunbridge Wells. He had lost weight but he looked well and it was great to be together again. There was much to be done before our wedding in August, and much that would involve my mother, Nea. Charles and I would both have preferred a registry office marriage, which would also have been easier for Nea (who bore the brunt of the preparations, as mother of the bride). However, Charles' mother, aunt and close family were Calvinistic Methodists, some of them deeply religious, and they preferred the idea of a church service. In the end we had the ceremony in mid-August at St Sepulchre's Church in London, and we were married by Mac, a friendly prelate known to Charles.

*Charles and Denise on their wedding day in 1957.*

After the wedding, we drove north to take up Edwin's offer to lend us his boat *Crystal II*, berthed at Oban, for the first part of our honeymoon. Mindful of my tendency to get seasick on Channel crossings, I was a bit apprehensive, but sailing in the relatively sheltered conditions prevailing just then in the Firth of Lorne did not make me feel ill. Here was a new activity which I found really enjoyable and I looked forward to exploring it with Charles, who was already a keen sailor.

Before lending us *Crystal II*, Edwin had, characteristically, stocked the boat with food and drink so that every time we opened a locker we would find a bottle of whisky or French wine for our enjoyment. This was the best of wedding presents, and we drank a toast every night to 'the old badger', as we liked to call him. Our first little cruise took us north, up the Sound of Mull, till we reached Loch Sunart, and made our way east past the Stirk Rocks and through a rocky inlet into Loch Drumbuie (Loch na Droma Buidhe). We anchored off its southern wooded shore, which was a delightful spot, though the midges were bad. Its northern shore was bounded by Oronsay, a rocky island which we explored on foot.

We were woken one morning by a southeasterly gale. The anchor dragged and, after failing to re-anchor properly, even with two anchors out, we were obliged to bring them in hurriedly. With the engine running, we shot out through the inlet and felt the full force of the wind. Minutes later the jib sheet parted and the jib tore to ribbons. Charles took in all sail while I manned the pumps. Leaving the Stirk Rocks close to starboard, we rushed back west across the Sound of Mull to Tobermory, which was partially sheltered from the east by Calve Island, and anchored in the harbour off the Macdonald Arms. After a rest, a rub down and a drink, we went across for a hot bath and a meal. We soon made friends with the crew of *Tarn of Tarbet*, a nearby yacht with a broken boom. They told us they had ventured out in the early morning and been caught by gale-force winds, after which they had been towed back into harbour by a trawler. I began to see that doing the wrong thing when sailing, as when climbing, could have unpleasant consequences. I had much to learn.

We sailed south again on another squally day and broke a forestay off Loch Aline, where we put in under engine to mend it. After motoring against a foul tide off Duart Castle, we made our way west to the entrance of Loch Spelve, went in and anchored in the northwest corner. The next day we forsook the sea and went up Sgùrr Dearg, immediately behind our anchorage. A day or two later, we made our way through the Dorus Mòr to the Sound of Jura and on down to Crinan. The combined effects of wind and tide in the narrows were spectacular – and this was a new and exciting experience for me. After exploring Loch Craignish, Charles and I sailed back to Crinan and left *Crystal* in the dock, ready for Edwin.

We then toured Skye by car. Staying first at Sligachan, we walked part of the main Skye ridge before moving round to Loch Brittle. On one occasion, when we were walking along the track that leads along the shoreline from Loch Brittle to Loch Scavaig, we came upon a woman well and truly stuck in a bog, from which her companion had been unable to extricate her. With extra help from Charles, she was eventually freed. This tour of Skye marked the end of our Scottish honeymoon.

CHAPTER 9

# *A Second Honeymoon – In the Himalayas*

After my introduction to sailing we settled into married life at Gwylfa, Charles' mother's house at Derwen, a small village a few miles from Corwen in North Wales. At this time Charles was still a surgeon, working as Senior Registrar at the Liverpool Hospitals, to which he commuted daily by car. Life in this sparsely populated farming community was something entirely new for me. With a small car and my French driving licence, I was able to drive into Corwen to shop, and I soon adapted to my new life. I actually enjoyed being cut off from the centres of civilisation, but there was a lot to learn about living in such a rural Welsh-speaking environment.

At Gwylfa there was electricity to power the cooker in the kitchen and to heat the bathwater for the bath upstairs, but there was no electric lighting. Instead we had oil lamps which needed filling and trimming. I was romantic enough to love the warmer, kindlier light they shed on human skin, giving one the feeling of being part of some Old Master painting. I was less happy about washing clothes and bedding in a wash-house, where a wood fire had to be lit under a great brass cauldron of water. Afterwards the clothes had to be put through a mangle, before being hung out to dry in the garden. I taught myself to cook, in what I hoped was an approximation to a French style – fortunately Charles was very tolerant. I could never master the wonderfully light sponge cakes that his mother Edith used to bake, but I could serve up a good steak, as there was an excellent butcher in Corwen.

For the second part of our honeymoon, in autumn 1957, Charles planned to take me to the Himalayas, where we would spend a few months exploring Sola Khumbu with the sherpas who had been with him on the Everest and Kangchenjunga

Expeditions in 1953 and 1955. I was looking forward to this wonderful opportunity. We set off from Tunbridge Wells in my mother's little Renault-Dauphine on 3rd October, and flew over France, then Switzerland, enjoying a wonderfully clear view of the Alps, particularly of the Bernese Oberland, with the Jungfrau looking just like a picture postcard. The Eiger was plastered with the first winter snow, and the Finsteraarhorn was looking loveliest of all, its long ridge in shadow and its sharp summit catching the evening light. Then we were over the Austrian Alps. Firm-looking knife-edged rock ridges threw spiky blue shadows onto brilliant snowfields. Crevasses looked like fine pencil lines and icefalls tumbled down into brown-green valleys, with minute villages at the bottom. As the mountains got lower, the snow thinned down to a sprinkling. 'Who would have thought,' Charles said, 'that there were so many mountains in Europe?' The sea of clouds reminded us of bare glaciers, and sometimes of ice-cap country.

When we reached Bombay, getting out of the plane into the hot, damp afternoon and undergoing the tiresome customs formalities made me feel that I would very soon suffocate. Fortunately the customs officer was put off his search through our baggage by some embarrassingly feminine items in my suitcase and we escaped. We were met by Shirley-Anne Cumberledge, a kind friend, and driven to Trombay House, which was right down by the sea in a belt of palms on the outskirts of the city.

When we went down to the beach for a swim, it stank of rotting fish and we had to cross mounds of drying jellyfish before we reached the water. The sea was thick, brown and very salty, full of things that tickled our legs. We went to inspect the catch that had just been landed, along with a mob of ragged children carrying little bags and baskets. There were all sorts in the net: prawns, eels, jellyfish, dogfish, a small shark, a ray and a host of brightly coloured creatures I had never seen before. A man got stung in the foot by a ray but his companion managed to get the sting out and proceeded to cauterise the wound with a burning cigarette end. They had also caught a sea snake, whose bite is apparently almost fatal. One chap summoned the courage to pick the creature up by its tail. His fingers were just closing on it when another fellow speared it with a harpoon, to the great delight of the crowd.

We boarded the Delhi train the following evening, and when we arrived it was still hot but not as unpleasant as in Bombay. Porters, dressed in red turbans and tops, whisked our baggage onto their heads, while our friend, Mary Hotz, took us out to her car and drove us through leafy avenues to our hotel, in the newest part of New Delhi. The Ashoka Hotel was an extraordinary edifice, built in the same red sandstone as Agra, in a muddled pastiche of Mogul and modern architecture with air-conditioning throughout. Poverty was not as obvious here as in Bombay, and the embassies and posh hotels had a veneer of westernised prosperity.

Arriving in Patna at 7am, we took a taxi to the air strip, and later climbed into a Dakota. We flew over the Ganges, here a dull, winding, muddy river, and then over the famous flat marshy jungle of the Terai. I imagined it to be full of wild animals: a dense grey-green forest intersected by dry, sandy riverbeds. I was allowed to sit next to the pilot for a view of the Himalayan chain sticking out above high-piled cumulus: the Langtang and Jugal Himal, Gauri Sankar, Everest, Makalu, Annapurnas II and IV. Most exciting. Then we chose a gap in the clouds and plunged down over high, terraced ridges onto the Kathmandu plain. The air strip looked very small and seemed to have a cliff at either end. We were met by Dawa and Urkien (another lead mountain guide) and one of the embassy staff.

Richard Proud was our host there for four nights. When we went shopping in Kathmandu we found almost anything was obtainable: primus stoves, typewriters, Tampax, family planning. We bought a primus, umbrellas, caps (hideous peaked things) and some Turkish towels; and Charles had a really good pair of cotton pyjamas made for him for 20 shillings. Kathmandu seemed to be a strange mixture of temple and bazaar, with poky little open-fronted shops and Nepalese wares strewn over the ground outside, along with drying chillies and other produce. With cattle wandering up and down at will, driving through the streets required much patience.

We set off on 13th October with Richard, who drove us in his jeep along a very bumpy track for 15 miles as far as Banepa. The seven coolies and four sherpas followed in a truck. Banepa was hot and dusty and we did not stop to look at shrines or temples. We were plagued at the start by a very dirty-looking crowd. A woman came after us moaning and begging, and a talkative Nepali kept up an incessant flow of questions for about half a mile along the hot, stony track. Richard was the only one who could understand him and his replies grew shorter and shorter. We passed through many little villages, with houses that looked as though they had been built and originally inhabited by more artistic, prosperous people. They were mainly whitewashed, though the lower part was sometimes reddish brown in colour, with very handsome carved windows, and steep red-tiled roofs with turned-up corners, like pagodas.

Richard left us after lunch, and we went down into a broad green plain and pitched camp by the Lepi Khola, where our coolies seemed afraid of catching malaria, and a school teacher came to practise his English on us. The next day, we made an early start, up over a col and down in the heat (a most harrowing descent) to Dola Ghat, where two big rivers join – the Indrawati and the Sun Khosi. Charles and I had a bathe in the former before the coolies arrived. Then we took photos of a small Hindu shrine with little stone bulls inside. I sat with my feet in the Sun Khosi for a while, and we camped up on a ridge between the two rivers under some large, shady trees.

On the 15th, we were off just as it was growing light, crossed the Sun Khosi and climbed 4,000 feet of much-terraced hillside. The first few hours were pleasantly cool. We bought limes for making 'lemje' and stopped for breakfast under a tree two-thirds of the way up. Charles did a good drawing from this spot, making the terraced fields and houses look much nicer than they felt. It grew very hot and the afternoon proved toilsome, despite our umbrellas. We got to the top of the hill at a resting place under some trees, to find the sherpas and coolies boozing with the locals.

The next day, we went up a wooded ridge and had a good view of the Jugal Himal in the early morning light, then went down to a river where we had a pleasant bathe before going up again to Risingo.

There we camped in front of a gompa, rather an attractive though squat building with turned-up eaves (symbolising a stylised cobra) and a verandah. The walls were covered with bright paintings of Buddhas. Inside were more paintings of Buddhas, some of them making love in the most uncomfortable-looking positions!

As 17th October dawned, we moved on to Mangal Deorali, which was rather a long trudge. Down by the river, the locals were hauling a great log, to a 'yo-ho, heave-ho' kind of chant. We had a wash, then went up to a windy col where it grew very dark and thundery. As the storm was accompanied by a colossal downpour, we decided to spend the night in a house. We simply marched up to it and Dawa called up to the verandah while the sherpas and coolies started clearing maize husks from the ground floor. It rained and rained but Charles and I were snug in our sleeping bags. Waking next morning, we saw a wonderful view stretching before us, from Gauri Sankar to Karyolung. We went down to a chain bridge, which felt as though it was coming to pieces in the middle.

Two days later was Charles' birthday, and we continued descending to the Bhote Kosi and across it by a suspension bridge built by Henderson's of Aberdeen, then up in the shade to Namdu. There we met some ladies who were puzzled by my sex, so Charles caused much laughter by declaring 'aime ho!' which means 'I'm a woman!' In Namdu a two-year-old girl was brought to Charles. She had become senseless after secretly drinking arak and there was nothing he could do for her. It was an insalubrious place and we went on in increasing heat to a Hindu temple, where we saw masses of tridents and took photos. (The trident is the three-pronged spear of the god Shiva, symbolising will, knowledge and action. People often bring miniature tridents as offerings.)

On 20th October, I almost had to hold my nose as we went through a village which was indescribably filthy and saw a cow being butchered in the street. We passed along a flat valley, before another steep ascent, finally reaching a col, where I lay down in the sun. Another knee-jarring descent brought us to Chyangma, our first Sherpa village. Below a gompa stood two stupas with large staring eyes and question-mark noses. The local people were preparing for a festival and decorating the stupas with strings of white, red and yellow flags.

We went down through meadows full of horses, past a tree with orchids growing on it, where Charles stopped to pick some for me, to a rather dirty campsite by a little stream. There we were pestered by hungry dogs and inquisitive people. I was very tired and could hardly stay awake long enough to eat my supper, and Charles decided the next day should be an easy one. Accordingly, on the 21st we only went as far as the Liku Khola, or Phedi, at the junction of two rivers. It was a lovely camp. Our coolies shinned high up the trees and lopped off large branches for firewood. I took a few photos of them silhouetted against the sky.

The following day, we went up to Seti gompa, another once-prosperous building with attractively carved windows, and an enormous highly decorated prayer wheel, housed in a little hut with colourful walls, which had been papered, then painted. This was a famous place where, some years earlier, all the men had been sent to prison for various offences, such as waylaying and robbing passers-by, leaving an entirely female community. Some of the men had evidently drifted back, for there were a number of quite young children around.

At first I was against breakfasting in the gompa as it looked dirty, but the cold soon drove me in. The old lady who kept the place, and lived in it, was most hospitable and laid a homespun rug on the floor for us. The sherpas cooked on her fire – as usual an open fireplace, against a wall, with a sooty, wickerwork frame for drying grain suspended above it. Smoke drifted up through the rafters to some sort of loft. The gompa was a strange mix of the domestic and the holy. There were some Buddhas bedecked with flowers on a sort of altar, with a few little bowls for offerings. A big drum hung from the ceiling and there were a few dirty prayer flags, looking more like smoky dishcloths, on the walls. In one corner of the dusty, wooden floor lay two pumpkins, which we later bought. In another corner, among the cooking pots and water pitchers, we noticed a cylindrical container which had been used on the Swiss Expedition to Everest.

After a good breakfast, we left with two little boys as porters, as one of our coolies was sick. We camped on a ridge in thick rhododendron forest and the sherpas slept inside a broken-down house with two tarpaulins across it. We must have been at about 12,000 feet and it was very chilly. We went to sleep fearful of leopards, particularly as we had been adopted by a mangy yellow mongrel dog, which Dawa thought had been up to Camp I on the Swiss Expedition. On 23rd October, we crossed the Lamjura Pass, where we saw masses of blue gentians in flower. Somewhere on our way to the pass we lost the dog, which was perhaps just as well.

Junbesi turned out to be much closer than we had expected, and after passing a rock with massive painted inscriptions, we rounded a corner and there, at the back of a valley was Numbur, rising high and white and triangular above reddish-brown foothills. Junbesi, with its stupas and gompas, shining brass knobs and prayer flags, looked attractive and we camped a little way beyond the village in an open meadow, with no terracing.

Above us rose a very steep cliff with another gompa perched high up, looking quite inaccessible. We paid off our coolies and hurriedly wrote letters so that two runners could take them back on the 25th. New coolies were engaged: Sherpa folk from Junbesi, who did not look as strong as our Tamangs, but seemed to manage just as well. We took on two old men, called gagas (meaning 'grandfathers'), one lad and three women. Passing through meadows of long grass, where quite a few Sherpas could be seen, ostensibly cutting hay, we followed a boy with a docile-looking bull up through the forest to a yak farm, and camped just above it. There were masses of rotten rhododendrons about, thick with moss, as well as rotten spruce and pinewood. We soon had a wonderful fire going and sat by it all evening, making it burn bright and sweet-smelling by adding juniper.

Next day we had a rather gruelling uphill trudge through the forest. My temper was not improved by falling into a stream after breakfast, when Charles kept me hopping from one verglas-covered boulder to another. We went up to a high col, where there were many chortens, before dropping down to Fook Dui, which was much nicer than it sounds, and where we were pleased to find a thriving yak farm, which promised plenty of milk and cheese. Here they interbred bulls with yaks, the result being a very sturdy, short-legged animal, with a gentle face, and surprisingly fleet of foot. We camped by another deserted stone house on a flat, silty plain under the mountains. Through the clouds we had an impressive evening view of Karyolung, which rose above us, immense. Mountains always appear much higher when their lower sections are hidden by cloud.

The next day was the last on our approach. We followed a long moraine right up to Dudh Kund, the holy lake that lay beneath the receding glaciers of Karyolung and Numbur. It was not milky, as the translation of its name implied, but a lovely semi-opaque fjord-like green. Numbur and Karyolung were both reflected in the water, in those rare moments when the lake was unruffled by the wind. We pitched our camp among the walls of some deserted, broken-down buildings, constructed by some benevolent holy men for the Hindu pilgrims who came up here in the summer months to offer tridents to Shiva. Innumerable small copper tridents littered the shores of the lake. The story went that some pilgrims had once been caught in a storm up here, and had all died of exposure. I could well believe it, for it was a windy spot with a kind of funnel at the end of the lake between the moraine and the cliffs.

The sherpas put a tarpaulin over one broken-down house and made themselves a cosy, if smoky, home. At first our tent was pitched inside the low walls of a house above theirs, but we found it too windy to sleep so we moved to another house by the lake. Our tent was walled and boarded in there and we were much warmer. It got cold very quickly in the evening and we were glad to crawl into our bags by 4pm. I felt lousy coming up to the lake and had some nasty headaches but the effects of the altitude were not as bad as I had feared, though I was sorry not to be able to sing merrily like Pemba Norbu, for whom this height was virtually normal.

CHAPTER 10

# *A Skyful of Himalayan Memories*

On 29th October, the day after our arrival, we went up the moraine at the north end of the lake and on to the glacier. The day was wonderfully fine, and we went as far as necessary to get a view of the col between Numbur and Karyolung. We could see a rock wall about 1,000 feet high, rising from the glacier to the col: a formidable-looking barrier. Charles and I both thought it would be worth putting a camp up on the glacier to have another look.

We left on 31st October with Urkien, to get acclimatised by climbing a rock peak up the valley to the east of us. On the way to a col south of the peak, we clambered tediously over snow-covered boulders for two and a half hours. There we found a chimney and chockstone leading to a ridge, about 'Diff' standard. Charles led up this to some very loose ground with a view on to an airy knife-edged ridge. I joined him there and found a terrace on the west side of the ridge. Urkien joined us, un-roped, and we continued. It was easy climbing, exposed in one or two places. We tied Urkien on and reached the top. By 3pm we were back at the col, enjoying good views of the Mera peaks. We thought ours might be about 18,000 feet. The descent was wearisome but we were in the camp by dark, seeing a ridge to the west wonderfully clear against the night sky.

Dawa arrived on 2nd November with Changjup who looked, as always, round-faced and beaming. I was still feeling queasy on 4th November and we stopped after two and a half hours in a green, flat valley near a frozen stream. It was east of the little peak we had in mind, known locally as Khatang, meaning 'Trident'. Dawa had marked out a route across the half-mile of rubble-covered ice with chortens, or cairns, at intervals. The next day I felt much better and we went on to camp on glacier-worn slabs and boulders beneath an icy feature on our peak, which we called the 'Yoyo'. Wearing crampons, Charles and I went up to it for a recce, via a steepish ice slope, but it looked vertical for about 30 feet and Charles thought it was too steep. We decided on a more northerly route and went back down. We had mutton soup that evening, with rice and alu (potatoes) with a sprinkling of hot red peppers.

On 6th November, we set off, trudging over rubble-covered rocks for an hour under Khatang's central, east rock ridge. When we reached the ice, we stopped to put on crampons and contoured the little rock cliff on our left, before climbing up a steep slope on firm snow. Dawa and Urkien went ahead, cutting steps, where necessary. Coming to the end of the rock, we went straight up to a little col or shoulder, where the wind was strong, and stopped for a rest, and some food and drink.

I felt rather listless, my feet were icy, and the wind was making it difficult to keep my balance. The summit ridge was corniced, but not badly, though at one point I thought I could see daylight through the holes made by our feet and axes. It was also taking much longer than I had expected, perhaps because I was moving so slowly. I was very glad Dawa and Urkien were ahead, cutting steps. These were not always necessary, but made for a slower pace, which I welcomed. On the left a steep rocky cliff lay below us, while on the right the ground dropped away equally steeply. Far below were gaping bergschrunds. However, the snow was so good that there wasn't much danger of slipping.

At the top there was no wind and we sat there for some time taking photos. To the west-northwest, we could see Gauri Sankar. Beyond the Numbur–Karyolung col, we could see a bit of Lhotse and some other lower mountains. The sherpas went down first and we followed, taking photos of them as they went down our beautiful ridge. We joined the boys at the col and ate sardines and chocolate. It had taken us about five hours coming up and less than two going down. By now I had scarcely any headache. We got back to camp by 2.30pm and spent another cold night, but felt happy and satisfied. On 7th November, Pemba Norbu and Nima Dorje turned up early, but now we felt lazy and did not leave till 10am.

We returned to Dudh Kund, our green lake, at a very leisurely pace. The ice on lake, which was our only source of water for drinking, cooking and washing, was by then a couple of inches thick, and made the most extraordinary wailing and cracking noises, particularly at night, though it no longer howled like a pack of wolves. When we asked Nima Dorje what accounted for the sounds, he said, 'The ice, it will be; he speaks,' and we couldn't persuade the sherpas that there were any ghosts. Urkien observed that the ice also speaks in the daytime, which apparently also meant it couldn't be due to ghosts. On the 9th, Pemba Norbu and Changjup went down to Junbesi for more food. Apart from some bouldering in the afternoon, with Urkien and Nima Dorje, both of whom climbed very well (particularly Urkien), we did very little. I was depressed to find that at 15,500 feet I could scarcely get off the ground, whereas Charles, who was much better acclimatised, managed quite well.

The next day proved to be our warmest. High up, a westerly wind had covered the sky with a white film of cloud which might have presaged snow, but for the moment the weather was much pleasanter as I sat in my shirt sleeves, squinting in the sunlight. While Charles was in the tent writing his diary, Dawa and I were busy patching and mending Charles' clothes. Dawa was a dab hand at sewing. We also sorted kit for going up towards Numbur for a recce. Thicker clouds soon began to drift up from the valley and the wind got up again. I began to feel hungry: a good sign. We had our afternoon tea in the sherpa house, which had become quite a habit. We would sit on a colourful rug by the fire until the smoke got the better of us. Charles had fixed a cardboard cylinder to the two-piece tarpaulin roof to act as a chimney, but it only worked on the very rare occasions when there was no wind.

On 12th November, we set off up the moraine at the end of the lake, and for a while I found it much easier going than the first time. Charles and I took a more roundabout route, while the sherpas shot straight up the rubble and disappeared over glacier-worn slabs. A high wind, seemingly coming from all directions, was blowing up on the glacier, which was very slippery in vibrams.

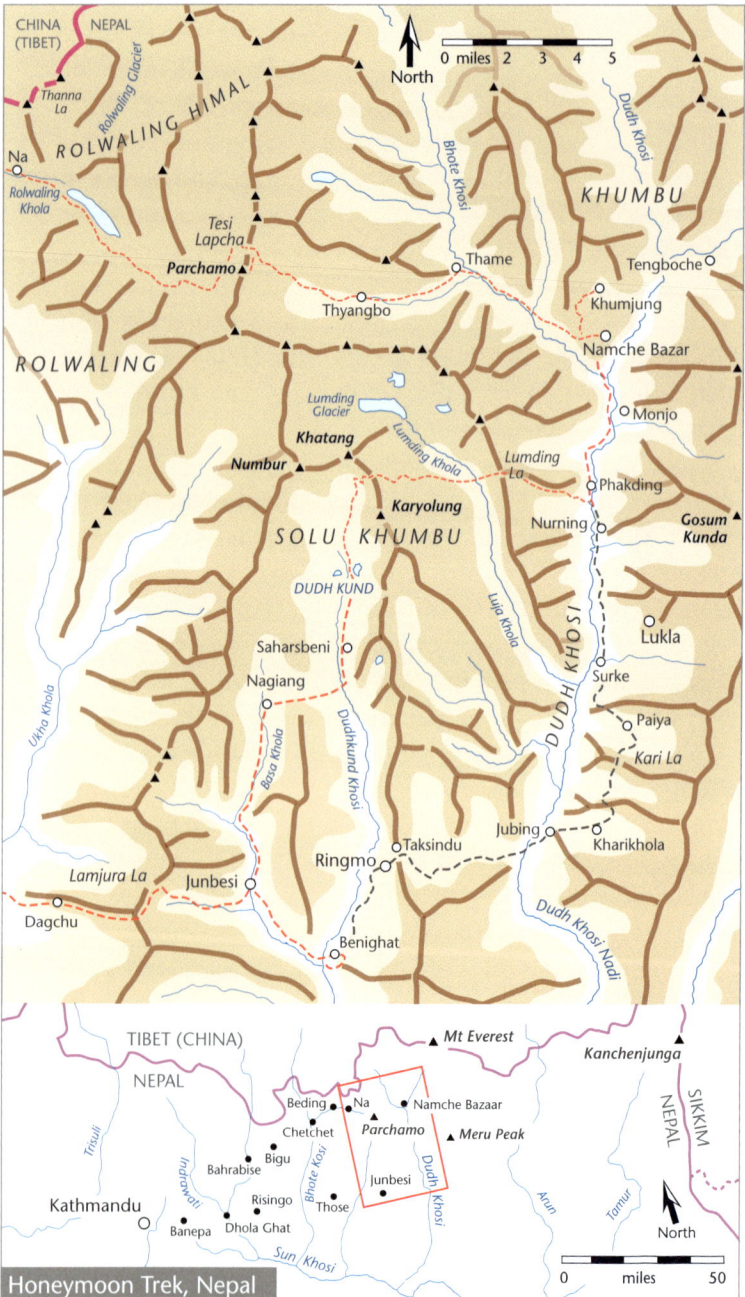

CHINA (TIBET)
NEPAL
*Thanna La*
*Rolwaling Glacier*
ROLWALING HIMAL
Na
*Rolwaling Khola*
*Tesi Lapcha*
**Parchamo**
Thyangbo
ROLWALING
*Lumding Glacier*
**Khatang**
**Numbur**
*Lumding Khola*
**Karyolung**
*Lumding La*
SOLU KHUMBU
*DUDH KUND*
Saharsbeni
Nagiang
*Ukha Khola*
*Besa Khola*
*Dudhkund Khosi*
*Lija Khola*
Ringmo
Taksindu
Jubing
Kharikhola
*Lamjura La*
Junbesi
Dagchu
Benighat
*Dudh Khosi Nadi*

North
0 miles 2 3 4 5

*Bhote Khosi*
*Dudh Khosi*
KHUMBU
Thame
Tengboche
Khumjung
Namche Bazar
Monjo
Phakding
Nurning
**Gosum Kunda**
DUDH KHOSI
Lukla
Surke
Paiya
*Kari La*

TIBET (CHINA)
NEPAL
*Mt Everest*
*Kanchenjunga*
Beding • Na
Chetchet • **Parchamo**
Bahrabise Bigu
Risingo
Banepa Dhola Ghat
Kathmandu
Those
Junbesi
*Meru Peak*
Namche Bazaar
*Trisuli*
*Indrawati*
*Bhote Kosi*
*Dudh Khosi*
*Arun*
*Tamur*
*Sun Khosi*
SIKKIM
NEPAL
North
0 miles 50

**Honeymoon Trek, Nepal**

58

We skated along to the moraine, where the Sherpas had pitched their tent in a little bowl, behind a cone-shaped moraine hump, and started pitching ours slightly higher. It was quite a job, as violent gusts snatched the canvas from our hands. We anchored it to huge boulders, and set about building a wall round both tents. Whirlwinds of stinging snow swept across the gentler slopes at the base of the mountain. There would be a slight lull before they found us, behind our little moraine, and dashed down on us like 'the wolf on the fold'. Our tent, an old one dating from 1953, lay more or less broadside-on to the wind and suffered a tremendous battering but, to my surprise, only the windward guy line was torn out. The gusts grew stronger as the night wore on and sleep came only in snatches despite sleeping pills.

Morning came uncomfortably, with undiminished wind. After breakfast, Charles, Dawa and I set off, leaving Urkien behind to mind the tents and build a higher wall. We wore crampons to go up the flat of the glacier towards the col, passing avalanche debris, some of which had come down from a high icefall on the middle peak, and some, much more recently, from a small hanging glacier on Karyolung. Both icefalls, bare of snow, gleamed in the wind. We also passed glassy blocks of polished ice, reminding me of the smooth bottle-green icebergs I had seen in Greenland. Having climbed up a ramp of snow-ice, we were almost directly under the cliff. Here, there was avalanche debris from both sides scattered about at the bottom and holes where the stones had sunk in.

The cliff, several hundred feet high, looked very formidable, rather concave in shape and overhanging at the top. The bottom and middle sections consisted of smooth, slabby, veined rock with no ledges, and some overhangs. The top section looked more eroded and rotten. Charles thought the top and bottom thirds looked possible, but the middle third looked doubtful, even as a climbing 'jaunt' (Charles' word), and pretty hopeless as a portage route to the col. We turned back about noon from the base of the wall, and had tea and an omelette in our high camp before going right down to the lake, very disappointed. Charles, Dawa and Urkien carried our camping equipment back down between them.

We had the windiest night ever down here, and decided to move on to the Lumding Khola.

I felt fitter at this camp than hitherto. After washing in hot water in the morning, we bouldered in the afternoon, going back to our favourite problem, the awkward traverse of a steep cliff immediately above the lake, using all manner of artificial means, including pegs, planks and other contrivances. Having retrieved our pegs, we had a happy evening sitting with the sherpas by their fire, watching Urkien making shakpa (a traditional sherpa stew) with chushia, a kind of brownish lichen, such as Charles had eaten with them back in 1954. We all built cairns to commemorate our visit.

On the morning of 16th November, the coolies failed to arrive, and Charles and I went up to the lower lake in the eastern tributary valley. It was part frozen, the water level down 5 feet since we'd climbed the rock peak. There were a lot of caddis-flies in the lake, and hundreds of very small crustaceans – a bit larger than a pinhead, looking like tiny prawns – some of them carrying half a dozen bright red eggs aft. Pemba Norbu arrived, but the coolies were still down at Fook Dui. Five coolies arrived the next day, including two small boys, Pasang Nima and Kipa Tsiri, with their stepfather. We left about 9am, went down to Fook Dui, and thence by a track to Lusipur, following Changjup. We then went on to a ghat above Thienga where we could see into the Dudh Kosi Valley and the many ridges, red in the evening light, Gosum Kunda, the spear-like ice peak and the Mera peaks beyond. We reached camp at dusk. There was a nice stream nearby and a great sense of height produced by the fall of the foothills beneath us and the sea of cloud stretching south as far as we could see. We enjoyed some wonderful sunset colours (mauve, and an arctic purplish-red, for a few moments in the east), before spending a very cold night there.

We left early on 18th November, got lost following a set of tracks, which turned out to be Urkien's, on his way back to Khumjung, and had to make up about 400 feet in height to reach a rocky col, where we sat looking at Everest and Thyangboche and the Kwangde zone. The northeast side of the col was all deep and powdery snow. We went down into the mist, feeling insecure in the furrow left by the coolies, and camped among rhododendrons below the snow, on a small saddle with a stream nearby. There was plenty of rhododendron and juniper about and we had our own fire. It was a lovely place and Charles lay back and looked at the stars while I sang French songs.

Next morning, we followed a path through steep rhododendron forest down to the valley floor. There was crisp snow underfoot, excellent in vibram boots but not so good in the bootees used for carrying loads, and Dawa and Charles were kept busy cutting steps for the coolies. There was bamboo growing there and I cut some to take with me, which was later appropriated by Pemba Norbu, to make cigarette holders. We came to the river bed, where the valley broadens into greenish pasture, and saw a few deserted yakherd huts here and there. Prayer flags on sticks fluttered over mossy boulders. We found stepping stones across limpid tributary streams, in contrast to the main, turbulent, grey-green glacier torrent. Charles went across a bridge held together with strips of bamboo – it was so rickety that I preferred leaping across from boulder to boulder.

From the valley floor, we made our way uphill again to the start of the Lumding Khola, which we reached about 3pm, when we paid off our coolies, making our camp near some houses. We sat outside our tent and when the clouds cleared later we looked at the Pleiades and Milky Way, wondering if there were other inhabited satellites. The next day, 20th November, we went with Dawa up a peak south of the camp, which was really a spur off Karyolung. It was longer than it looked, with a rise of 3,000 feet, and I got very tired. However, the view from the top was very good, both of the Karyolung col and of the peaks north of the valley. We decided to camp at the head of the valley and see which peak we might try.

We left the next morning with our four sherpas, Dawa, Changjup, Pemba Norbu and Nima Dorje, and went up the valley floor for nearly 2 miles to the slabs and waterfalls. Going up the true left bank, we reached the upper cwm, with moraines and glacier in mist and cold wind, about noon. Soon it began to snow, while – much to my disgust – the sherpas scattered to look for the famous cave. After half an hour Pemba Norbu appeared, having found it further north. The sherpas were by now scattered far and wide, and we went up for another 15 minutes. The cave turned out to be a small, slightly overhanging boulder, forming a sort of kitchen, with two low, stone walls, an old fireplace and a bundle of firewood, which was the only cheerful thing about it. When Charles and I arrived, the sherpas were busy levelling the uneven ground on the lower, windward side of the boulder. Fortunately we were in time to get them to begin again on the leeward side, which was flat. Changjup got going with the kitchen and we were soon drinking tea. Pemba Norbu and Nima Dorje had some tea and tsampa, before handing their half-smoked cigarettes to Dawa, and leaving to go back down into the valley.

On 22nd November, we woke to a very fine morning with a thin covering of fresh snow everywhere. We decided to move one tent, for Charles and me, to a higher place, from which we might try an easier-looking peak to the east. Dawa and Changjup came up with us and in a couple of hours we had found a pleasant, sandy site among polished, slabby ridges of glacier-worn rock. Once we had pitched the tent, we sent the sherpas back to the 'cave'. We had a lazy, sunny afternoon, made some tea on a butane cooker, and ate some sardines and chocolate, getting hungrier as the afternoon wore on. Alas, we had very little food with us and supper consisted of a very small omelette (more like scrambled egg), fried on the billycan lid. We also had a tin of sardines heated on the stove, and one potato, also heated on the lid and mashed with butter. We then broke up two bars of chocolate into mugs to make our cocoa, which was excellent. This was the one occasion when we cooked for ourselves, and a very happy one despite our hunger. From our vantage point, we could see the two sherpas lying stretched out in sunshine down at the cave camp.

Next morning, the little lake, which had been our water supply, had frozen over, and it took ages to melt ice to make tea. Dawa arrived long before it had turned to water. After some tsampa and two more eggs, we moved over the glacier to the foot of the southwest ridge, which proved to be both shattered and difficult to bypass, except on the south and east. There we went about 1,000 feet up a boulder slope, the ridge hundreds of feet above us on our left, and climbed a buttress of sorts to reach the southwest face, a very wide, loose zone. Dawa went up an exposed groove of ice and rock. Charles and I, who were behind, chose a chimney leading to a gully. This was easy but exposed to stonefall. Once on the face, we saw a route up to a shoulder of the southeast ridge, but still way below the final snow ridge. The face was high and there was a danger of stonefall so we came down, Dawa using our route. When we got back, Changjup was installed with the other tent and we were waited on again.

On Sunday, 24th November, we aimed for the ridge northwest of the mountain, again with Dawa, and decided to try another route up the middle peak. All went as planned for some time. We crossed the glacier, traversed the smooth slabs and scree under the west face, went up a little gully between the icefall on the left and the face on the right, where we put on our crampons, and went up an easy snow basin. The snow was crisp and firm, lovely to climb. We went up a cone of snow, between the rock and the ice, until we reached a ledge on the left in a band of rotten, reddish rock. Just round the ledge there was scree; but not far above, it steepened into very unpleasant, rotten ground. There was no belay and Charles said he needed 100 feet of rope to reach the band of grey rock above. This also looked very rotten; and it remains uncertain whether or not we could have reached the rocky stance above.

We returned to the ledge and directed our attention to another steep snow-cone. Dawa cut steps in this while Charles belayed him from a peg he had knocked into the rock. Dawa eventually belayed to a large, loose, grey boulder, but the grey band of rock looked even worse now, with huge grey-white rocks poised, lying on a slabby face, and we decided to retreat. We were disappointed not to be able to see over the top at least; but even if we had, the northwest ridge of the mountain would have proved too much for us.

Pemba Norbu had come up for the night and the next day we packed early and came down to the Lumding camp, sad at having to leave our high camp. Urkien was back with only one coolie; but the sherpas were able to carry everything down on the 26th. On our way up to a pass we found bear tracks, which were new, since one of the coolies had been that way five days earlier. It must be red bears, the sherpas said, as black bears would have been hibernating lower down by now.

We descended along a ridge, sometimes on the north and sometimes on the south, with intervals of climbing uphill, before moving steeply down in cloud to a camp above Rimijung, near a gompa in pleasant pine forest. On 27th November Dawa and Changjup left early to do business in Khumjung. Two coolies came up from Rimijung and Charles and I had a very happy and enjoyable walk up the Dudh Kosi, crossing it three times. It was sunny, we both felt well, and we had leisure. We saw the mills and the big cave at Monjo, and stopped to wait for the coolies just below the junction of the Dudh and Bhote Kosi. There was flat ground there and enclosures of pine branches where men from Sola Khombu (Pemba Norbu among them) had lived in June while building a new bridge. When it was almost completed, flood water had apparently washed it away, and the work had been abandoned. Pemba Norbu had seen Dawa's wife drowned there. She fell into the Bhote Kosi and was seen near the eastern pier, but was never seen again. Pemba Norbu and Urkien had searched down river but found no trace of her.

The next day we went up the east bank and over a bridge to Namche, where we were met by the checkpost officer and his blokes, all pleasant, rather fat and very friendly Indians, who spoke English. They took us straight to the wife of a headman, who had been having a nosebleed since the small hours. Charles asked if the headman's wife hadn't died three years ago. 'Oh, this is another headman, here there is many headmans….,' he explained. 'Here, there is no difference between rich man and poor man, only rich man has more money.' But they dress the same, and their children have no schooling. A rich man might be worth as much as five lakhs or half a million rupees. Charles plugged the woman's nose with a bandage soaked in novocaine adrenaline, but he was not happy about it and they promised to give him a report on her condition later.

After some refreshment, we went up the steep track that led from Namche to Khumjung in swirling mists. Now we had an escort of small children, who had been sent down to welcome us with bottles of chang and arak, which had to be sampled at every stop. After a while we began to feel rather squiffy. Khumjung, or rather its fields, lay in the bed of an old lake, while the houses were built in a wide arc on the hillside behind. The fields were bare and grey, as were the stone walls surrounding them, and the houses looked drab in the dull light. Apart from yew and overgrown juniper, there was very little vegetation.

Our tent was pitched in the field beneath Dawa's house. We had tea with him, looked at some colour slides and were pressed into taking more chang and arak. It grew very chilly and I went down to my tent to warm up in bed. Soon after, a message came up from Namche to say the woman was much worse, she was losing blood again and her pulse rate had gone up significantly. Charles set off with Changjup for Namche, armed with morphia and bandages. I stayed in Dawa's house for the evening. The company was numerous and included Dawa's son, rather a slick type who wore a traditional Tibetan hat edged with gold braid and spoke English. He was playing with a little black Tibetan terrier bitch called Nagri, which we later bought from him to take back to Britain for our friends, the Hendersons.

In one corner sat Dawa with three monkish gentlemen clad in traditional dull red Tibetan homespun. One of them was a servant of the head lama of Thyangboche. Dawa appeared to be handing over wadges of notes worth hundreds of rupees to this individual. The notes were counted, and carefully inspected by holding them up to the paraffin lamp. Much chang and arak were drunk and much food was eaten while they spoke about the money. It was hateful to me to see the way they were fleecing poor old Dawa. After the money had been paid over, one of the monks drew out some little paper bundles tied up with red string. Each strip of paper had writing on it which I took to be prayers for Dawa's wife. I wondered if Dawa really believed in the efficacy of these prayers.

Next morning, 29th November, we had breakfast first with

Urkien, then with Changjup, who entertained us in his new house, which looked a bit cleaner than the others as it had not yet acquired its lining of soot. Changjup made the meal himself, while his wife went round pouring chang out for everyone. I was given some very salty Tibetan tea, and found it most unpalatable. Having managed to break away from a throng of sherpas who were again pursuing us with glasses and bottles, and after donning the traditional white scarves, Charles and I went down to Namche. (Before we left, we told Dawa to start for Thame not later than 1pm, with the sherpas and coolies.) When we got to Namche, we found the headman's wife well on the way to recovery from her nosebleed and she gave us a welcome present of rice and eggs. We hurried on through the next village, fearful of having to stop for another medical emergency. Charles told me that in this part of the world people often died of a broken leg, for example, when gangrene set in due to lack of proper treatment. I seemed to hear a voice in my head saying 'Welcome to the real world!'

We now had a relatively easy walk up the side of the true left bank of the Bhote Kosi Valley. On the way to the Tesi Lapcha, a high pass, we met several sherpas who had been with Charles on previous expeditions. Among them was Dawa's son-in-law with a yak caravan which had come over the Nangpa La on its way back from Tingri over the border in Tibet with salt, wool and china cups. As darkness was falling, and with the sherpas far behind, Charles and I chose a campsite near the bridge over the Bhote Kosi, a nice flat place among boulders. We collected firewood, and sat by a good fire, while I stroked Nagri, the little black pup we were bringing home for Jill Henderson. Eventually Dawa, the sherpas and about six sherpanis arrived. Changjup charged past in the dark, and had to be retrieved from Thame gompa. The atmosphere was not good as Charles was cross with Dawa for bringing women coolies and arriving late.

We made a leisurely start on 30th November and walked up to Thyangbo, where we camped early, as we were unsure about the supply of water higher up. As we ascended, the valley looked lovely, and we enjoyed views of Ama Dablam and Makalu far behind.

When asked about the distance from there to the col, Dawa said we could do it if Charles and I got up earlier: a remark which angered us. Dawa had previously spoken a lot about Angtharke and Tenzing's success and had sounded discontented and unhappy.

On 1st December, we were all off before 8am and climbed in sunshine up to the start of the moraine. After Dawa's remarks I was determined to keep well ahead, despite stomach pains and diarrhoea. Above the meadows there were some tedious moraines to cross. The ice was bare and slippery and as our crampons were packed away we kept to the stones. Then came some very polished, hard-frozen snow, also very slippery, where the sherpas cut steps for the coolies, followed by another very loose, steep moraine. Now came a choice. One route, for the yaks, lay up a couloir; the other up some glacier-worn slabs at the edge of the rock and ice; above it some huge rocks were precariously perched on pillars of ice.

Dawa said they were going to take the sherpanis up the couloir, so Charles and I made good speed towards it. Just then came a small stonefall down the gully, which seemed very dangerous. The sherpas, scared perhaps by the stones, had decided on the other route. We joined them and found the slabs quite easy. There was just one step where Charles gave me a boost from behind, and the sherpas did the same for the sherpanis. After a few more ice spikes we were there, at the Tesi Lapcha campsite. The mountain immediately north of the pass rises in a sheer cliff, overhanging at the bottom and providing a very small space protected from stonefall, enough for a couple of tents. The snow 30 feet out from the cliff was peppered with stones. By driving in pegs on the overhanging wall, the sherpas managed to fix up a tarpaulin for the coolies.

The sherpanis were all complaining of headaches, which surprised me, and I was pleased not to have one myself any longer. Charles doled out aspirin to the women and some cough sweets for Lakpa Tsering's wife, who had completely lost her voice and should not have been up there. Curiously enough, the evening felt warm, and we slept well. Next day, Charles and I set off at 8am for the snow peak immediately south of the pass, Parchamo (6,273m), which was first climbed by Dennis Davis and Phil Boultbee in 1955. Meanwhile, Dawa went down to the Rolwaling with the coolies, cutting a fair number of steps in hard snow below the pass. We found the snow in excellent condition for crampons and reached the summit ridge, below the corniced part, in about three hours. It was fun to be climbing just with Charles.

As we gained height, however, we got progressively colder. The slope got steeper and we belayed each other, Charles cutting steps while I waited. We were completely in the shade on this face and I soon began to lose feeling in my toes; by the time we reached the ridge I felt half frozen. Charles could certainly have gone on but I was becoming something of a liability. I felt very downcast but grateful for the experience. We kept our crampons on until, way down on the far side of the Tesi Lapcha, we got off the ice on the right-hand side of the glacier, under an ominous-looking cliff, where stones might come rattling down from the slopes above. The sherpas told us later that somewhere in this vicinity they had come across a dried, mummified man crouched under a stone. They weren't sure how he had met his end. Some said stonefall and some that he had died of exposure.

Lower down the glacier, Pemba Norbu, Nima Dorje and Urkien waited for us, camp already pitched. The mountains of the upper Rolwaling are most attractive and I should have liked to stay, but the next day, alas, we needed to start making our way down the giant furrow that gives this feature its name, keeping to the true right bank. This entailed climbing almost to the level of the Tesi Lapcha, up some rocky cliffs, before descending them again over very exposed ground. I was shattered to think they took yaks over places where I had to use my hands and felt dizzy when I looked down. After a 'moderate' rock pitch we traversed into a nasty-looking gully, exposed to stonefall, by means of a dust traverse, beneath which the cliff dropped away unpleasantly. We went down the gully as fast as we could and exited on the far side via another frightening dust traverse. At this moment, as if to emphasise the peril, one of our aluminium pans broke free from the top of a load and went tink-tonkling down into the chasm.

When we eventually reached the valley floor, we trudged along the lateral moraine for hours, it seemed, and only just managed to reach a little dried-up lake by nightfall. There was no water anywhere, and we had no provisions, so Changjup and Pemba Norbu went down to look for Dawa's camp, which was not far ahead, and brought back some food. Meanwhile we had found a lovely, grassy spot for ourselves, with a pleasing smell of juniper and dung. On 4th December we made a late start. As we went down, a valley opened up on the right, at the far end of which lay two passes into Tibet. While the sherpas continued along the track, Charles and I went up a moraine to get a good view. We took photos and trundled boulders and enjoyed the sun for a long while before going down to Dawa's camp.

The next day, we went through Na, a deserted summer village, and on down through Beding, where there were very few people about. We stopped for breakfast under a fantastic waterfall that had worn the cliffs into strange funnel shapes. Charles and I were in great good humour at finding ourselves so low in height and therefore so much more energetic. We actually ran and bounced down the gorge until we came to a side stream flowing down from the Gauri Sankar massif. There, we camped by the clear, rushing water on a sandy beach, and Charles made a really fine fireplace, where we had our best fire yet. We washed ourselves, wrote up our diaries and sat by the fire while Changjup and Pemba Norbu washed our socks.

On 6th December, we went right down the Rolwaling to yet another Bhote Kosi, on our right, which flowed down from Tibet. We had been going for an hour or so when our path, now on the left bank, which was being rebuilt, suddenly faded out before a steep, holdless wall. Workmen were piling logs up against it. Charles got up it in a trice. I was handed yakhair rope by one of the workmen, and was soon up. Dawa hauled himself up, clinging perilously to a bamboo shoot. Then all the loads came up and finally the sherpas. Our path now turned into one of those irritating up-and-downers and round-abouters before it finally decided to go down, but then it went right down. By about 4pm, Charles and I had reached the main river, and crossed it over an impressive bridge with rather gappy side-rails. We found a campsite in a stubble field on the far side. We had left the sherpas in the last village, and they did not appear until dusk, when they straggled in as tight as coots. The sherpanis had also been boozing and had to be led across the bridge. Dawa began raking up the stubble in his characteristic manner. Urkien arrived last, wild and dishevelled.

We asked that evening for 'rumble-tumble' and enquired whether Urkien knew how to make it? Of course he could make rumble-tumbles; he could make several if necessary, he said. We hadn't realised that the rascals had brought booze with them in their water bottles, and the whole company got more and more sozzled as the evening wore on. The rumble-tumble eventually appeared, a horrid, mashed-up pancake affair. Disgusted, Charles went and made some proper scrambled egg. Urkien took great offence and when we asked for cocoa, he said if he couldn't make rumble-tumble, he couldn't make cocoa either and he wanted to go home in the morning. He was in a high old state, but Changjup was worse. For some reason he kept insulting Urkien and we feared they might come to blows, but they were too drunk for that. The last thing we heard that night, when everyone else had settled down, was Changjup, flat on his back, ranting at the heavens.

The next morning, a rather subdued atmosphere prevailed. Urkien apologised for getting drunk and all was forgotten. We spent the day going down the Bhote Kosi from Chetchet, and ended up somewhere short of Bulung. At first we were in jungle and followed the river closely, climbing up and down, and passing through a troop of brown monkeys with their young. Then we left the river and contoured innumerable hillsides. We kept getting lost and eventually had to stop for the night on a terrace. There was a thunderstorm with a lot of rain. The next morning was fine and hot and we eventually passed through Bulung, but we were still unsure whether it was a town or simply a region. Having gained height, we eventually came to some pleasant jungly ground above the terraces, with wonderful cross-valley views. We could see right down to Dolalghat or the ridge above it. Our next search was for Bigu.

This part of Nepal was much more attractive and prosperous than the country we had been through on the Junbesi route. We passed flourishing, whitewashed farmsteads, where we were accosted by some well-to-do farmers who wanted us to mend their wireless. We escaped and concentrated on getting the sherpas out of a chang house. It was getting on in the afternoon when Charles went into one of these houses and told our boys to stop drinking, whereupon one of the sherpanis started to hand round a fresh bowl of chang. Charles got angry and threw the bowl out of the window. Still cross, he led the way across the hillside and, when the path ran out, he barged on through the prickles. Soon we were in an inextricable position: Charles, myself and Changjup, who had been saying, in increasingly feeble tones, that the path lay beneath us. We had barely started to claw our way through rhododendrons and thorn bushes when I too got angry and hurled my birch stick down the slope. Changjup, who had already retrieved it for me a couple of times, looked at me in amazement and said 'Sorry!' He then fell down on to me, and I fell on to Charles. Dawa came to our rescue and hacked a way out. Tempers were restored when we found a delightful campsite by a stream.

On 9th December, still looking for Bigu, we went right up the valley, a tributary of the Bhote Kosi, and crossed the river at a place where the old bridge had been partly swept away. We stayed there for lunch, while the main caravan moved on, and had not been there long when a gentleman came over the bridge carrying his shoes. The fact that he had shoes, a pen and a certain swagger showed that he was an important Nepali. It turned out he had a government job in the Ministry of Education. He came over and told us that he lived in Bigu and invited us to spend the night in his house. He said that he too would be heading over the Ting Sang La the next day, on his way to Kathmandu, and would accompany us.

Not wanting to take up his offer, Charles and I went up the track towards Bigu, passing a little rock-hewn retreat, where Charles took some pictures. We soon came to a big house with attractively carved windows and a big yard, where skins lay drying: the house belonging to the important Nepali. We found our sherpas busily drinking chang there and made haste to get them out. Charles and I now fairly raced up the valley but found no suitable campsite. Eventually, at dusk, we stopped on an earthy terrace high above Bigu, where the sherpanis slept under some sort of a cave. It came on to rain and everything was soon very wet.

The next morning, we went up through a pleasant forest of pine and rhododendron to the Ting Sang La, a 12,000-foot pass. It grew chilly and there was snow lying on the ground. In the woods we saw many langur monkeys in their winter colours: grey, with white-rimmed faces and a blob of white on the ends of their tails. We also saw pine martens, stripy and fleet as squirrels, running along pine branches. Having stopped for lunch in a clearing high up, Urkien lit a fire in a shepherd's shelter and we huddled round it. We found some whitish stones, which Charles remembered finding the last time he had been here. I thought it must be soapstone, as it was soft enough to carve. The sherpas told us the schoolchildren used it as chalk and we brought several lumps back with us.

During our lunch halt, I changed my gym shoes for boots, as the snow was a foot deep on the pass, while Charles struggled on manfully, with his toes poking out through his gym shoes, taking photos of the wintry scene. We would have had a splendid view of Gauri Sankar if it had been clear, but we could only see high-piled clouds. We lost our way coming down the other side of the pass, following the tracks made by the sherpas, who had lost theirs. Finally, after a steep and slippery descent, we caught up with them in the meadows. We found a very pleasant campsite at the edge of a forest, with a shepherd's hut a few hundred yards away, where the sherpas bought a leg of mountain sheep, which had been killed by a leopard the night before. There was plenty of wood and we had our last really big fire. I could think of nothing but leopards all evening and was frightened to go more than 20 yards from the camp.

That night Charles said I was to wake him if I heard a leopard. At about 2am, I heard a peculiar sound, which I first took for a saw: grr-donk, grr-donk. It was an unlikely time to be sawing wood, and the sound seemed to wax and wane. I went off into a doze and some time later the sound came again, so I woke Charles who thought it did sound like a leopard. I felt scared and snuggled up to him. By dawn the sounds had ceased. The sherpas, who had been sleeping out in the open, heard nothing. Strangely enough, back in Kathmandu, we came across a reference to the 'sawing' noise made by a leopard in a poem of Eliot's!

On 11th December, we descended, through villages that began to look more like Sherpa dwellings. We stopped in a gompa where we found, amongst other things, some comics and some 1937 newspaper cuttings, including a photograph of Snowdon, seen from Capel Curig on a snowy winter day. Neither of us knew then that we would one day be living in that same village. Dawa, Charles and I were ahead of the others when the thump of stones falling from a steep, vegetated cliff with an overhanging and crumbling cornice, brought us to a sudden halt. We had disturbed a family of monkeys; and as they fled in panic, they dislodged quantities of loose rock. We ran for it, stopping out of the line of fire to warn Changjup, who was some way behind. Just then a stone came spinning down, cutting straight through thick, bushy vegetation to land on the track. No-one was hit and we proceeded, lunching by a little side stream. It was hot and Charles bathed in a small pool with a waterfall while I sat and washed. Pemba Norbu, who was carrying Charles' kitbag, was called back and was much embarrassed by the sight of Charles in the nude.

We went on down a broad and pleasant if populous track to Barhabise where the sherpas had already pitched camp, against Charles' explicit instructions, in the trees near some evil-smelling hovels. We uprooted them and moved down towards the Sun Kosi, where there was a broad expanse of grazing ground under a large tree. Though there was not much wood about, it was a pleasant spot. A large crowd of Nepalis began to gather round and we were back in the old staring match again.

The next morning, it was raining heavily. We went down the big river under our umbrellas and we were soon overtaken by a band of musicians carrying an assortment of drums. Presently, by the water's edge, we saw a gathering, complete with musicians, corpse and funeral pyre. I would have liked to stay but Charles hurried me away. It came on to rain very hard again and we took refuge in a cattle shed. Smoke from our fire drove a lot of wasps out of a nest. They were huge and horrible, more like hornets, and one of them stung poor little Nagri, who howled piteously, though she soon recovered. The village was full of Tibetan traders, who came to exhibit their wares. We bought a marmot-skin rug for 40 Nepalese rupees (Dawa having beaten them down from 50) and a green stone, purportedly turquoise, for 3 rupees. The rug smelt a bit but we thought we could get it properly cured and lined at home.

On 13th December, we crossed the fine suspension bridge over the river that comes down from the Jugal Himal, and went up the hill on the other side to a high, pleasing ridge. We went along it, passing a school which sounded like the Tower of Babel. In Nepal, learning apparently consisted of chanting everything out loud – hence the noise. Meanwhile the school teacher, a gangling, loose-breeched fellow, sat apathetically in the doorway. The sherpas stopped here for chang while Charles and I, with Urkien and Nima Dorje, went on, but we found no pleasant stopping place and continued right down to the Indrawati. It was an uncomfortable descent; the knobbly, rolling stones made our feet very sore and we were sorry, once again, not to have our boots on.

We passed through a water mill and eventually came to a ferry. I had been looking forward to this all day. The 'nau' was a long, hollow dugout that could seat several people and was propelled by two small boys pushing it upstream for about 30 metres. They then gave it a shove into the stream, which bore it down and across to the other bank. Later poor little Nagri was given a bath in the river and Dawa was quite unpopular with her that evening as she shivered by the fire.

The next day, Dawa left early enough to reach Kathmandu that same evening to arrange our transport back. We, meanwhile, left at about 9am. First we had to go quite a distance up the true right bank of the Indrawati. This involved a great deal of wading and bank-hugging at the water's edge. We eventually left the river to find ourselves on a broad, humpy sort of ridge. It was hot in the middle of the day and the countryside relatively treeless. Little

Nagri got very tired and had to be carried. Soon we were in another village and by now it was almost too dark to see. We stopped at a rest house and pitched our tents on a stubblefield above. This was our last night in a tent and I was sorry that our expedition was coming to an end, though I was looking forward to the comfort of sheets and good food. It was particularly sad to have to say goodbye to our splendid sherpas. They have very few faults, apart from their addiction to chang, and they are without doubt the best companions in the world.

On 15th December, we went up to the last pass. Before us, above the Kathmandu plain, stretched a thick, woolly sea of mist. Here and there, shoulders of terracing, crowned with huddled houses, rose out of it, catching the sunlight. Behind us stretched our mountains, a white, jagged banner, from the Langtang to far-off Karyolung. It was the best view of the whole trip. We looked and looked, wishing we could stay and begin all over again, before going down into the mist-filled plain, with a skyful of Himalayan memories.

## CHAPTER 11

# *A Trip to Russia*

Charles' Himalayan expeditions had attracted the attention of Russian mountaineers and he had accepted an invitation to give a series of lectures in Moscow, Leningrad, Kiev and Tbilisi in spring 1958, to which I was also invited. We arrived at midnight, local time, and were met at the airport by a group of mountaineers, headed by Eugene Gippenreuter and his wife, who presented me with a bunch of flowers. They were all wearing greatcoats and fur hats and there were banks of snow on either side of the road. We went straight to the Hotel Metropol and had dinner with the climbers. By now it was 1am but the restaurant was still very busy. I sat with Eugene on one side and an elderly-looking Vitaly Abalakov, one of Russia's most distinguished mountaineers, on the other. He spoke German so we were able to converse. He had lost several fingers and toes while climbing in the Pamirs, which I began to think of as the Russian equivalent of the Himalayas. Abalakov was an 'Honoured Master of Sport', a distinction conferred on only the very best climbers.

We were plied with vodka, Georgian wine, caviar and many other dishes. A speech of welcome was delivered and Charles responded. Drink flowed, tongues loosened. Abalakov told me that Russians did not use vibrams, only nailed boots. Later Eugene confirmed this. He said that for a long time Russians had been sceptical about vibrams but now they were beginning to think they might be a good idea. Knowing that the Russians used organised camps, not unlike the French, we asked if it was possible for individuals to climb independently. Eugene replied that it had not been, but they were now 'developing it'.

We retired to bed at about 3.30am and slept rather badly, partly owing to the central heating and the impossibility of opening any windows. Our vast apartment looked out on central Moscow, not far from Red Square, where the embalmed bodies of Lenin and Stalin lay, open to view, in a specially built mausoleum. Eugene took us there next morning but, as we were too late for the time specially allotted to foreign visitors, we had to join the general public in an enormous queue that stretched right across the square, with militia marshalling us into line. This queue was longer, slower and drabber than any I had ever been in. The people looked sombre and the men wore thick greatcoats, felt or leather kneeboots and fur hats with flaps. They were generally short, sturdy people; the women were stocky and powerful too, with round faces and snub noses, reminding me of our Polish servant Maria, in pre-war Paris.

We then had lunch, which took two and a half hours, due to prolonged waiting between courses. I had already noticed a very relaxed attitude in Russian restaurants with regard to timing. Charles gave his evening lecture in a lecture hall that seated 800 and was full to bursting. There were a lot of delays, as the projector was too big for the slides. They were slipped into cardboard holders, which hid half the picture and invariably appeared backwards or upside down, but the audience did not seem in the least put out. Afterwards written questions were sent up to Eugene, who translated them for Charles. They wanted to know what Charles thought about the Yeti, and were a little disappointed that he hadn't actually seen one. Eugene told us that no fewer than four Russian expeditions were going out to look for the fabled 'snow-man' this year. Somebody asked me why I let Charles go on expeditions and I replied that I too enjoyed climbing and hoped he would take me along with him one day.

One of the most striking differences between the streets of Moscow and those of other capital cities was the absence of cars. As far as I could gather from Eugene, the Russians imported no cars but manufactured their own two or three makes, including a 'Zim', a roomy, high-powered machine. There were long waiting lists for these, as cars were difficult to obtain. There was also an absence of advertisements, except for a few state-sponsored ones. As there was no incentive to create attractive window displays, the shops looked uniformly drab. One very welcome difference was the absence of smoke- or grime-blackened buildings, compared with London or Liverpool. With plenty of space available, the Russians clearly kept their industries well away from their city centres.

In the afternoon Charles went off to a press conference while I had a rest. When I reached the press bureau, we were shown a 20-minute colour film of the traverse of Ushba. There was a commentary by a woman who was supposed to represent the mountain itself. She warned the four climbers who set off for the traverse not to pit their puny strength against her. It sounded so indescribably corny it made us both cringe. When they finally reached the summit, she came on again to explain the moral: try to act in everyday life as you would on the mountain. Great stress was laid on the importance of friendship and comradeship. Technically, it was a good film. The colours were realistic and it looked a lovely climb, which would normally take three days, with two bivouacs. The snow and ice climbing looked quite hard, the rock climbing rather phoney. So far we had not seen a Russian rope. Eugene said they made them of something resembling nylon, though the ones in the film looked much like ours. We learned that in the Caucasus everyone does their own carrying.

In the evening we went to the Bolshoi Theatre to see Eugene Onegin, a rather long-winded opera with a gloomy ending. The heroine was played by an ample matronly figure, the incarnation of Mother Russia. Eugene had slipped away during the third act, to go home and do his packing. In the Ladies, I was addressed by another woman of ample proportions in a black velvet dress. When I said, 'Niet Russki,' she looked at me and by her gestures I gathered she was saying: 'I can see you aren't Russian: you're not the right size,' or words to that effect.

We arrived in Leningrad on 4th April and were met on the platform by some of the Leningrad mountaineers, a lady secretary, Biletski, Budanov, and others, who took us to the European Hotel. Our English-speaking guide, an attractive young woman called Mariana, pointed out the various Tsarist palaces, monuments and places of interest, including the Museum of Religion and Atheism.

We saw the fort and the church within it, with its tall gilded spire, climbed the previous year by Budanov to help re-gild it. This was the political prison of the tsars, where Peter the Great imprisoned his own son, and where he himself was buried. We saw a statue of him on the river bank by the Winter Palace as 'the bronze horseman'.

Having driven through drab surroundings to visit the new stadium by the sea, we were told that it could seat 100,000. Mariana was full of statistics. There was a shabby grandeur about Leningrad and so much of the past still seemed present. I had the impression that Russians were rather proud of their old tsars, once they were dead and gone. Remembering the tedium of the Kremlin, where the huge size of Peter the Great's kneeboots had briefly held our attention, we astutely avoided a museum of Russian painters, and instead invited Mariana to lunch. She spoke English very well but had never been to England. After lunch, we drove to the Geographical Society, which had branches throughout the USSR and encouraged teachers and explorers, had a library and also published explorers' reports. At 7.30pm Charles lectured to a packed hall, with over 800 present and another 200 in an adjacent hall with a loudspeaker. His lecture went much more smoothly than in Moscow, taking just two hours. Here, too, the audience were remarkably friendly and interested. Afterwards there were questions and we were each presented with a book of photographs of Leningrad.

On 6th April, we were up late and tried once again to buy fur hats, without success. Biletski and others came to see us off, and brought snaps of our visit. We took off in a twin-engined Ilyushin for Kiev, calling after nearly three hours at Minsk. There was no insistence on seatbelts, but the navigation was spot-on. We came down to about 300 metres before seeing anything in the cloud and then flew straight in and landed smoothly. Every few minutes beforehand our air hostess came into the cabin and looked at the altimeter on the cabin bulkhead and then disappeared, presumably to report on our height to the crew. At Minsk, she told us we had a half-hour wait, so we went for a glass of beer but were almost immediately called back to the plane. 'No hurry!' said Eugene, but when we got on to the field the plane was taxiing off and had to be recalled by radio. It was snowing and rather miserable and we were glad not to have been left behind.

In Kiev, about twenty people had come to greet us with bouquets of wild flowers. We drove to the Intourist hotel where, with Eugene, we had caviar, vodka and Ukrainian chicken croquettes in melted butter. We slept badly! Eugene and his Kiev friends wanted to show us 'live monks' in the Kiev Monastery. They also wanted to show us mummified monks in the catacombs. These have been preserved for centuries by the action of the soil, they say, and are occasionally brought out and dusted. What Charles wanted to see was a hospital and we had a rather fruitless argument which ended in our not seeing a monastery or a hospital. It made us wonder if hospitals and homes, except those that have been carefully prepared, are off limits for visitors. Eugene told us that a 'home visit' could probably be organised in Tbilisi. The fact that it had to be 'organised' spoke for itself.

Charles lectured in the evening, after walking alone in the streets round the hotel to see if he was being followed. He did not seem to be, but generally had the feeling that he was. I had also been conscious of this feeling ever since our arrival in Moscow. His lecture took place in a large hall in the university. The words of the first speaker, who introduced Charles, sounded more like a peroration, and I began to feel slightly uneasy, and more conscious of a politically hostile environment, though all the mountaineers we met were extremely friendly and sympathetic. After the Kiev lecture we all repaired to the Intourist hotel for supper, which was more like a thé dansant, where I was taken for a spin round the dance floor. We were then presented with an ice-axe and books of photos.

Next morning, we were up at 6am to catch a plane. We made three harrowing intermediate stops before a place near Poti on the Black Sea in virtually nil visibility. On a couple of these stops we thought we would have a snack but each time our meal was cut short and we had to hurry back to the plane. We passed over many collective farms, which were peasant-run with an elected chairman. Strips of land had been replaced by huge fields and mechanisation. They explained to us that the peasant took part of his income in farm produce, and part in money. The state bought the produce at a favourable rate, and the farmer paid a sort of income tax.

During the later part of our flight, we were over the Black Sea, just off the coast, with its winding road, and the Caucasian foothills 11,000 feet above us. Snow cover started at 6,000 feet. Our last stop was the nicest, at a town on the Black Sea, from which you could fly to mineral waters en route for Spartak Camp. These camps were 'dry' (alcohol-free) because they were used for athletic training. Here it was warm and felt almost Middle Eastern. We flew in to Tbilisi and were met, as usual, by a delegation bearing flowers, including Nicolai Nicolaivitch, President of the local Alpine Club, and Alexandra Japaridze, a sad, grey-haired woman in black (the first woman to climb Ushba in 1934), and a younger woman, Maria, who had also been up it, and many other Georgian climbers. Alexandra had spent nine years looking for a brother lost on the Ushba range; all her family were good climbers. We were taken to the Intourist hotel where it was announced that a film and supper had been planned for us.

While I went to bed, Charles and Eugene went to see the films. They saw a bit of Georgian ballet, then a climbing film of Lenin Peak, then tourist information about Georgia, and two more climbing films: the traverse of seven 6,000-metre peaks and Stalin Peak. Charles thought the general standard of rope work and rock climbing was low, with much use of the rope as a handrail. We had already made it very plain that we wanted a trip into the mountain country but getting our hosts to agree to this was amazingly difficult. Instead they wanted to take us to a champagne factory, to museums, to buildings of historic interest, to their Alpine Club, but in the end we won. We had to spend 15 minutes in their Alpine Club headquarters on the way, as they had already gathered people there to receive us, but we did see some interesting letters from Douglas Freshfield to Professor Nicolaedze, deceased, who had lectured in London in the 1930s.

Then we drove up a valley, along the trans-Caucasus military road, through lovely, wooded hills with gravelly rivers, and hilltops crowned by eleventh-century churches and forts. We went through deciduous forests with apricots in flower. Up the side valleys we saw snow lying quite close and eventually we got stuck in deep mud in a place where there had been a landslide; after much waiting in the rain, we were towed out by a lorry. The whole outing was immensely enjoyable and restful – a breath of freedom after the last few days when we had felt compelled to fit into a pre-ordained plan.

Coming back from the drive with nine people in two cars, we stopped for 'dinner', as they call the mid-afternoon meal, at the junction of two rivers at a favourite climbers' restaurant, where Freshfield once stayed. Here, we heard many toasts, with much Georgian wine. Charles could not remember how many he proposed, but certainly fewer than those proposed by Nikolai Nikolaivitch, who was voted chairman of the table. Afterwards we hastened back to Tbilisi. On the way Alexandra had to stop on the road to be sick and by the time we got back to the hotel I decided I'd had enough and went to bed, so I missed Charles' lecture which, I later gathered, was not one of his best. The Georgians had no clue about projecting the pictures, which appeared upside down, back to front, in the wrong order, and out of focus, with the projector snatching the film every few feet, and probably ruining it. Furthermore, they were the worst audience of the four. They talked a lot, were slow to grasp jokes and by the end Charles and Eugene were tired out.

I was resting in our bedroom when the latest floral tribute was brought in. It was about 3 foot square and 3 foot high and contained two drinking horns, one for each of us. This was our last evening in Georgia and I felt I must make the effort to join the party below. It all started up again at 11pm with innumerable toasts, against a pageant of Georgian singing and dancing. We fetched our drinking horns and more speeches were made. Everyone round the table had to drink to our married happiness and our many children. Eventually, by 2am, it was all done and Charles told Eugene he would murder him if he called us before 10am.

On our last day, we had been promised a visit to a Georgian home and, after getting up at 10am, we were taken to an attractive top-floor flat, where last night's chairman lived, for breakfast. Everyone who had been at the previous night's dinner was there and the table was piled high with cooked cheeses of various kinds, hors d'oeuvres, caviar, fish, a roast suckling pig, three glasses to each place, and bottles of wine and cognac. The very sight, after the previous night, made us feel sick. There was a side table too, heavily laden with cakes and sweets. Our hosts were a bit offended that we couldn't tuck into it all. Charles sampled the wine, while I kept to mineral water, and there were more toasts.

We got away at last, with little time left to see the promised hospital. As we drove in, the patients seemed curious to see us, and we felt for the first time that we were witnessing something unplanned. The doctors were unshaven and things looked generally scruffy. The wards were small with several low beds in each. The corridors were also full of beds because a wing of the hospital was under repair. We visited the operating theatre, which resembled one you might find in a poor cottage hospital, where a chap was having his appendix out under local anaesthetic, and not liking it much. The orthopaedic splints looked antique; washing facilities for surgeons were rudimentary; lighting was poor; and anaesthetic apparatus archaic.

By 1.30pm we were at the airport, where we had to wait three hours because our plane was late arriving from Moscow. It was fun covering 1,000 miles in a couple of hours. The Toupilev had only two engines, so there was a fair bit of noise and rather erratic acceleration and deceleration on take-off and landing. But we saw glimpses of the Caucasus below; and high up, at cruising height, we had the feeling of being beyond our world.

*Denise climbing with her mother, on her eponymous route* Nea (VS 4b), *a classic climb of the Llanberis Pass.* PHOTO JOHN CLEARE

CHAPTER 12

## *Early Years in Bangor*

After the part played by Charles on the 1953 Everest Expedition, and his leadership of the successful 1955 Kangchenjunga Expedition, he wrote a book (*On Climbing*), which attracted the attention of certain members of the Welsh intelligentsia. They were on the look-out for a new Principal for Bangor University College, one of the four constituent colleges of the University of Wales, as Sir Emrys Evans was about to retire. Charles was offered the job and accepted. I was rather dismayed: I thought I had married a surgeon, in a profession which I admired, and now he was turning into an academic, a role about which I was much less sure. Looking back, I wonder if he perhaps had some inkling that he might not, at some stage, be able to practise surgery.

We called on Sir Emrys and Lady Evans, who lived in Bangor at Bryn Haul, in Victoria Drive, in a house belonging to the college, where we would be expected to live. It was a large draughty, semi-detached house, with three floors but hardly any modern amenities and needed to have central heating installed and a totally new kitchen. It would not be ready for us to move in at the beginning of the academic year, in autumn 1958, so we were housed meanwhile in a flat belonging to Lady Artemus-Jones, at the other end of Victoria Drive. I became aware of the University Wives Club, and was soon sent an invitation to one of their coffee mornings at a house within walking distance. When I reached it, I looked up at the first-floor windows and saw a row of heads, all wearing hats, and began to feel embarassed by my hatless attire. But once introductions were over, I felt more at ease and knew that I would soon be able to find friends within this group.

Charles, his mother Edith and I all thought it important that I should learn Welsh, but for different reasons. Edith wanted a daughter-in-law who could chat to her in Welsh, whereas I was more interested in learning the history and grammar of the Celtic language. It so happened that the man living in the flat above ours, Geraint Gruffydd, was in the Welsh department and he agreed to take me on. I could not have found a better teacher. He showed me the derivations of words so that I gained a thorough grounding in the language. I was also given a set of records of spoken Welsh, which helped with pronunciation, but I could never master the vowel sounds in 'Rhyd-Ddu', much to Charles' amusement.

During the fine spring weather in 1958 I was also able to get up into the hills to climb and walk. One day I had a phone call from Jennifer, a girl from the home counties, who wanted to start leading climbs, and asked if I would help her. I agreed to take her with me to climb in the Llanberis Pass. On a warm, sunny day we left our sacks at the bottom of Dinas Cromlech and I led off up *Spiral Stairs* with Jennifer following quite easily and clamouring to be allowed to lead. As we moved across the cliff on a traverse line, I noticed a sunny wall, with which I was not familiar, which turned out to be part of *Pharaoh's Wall*. I had stupidly left the guide in my sack and so was unaware that this climb was actually graded VS. It looked inviting and I decided to give it a go. The wall was steep but there were plenty of holds and we were both soon at the top of the pitch, where there was a broad ledge and good belays. The route above appeared to lead towards a corner crack. Here I suggested that Jennifer might 'have a look' at the start of the next pitch, but to come down if she felt uneasy. This was easier said than done, as coming down can often be harder than climbing up. And so it proved. Jennifer was barely 10 feet above me when, moments later, her hands suddenly gave way. She fell backwards over my head to land 40 feet below in a shallow niche, as the rope tore painfully through my hands, and brought her to a stop. When I shouted down, Jennifer told me she had broken her leg and could not move.

The sounds of her fall had been heard by other climbers nearby, who soon came to our aid and got Jennifer off the cliff and down to the road, where she was taken by ambulance to Bangor Hospital. Here I was able to get in touch with her mother, who came up by car, and I arranged for her to stay close to the hospital so that she could visit her daughter till she was well enough to be driven home. This was an accident for which I was almost entirely to blame and the sense of guilt lives with me still.

After our honeymoon cruise on Edwin's yacht *Crystal II*, I wasn't surprised when Charles set about finding a boat of his own. He eventually located *Triune of Troy*, a 37-foot Channel Class cutter, lying on the River Hamble in South Hampshire, and decided to buy her. We drove down together for a final inspection on 7th July 1959 and, with the help of Yuren, a hand at the local boatyard, we sailed across to Cowes and back in a moderate easterly breeze, force 3, under mainsail and small jib. By this stage I was heavily pregnant and amused when steering to hear Yuren saying 'Keep her full, Madam!' Looking towards the Needles Channel, we felt a strong urge to go out westwards there and then.

The next few weeks were spent introducing family and friends to the boat. I joined in as often as I could, between appointments with Mr O.V. Jones, our gynaecologist, and trips to the hospital for tests. All went well and by 23rd August, my own birthday, the arrival of my firstborn was imminent. My mother was staying with us and came with me for walks in the nearby Anafon Valley. My idea was to hurry things along by walking up a broad, grassy track before turning and gently jogging back down. It seemed to do the trick: I woke at 4am the next morning as my waters broke, and Nea lost no time driving me to St David's Hospital. She then tried to locate Charles, who was sailing with his cousins somewhere off the Anglesey shores in strong to gale-force winds, which had caused the dinghy they were towing to overturn. Fortunately Charles' cousin Tudor was able to right it.

Nea eventually found them beating up the Straits to the mooring at the Gazelle and Charles was back in time to hold my hand for the arrival of our first son at about 4pm, with Mr O.V. Jones officiating. We decided to call our boy Chuck, which had been Charles' nickname in the States, but his proper names were John Meric Charles, and he was not baptised. For the next few months my main preoccupation was breast-feeding Chuck, and long after I got home, which at this stage was Lady Artemus-Jones' flat, I spent happy hours weighing him almost every day, concerned that I might not be giving him enough milk. At this point, Charles brought in a nurse who was only too ready to bottle-feed our baby at any time, day or night. We need not have worried: in a very few weeks Chuck had doubled his birth weight. He was a good trencherman from the start, and was soon taking solid food.

Meanwhile Charles was busy finding the right academics to head the new departments at Bangor: a rewarding but difficult task, due to the competing claims of the other constituent colleges. He was friendly with his opposite number in Cardiff, Principal Bevan, whom we knew as Bill. They both shared a fundamental belief that their colleges should become separate universities. However, there were a number of diehards among the elders on the University Council who were keen to keep the concept of 'The University of Wales'. The old men said of Charles and Bill: 'We thought they were GIANTS and now we know they are DWARVES!' Well, in the end the dwarves got their way, but not for a number of years.

*Denise with Chuck as a baby*

*Denise leading Nea on Nea, (VS 4b), Clogwyn y Grochan, Llanberis Pass*
PHOTO JOHN CLEARE

Charles spent the next few weeks taking family and friends for short trips round the Anglesey coast in *Triune*. I joined in as often as I could, and remember with pleasure how delighted Charles' elderly mother Edith and her sister Dora were when we took them through Puffin Sound in quite boisterous conditions. By 1st October, it was time to lay the boat up for the winter and Charles, Ken Lawrence (our College Registrar) and his son David motored Triune across to Dickie's Yard. Our association with this yard was to last for many years.

The years following Charles' appointment as Principal corresponded to a period of university expansion in Wales and across the country, with a number of new departments created, mostly in the sciences, and particularly in the marine sciences, for which a new marine biology boat was also needed. Eventually *The Prince Mado*g was acquired and moored at Menai Bridge. As well as becoming familiar with the wider academic world, it was important to mix with notables living in Gwynedd and Anglesey, and elsewhere in North Wales, some of whom we already knew. We soon had invitations from Sir Michael Duff, who lived at Vaynol, and from Lord and Lady Anglesey, who lived at Plas Newydd and were keen supporters of music and the arts. I always felt hopelessly inadequate in social situations, a trait inherited from my French father, who, when small 'n'ai pas aimé dire bonjour à la dame', but of course we had our own special friends.

I don't remember exactly when I first met Julius Boenders, but it was probably at a college concert, as he was known to be very musical and, more generally, a lover of the arts and a friend of the Welsh landscape painter Kyffin Williams. We never knew much about his origins, beyond the fact that he was Belgian and a Francophile, or how he came to be living on a farm in Anglesey. But he and his French companion, known to everyone as 'Mads', gave us both a very warm welcome, which grew over the years into a very special friendship. An evening with Mr B and Mads was like dropping the hook in a sheltered French anchorage!

Frank Thomas became a good friend and a frequent visitor over the next few years. He was not only an accomplished pianist but also a keen photographer, who specialised in taking pictures of young children, including a wonderful series of our own three sons, as they grew up. Our second son, Robin, was born in 1963 and Peter, the youngest, in 1965. On one occasion Frank came to photograph Robin and Peter while I slipped out on an errand, and they were all so relaxed that Frank failed to notice the boys busily filling the petrol tank of our new green Rover with water.

In our early days at Bangor, Charles and I spent time walking and climbing together, and with friends, in Snowdonia. I had been looking forward to introducing Charles to the ski resort at Serre Chevalier, in the French Alps, where my brother Ian and I had learned to ski with Micheline, and I was delighted when we were finally able to get out there together one January, taking Charles' old friend Edwin with us. While Charles and I were soon improving our technique on the pistes, Edwin was attracting the interest of other skiers by performing telemark turns, a style of skiing that originated in Scandinavia; it was no longer practised much, but fun to watch. Charles and I were so pleased with our own progress that we decided to go skiing again the following year.

This time we chose to go to Zürs in the spring, and we took with us Charles' wartime friend and commanding officer out in Burma, Major Haden, whom we knew as Bill and who had done little or no skiing previously. Zürs is situated on a high pass in the Arlberg in Austria, and can only be reached by motorised transport, and we first had to fly to Zurich, where we spent the night with friends. The pass is a windy place and the surrounding open snowfields provide a wide range of pistes, one of which leads down to the neighbouring resort of Lech.

Charles and I had both looked forward to the moment of getting back on our skis, but to our great surprise and distress it became clear that something was wrong with Charles' legs, as he now seemed unable to control his skis. After protracted efforts he did a little better, but it was clear that something was radically wrong. As a doctor, Charles was the only one of us who could hazard a guess at the cause of the problem. It was clear that he needed the help of experts, but after some days he managed to retrieve enough mobility to accompany me down to Lech on his skis, before taking the lifts back up to Zürs. Back in Bangor, Charles lost no time in consulting doctors and I was soon driving him down to Queen Square Hospital in London for a series of tests.

In the first few months of Chuck's life, while we could still carry him around, I had a lot of help from Nea and Charles' mother Edith, but as soon as he became mobile I needed more help and we decided to get an 'au pair'. We were very fortunate with our first helper, Giesela, whom we all called Lala (Chuck's name for her). She was a capable German girl who was kind and strong and a good companion. She also liked hill walking, and on her days off I would drive her up into the hills. I was keen to get back to rock climbing and to leading climbs. Since Chuck's birth, I had become both heavier and weaker and it took months to get my fitness back. One fine summer morning, after driving Lala to Pen y Pass, I thought there would just be time, before rushing back to Bangor, to try the first few moves of *Spectre*. This was a climb I was familiar with, but now wanted to lead. Pulling up at the start of the climb on an initial hand jam, with no tell-tale tremors in my leg muscles, made me feel that yes, I was now fit enough to lead it, so I traversed off and sped back home.

For a week or two there was no opportunity because of rain. Then Charles went away with the car and I was left in Bangor with no transport and no second. I rang up Plas y Brenin and asked Don Roscoe, an instructor there, if he would 'second me'. He said yes, but not till after work. I hired an ancient black and green Austin with unpredictable indicators and gears and met Don one fine evening when the three cliffs in the Llanberis Pass were all bathed in sunshine, making the climbs on Clogwyn y Grochan look friendlier than usual. All went well until the crux, on the third and most strenuous pitch, which consisted of an awkwardly overhanging crack in which, at about 8 feet, there was a slot which would just admit the human frame. The problem was to pull round into it, in my case by a strenuous layback move on the left-hand edge, for which a big effort was needed. Once installed, I was able to put in a runner at the back of the crack and to rest, before moving up with good jamming holds as the crack narrowed, and I found small footholds out on the left wall. It was immensely reassuring to have Don as an encouraging and patient second, and I was very grateful to him. The final pitch traversed the steep face to the left of *Nea*, following an exposed but relatively easy line to the top. I felt that I was now on my way back to rock climbing.

Meanwhile Charles, who was planning to sail across to Norway shortly, was busy taking *Triune* up the west coast of Scotland again, with friends, before going through the Caledonian Canal to Inverness. When he rang from the Muirtown Basin, I was able to tell him about my climb, and soon after to join him there, along with Roger Orgill.

*The Pinnacle Club 1962 Jagdula expedition to Nepal made first and second ascents of Lha Shamma, Kagmara 1, Kagmara 2, Kagmara 3, Triangle Peak and Twin Peak. The team: Dorothea Gravina in front, (L to R) Nancy Smith, Jo Scarr (now Peacock), Denise Evans, Barbara Spark (later Roscoe), Pat Wood*

CHAPTER 13

# *The Jagdula Expedition, 1962*

Some time in 1960, Dorothea Gravina (who was by now a member of the Pinnacle Club) and I started looking for a suitable Himalayan peak for members of our club to tackle. Ours was not the first enterprise of this kind undertaken by members of the Pinnacle Club. Monica Jackson and Betty Stark had already made the first ascent of Gyalzen Peak in the Langtang in 1955, and Eileen Gregory had made first ascents in Kulu in 1956. What we wanted was something not too high, attractive in shape and difficult enough to be interesting, in a region that was not already well-known.

Looking through Marcel Kurz's *Chronique Himalayenne*, we came across a photograph taken by Tichy of an unnamed mountain in the Kanjiroba Himal in West Nepal, thought to be about 22,000 feet high. Described by Kurz as a fine pyramid, it looked most attractive, without seeming too formidable; the sort of peak which could be tackled by six women. The approach march would be a long one, but we were prepared to put up with that to find an area off the beaten track. On his return from an expedition to this part of West Nepal in the spring of 1961, John Tyson gave us a great deal of useful advice. He thought we might be able to reach our mountain from the east, but just before I was due to leave India, in March 1962, he sent me a photograph taken from the Jagdula Lekh, showing a possible line of approach from the west, up a hanging valley that dropped into the Jagdula Khola. The mountain was in fact called Lha Shamma (modern spelling is Lhashamma), a local name meaning 'peak festooned with hanging glaciers' and its height was estimated to be 21,038 ft (6,412 m).

The six members of our expedition left for India in three parties. Jo Scarr and Barbara Spark drove out in a Land Rover in July 1961. After a private expedition to Kulu, where they made

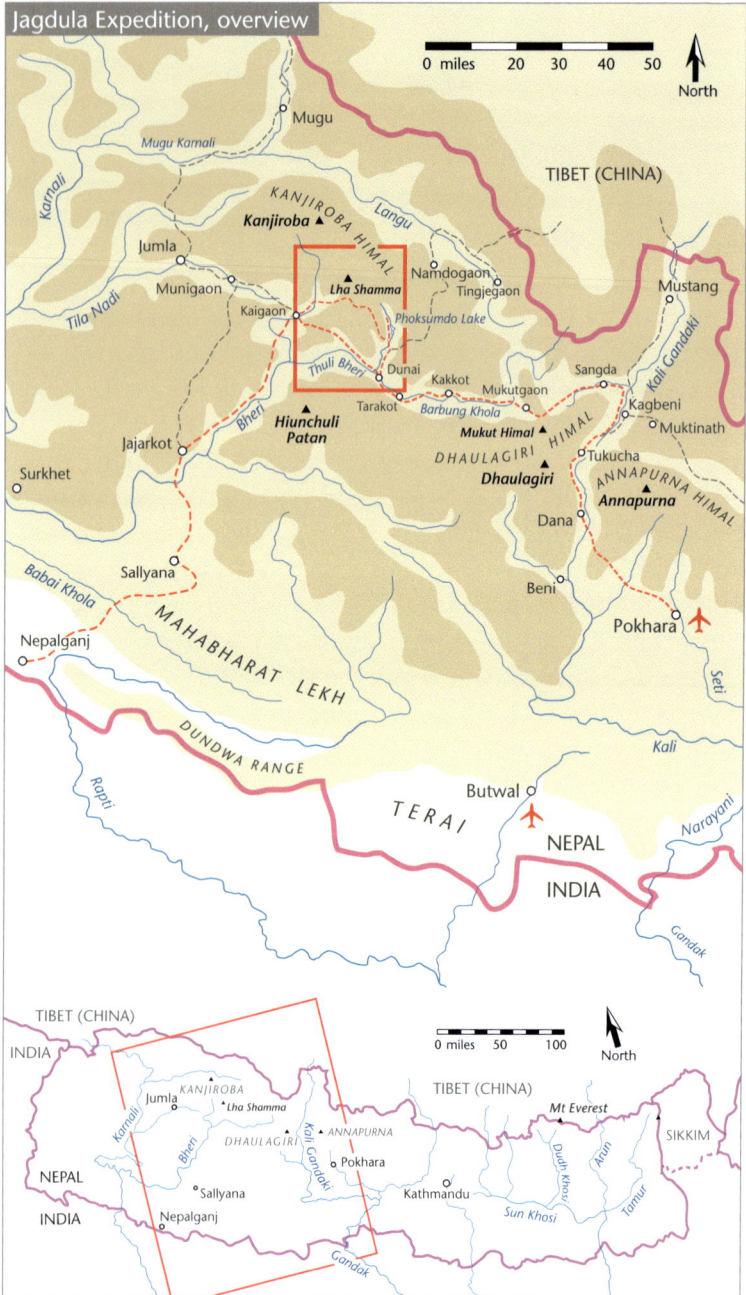

Jagdula Expedition, overview

0 miles   20   30   40   50

North

TIBET (CHINA)

Mugu

*Mugu Karnali*

*Karnali*

KANJIROBA HIMAL

*Langu*

▲ **Kanjiroba**

Jumla

Munigaon

*Tila Nadi*

Kaigaon

▲ *Lha Shamma*

Namdogaon

Tingjegaon

*Phoksumdo Lake*

Mustang

*Bheri*

*Thuli Bheri*

Dunai

Kakkot

Mukutgaon

Sangda

*Kali Gandaki*

Kagbeni

Muktinath

Tarakot

*Barbung Khola*

▲ **Hiunchuli Patan**

▲ *Mukut Himal*

DHAULAGIRI HIMAL

Tukucha

ANNAPURNA HIMAL

Jajarkot

Surkhet

▲ **Dhaulagiri**

Dana

▲ **Annapurna**

Sallyana

*Babai Khola*

Beni

*Seti*

Pokhara

Nepalganj

MAHABHARAT LEKH

DUNDWA RANGE

*Rapti*

*Kali*

T E R A I

Butwal

Narayani

**NEPAL**

**INDIA**

*Gandak*

TIBET (CHINA)

INDIA

0 miles   50   100

North

KANJIROBA

Jumla

▲ *Lha Shamma*

DHAULAGIRI

*Karnali*

*Bheri*

*Kali Gandaki*

▲ ANNAPURNA

Pokhara

TIBET (CHINA)

Mt Everest

*Dudh Khosi*

*Arun*

SIKKIM

NEPAL

INDIA

Sallyana

Nepalganj

Kathmandu

*Sun Khosi*

*Tamur*

*Gandak*

a number of first ascents, they took jobs in Delhi until we came out to join them the following spring. Dorothea and Pat Wood also drove overland in a Hillman Husky, in February 1962. Nancy Smith and I flew to Delhi in the middle of March. Meanwhile our baggage had been sent by sea to Bombay, where it was put on a train for Nepalganj, on the border between India and Nepal.

We arrived at Rupaidiha, on the Indian side of the frontier on 20th March, and spent the next few days at the American Mission with Miss Thomasek, whose kindness and hospitality were proverbial. Our sherpas were waiting for us on her verandah, sweltering in their thick clothes. I already knew Dawa Tenzing (our sirdar) and his cousin, Pemba Norbu. The others seemed to change in number and appearance every time we saw them, and we only realised later that there was a plot afoot to smuggle in two extra sherpas. We had asked for seven but Dawa had also brought along two younger ones, Pasang and Pasang Sonar, in the hope that we could employ them. It was a difficult situation as we had neither funds nor food enough for two extra men. We agreed, however, to employ them as coolies. In fact they proved invaluable. The others were Mingma Tsering, who came as cook, Ang Pema, Ang Temba (who had been with Tyson in 1961), and two 'new boys', Pemba Norbu II and Kachiri.

It took us several days to clear our baggage through the Nepalese customs, to sort our loads and come to terms with the ponymen. The Bara Hakim (senior government official) of Nepalganj very kindly allowed us to do all this in his garden. When he realised that we had brought no guns with us, he lent us two armed guards to protect us not only from the dacoits (bandits) of the Terai but also from rebel troops who had been making trouble recently in the Sallyana district. Our sherpas and our liaison officer, Krishna Rana, went ahead with the 45 ponies composing our baggage train, while the six of us followed on 26th March and drove through the Terai in Jo and Barbara's Land Rover, thus saving ourselves two very hot days' march.

We caught up with our ponies in a jungle clearing some 30 miles from Nepalganj, to find a third of them missing, along with

Dawa and some of the other sherpas. This was a phenomenon to which we soon grew accustomed, for two-thirds of our ponies were from the plains and one-third were from the hills. Not only were the plains ponies much weaker than the hill ponies, but the latter were homeward bound. Furthermore, the plains ponies preferred to travel by night, keeping to the valleys and fording rivers, while the hill ponies travelled by day, and had a marked aversion to water but scrambled nimbly up steep hillsides. We always seemed to be somewhere between the two groups and either went without our breakfast or without our tents. Dani Ram, the nervous little man in charge of the plains ponies, was often in trouble with Dawa, who could be heard shouting an angry and imperious 'Ho! Dani Ram!' as some wretched beast cast off its load.

The three weeks' march to Kaigaon, following the same route as that taken by Tyson in 1961, passed almost without incident, and by the time we reached Sallyana we were beginning to wonder if armed guards were strictly necessary. That very night, however, we were woken by a fearful altercation. Voices rose and we could soon hear the dull thud of blows. Rushing out of our tents with axes at the ready, we found that our escort had made a capture. The offender, who was three parts drunk and gabbled incoherently, had been found prowling around our boxes, and our policemen promptly tied him up for the night, threatening to take him before the local Bara Hakim the next morning. By then, however, tempers had cooled and he was eventually released. As the two policemen had to return to Nepalganj at this stage, we accepted the Bara Hakim's offer of another armed guard.

Apart from meeting streams of men with muzzle loaders, nothing untoward occurred till we reached the hill fortress of Jajarkhot, where 'rakshi' of an inferior kind was available and our guard became very drunk. To our alarm, he began to show us how his rifle worked. It seemed sensible to remove his ammunition, and Dawa contrived to do this without arousing suspicion. It was returned to him unobtrusively next mrning, but we decided that from now on we would rather take our chances with rebels and thieves, and the armed guard was sent home.

After following the magnificent Bheri gorges for a week, we reached the small village of Kaigaon on 14th April. Here 20 coolies were enlisted for the last stages of the approach. Most of them had been with Tyson and were keen to enlist, but Dawa commented that they were 'very danger', meaning 'unreliable'. Our plan was first to go some way up the Jagdula Khola to find the hanging valley in Tyson's photograph, to see whether it would provide a western approach to our peak, and if not, to follow the Garpung Khola, to the northeast in the hope that the east side of the mountain would prove more accessible. While the main caravan followed more slowly from Kaigaon, Nancy and I went ahead on a three-day reconnaissance up the Jagdula Khola with Mingma Tsering, Ang Temba and Ang Pema.

From the junction of the Jagdula and Garpung Kholas, we reached Tyson's Base Camp in a day. As we followed the path, which was very exposed in the lower part of the gorge, memories of Tyson's film came to mind and we wondered how the coolies would manage. There were a number of hanging valleys overlooking the east side of the gorge, and there was one, opposite Tyson's Base Camp, which seemed to correspond to the one in his photograph, but they were all extremely difficult and dangerous, being cut off from the valley floor by formidable rocky walls, whose steep, snow-filled gullies were scoured by falling stones.

It looked as though an approach from the west would be impossible, unless there were more accessible lateral valleys further up the Jagdula Khola. We decided to go on up the gorge the next day, to find out. We set off very early, first climbing to a cairn on the ridge named the Belvedere by Tichy, and then contouring along the west side of the valley at a high level. It was exhausting, as we were carrying tents and food, there was no path and the ground sloped steeply. In some places there was snow and in others a surface tangle of brambles and birch branches. There was little fresh water and we tapped into birch trees to slake our thirst. After some hours of backbreaking work, we reached Tyson's next camp up the valley, at a point where it was joined by a side valley on the west.

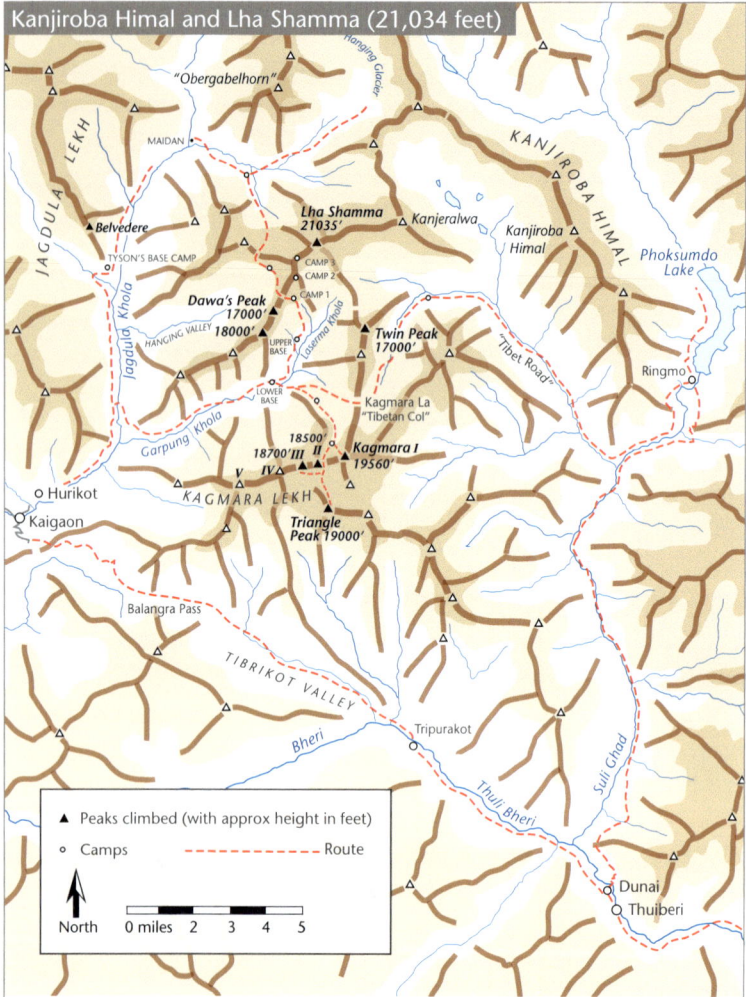

Kanjiroba Himal and Lha Shamma (21,034 feet)

"Obergabelhorn"

Hanging Glacier

MAIDAN

JAGDULA LEKH

KANJIROBA HIMAL

Belvedere

TYSON'S BASE CAMP

Lha Shamma
21035'

Kanjeralwa

Kanjiroba
Himal

Phoksumdo
Lake

CAMP 3
CAMP 2
CAMP 1

Dawa's Peak
17000'
18000'

HANGING VALLEY

Lasema Khola

Twin Peak
17000'

Tibet Road

Ringmo

UPPER
BASE

Jagdula Khola

LOWER
BASE

Kagmara La
"Tibetan Col"

Garpung Khola

18500'
18700'III  II
V    IV

Kagmara I
19560'

Hurikot

Kaigaon

KAGMARA LEKH

Triangle
Peak 19000'

Balangra Pass

TIBRIKOT VALLEY

Suli Ghad

Bheri

Tripurakot

Thuli Bheri

▲ Peaks climbed (with approx height in feet)

○ Camps        — — —  Route

North    0 miles  2   3   4   5

Dunai
Thuiberi

CHINA

INDIA

KANJIROBA
Lha Shamma

Jumla

Karnali

DHAULAGIRI

▲ ANNAPURNA

TIBET (CHINA)

0 miles    50      100

North

Mt Everest

SIKKIM

Kali Gandaki

Pokhara

Dudh Kosi

Arun

Tamur

NEPAL

Bheri

Sallyana

Pokhara

Kathmandu

Sun Khosi

INDIA

Nepalganj

Gandak

The sherpas were keen to stop here and Ang Temba, who had been with Tyson the year before, maintained that there was 'no road' further up. Nancy and I had no reason to doubt him but we felt that if we were going to give up the idea of approaching our peak from the west, we must be sure that to do so was impossible. Leaving Ang Pema to pitch camp, Nancy, Mingma, Ang Temba and I went on over even worse ground. The crest of the ridge above us looked more like a rock climb in the Dauphiné than a possible coolie route, as every few hundred feet a buttress of rotten rock barred the way. After surmounting a few of these, we turned back.

The next day we returned as quickly as possible to Tyson's Base Camp, where we found Pat and Jo. We were tempted to stay and climb some peaks in the Jagdula Lekh, but felt we must lose no more time in finding a way up to the Garpung Khola. While Jo and Barbara set off on a reconnaisance up the Garpung Khola with Mingma and Ang Temba, the rest of us followed slowly with the coolies. The Garpung Khola was a lovely valley, neither as steep nor as difficult as the Jagdula, but very wild and desolate. Much of it was still buried under winter snow. High up on the south side of the river rose one of the glittering peaks of the Kagmara Lekh. The track we were following was known as the Tibet Road, as the Tibetans brought their herds of yak along this route into Nepal during the summer.

On 23rd April we climbed over a rise and looked down over the last few miles of the valley, which was now wide, flat and grassy. Jo and Barbara had put a camp (later known as Lower Base Camp) under a cliff at the far end of the valley, on its south side. At this point the valley forks, and the left-hand branch, known locally as the Lasurma Khola, runs roughly northeast up behind the Kanjiroba Himal. Jo and Barbara had explored this branch and were certain we would be able to find a way on to the peak from this side. They had also found a site for an Upper Base Camp, at a height of 13,500 feet on the southeast flank of the mountain.

Dorothea nobly went back down the Garpung Khola to make sure the coolies came up again with the next set of loads, while the rest of us made a carry to the Upper Base Camp. It was a good spot with a clear stream running close by. While the sherpas built a kitchen shelter and levelled platforms out of the sloping meadow, we climbed higher with Dawa till we could get a view of the peaks above us. Some of us thought we would stop at this point, but it was soon clear that Dawa had other plans for our acclimatisation. Above us and to the northeast, we could see our mountain now and again as it emerged from the clouds. Immediately above us, on the Kanjiroba watershed, was a small, pyramidal peak with a long snow ridge leading up to it.

Nothing was said but we knew we would all have to go up it. We were unused to the height and puffed and panted in the deep, soft snow. From the summit, at nearly 17,000 feet, we looked down on the west side of the Kanjiroba range into the famous 'hanging valley' of Tyson's photograph. We were glad we had not come up it, even if it had been possible, for the west face of our mountain looked horribly steep in the swirling mists. The cloud obscured the view and it was difficult to see how we could best reach the foot of the prominent triangular snow-slope that led to the summit ridge.

The last few days of April were spent measuring out a base line for Jo's survey, and climbing one or two smaller peaks. On the 29th, Nancy, Dawa and Dorothea, who had by now come up with the rest of the coolies, went up to find a suitable site for Camp I, taking a load of tents and food. The weather was bad and on the way back Nancy fell down a gully and arrived in camp looking battered, though fortunately not badly hurt. It snowed heavily all next day but by 1st May it was brilliantly fine. Jo and I, who with Mingma and Pemba Norbu II, were to do the preliminary work on the mountain, left for Camp I. Dorothea and Nancy thought we should try the ridge rather than the icefall. We set off towards it with Mingma and Pemba on 2nd May. The ridge itself was quite easy till we reached some gendarmes, which separated us by only a few hundred yards from the base of the triangular snow-slope. We had spotted these gendarmes from the other side of the Garpung Khola and guessed they might give us trouble, for we had already discovered that the rock in these parts was very loose. We decided against pursuing it as altogether too dangerous.

As I rejoined the others, I could hear raised voices. The cause of the disagreement was the question of who should do the leading. The sherpas naturally felt reponsible for us, and did not like the idea of women in the lead, but we very naturally wanted to lead. It was useless to pretend that we were as strong as the sherpas, and it would have been stupid not to take advantage of their strength and experience, but we did not want to have everything done for us. Disgruntled but sure we would reach a compromise, we made our way back to Camp I, where we were joined by Pat and Nancy.

The next day the four of us, with our sherpas, went up the icefall, keeping quite close to the cliffs we had been trying. Although it was hard work, there were no obstacles. Early afternoon found us at a height of 18,300 feet, looking for a safe campsite. A platform was levelled on a projecting spur of snow, which would give us some protection from avalanches. Pat and Nancy and their sherpas went down to Camp I, and Jo and I went with Mingma and Pemba, with whom relations had now improved, to investigate the steep snow-slope above Camp II. It was really an ice-slope covered with snow, and lay at an angle of about 50°. Fixed ropes were later put up on the middle section. Over 1,000 feet above us, plumes of snow were being whipped up by the wind on the crest of the long ridge leading to the summit.

The next day I felt unwell and stayed in camp, watching Jo and the sherpas very slowly climbing the long ridge to vanish over the top. Pat and Nancy appeared with more food and tents, and late that afternoon the others came down with the exciting news that they had been some way along the ridge and had found a good spot for a third camp. The ridge appeared to be very long but they thought we could probably reach the summit from a third camp unless there were unforeseen obstacles.

The next morning, Pat was suffering from altitude sickness and we left her in bed at Camp II, knowing that Dorothea would be coming up later. Meanwhile Jo, Nancy and I and the sherpas carried a camp up to the ridge. When we reached it, after three hours' hard work, we found that it was narrow and corniced, with the ground dropping away steeply on both sides; and the snow was unpleasantly deep and soggy. The site Jo had chosen for Camp III was almost the only place wide enough to hold a camp. It was a small saddle below a step; beyond this the ridge described a sharp bend to the east. It was windy and cold and the altimeter put us at 19,500 feet. We pitched a pair of two-man tents – one for the sherpas and the kitchen, and one for the three of us. We slept very badly and had a late start next morning. The ridge continued airy and exposed; most of the time we were kicking steps on the crest itself, sometimes to one side, because of the cornice. Occasionally steps had to be cut in the ice beneath, but mostly we were moving through very soft snow and were scarcely ever able to get a good axe belay.

Unlike Jo, I found that I had not yet acclimatised and that I needed increasingly frequent rests. My ciné camera, which weighed only 5 pounds, felt very heavy indeed. By about midday we had covered two-thirds of the way and were still hoping to get to the summit, when we came to an ice-pinnacle, which we had seen from afar. We knew that we would have to contour it on the north face of the mountain, where the ridge was joined by the top part of an icefall. The weather had been deteriorating rapidly, and soon we were enveloped in cloud and it began to snow. While I sat in the snow having yet another breather, the others stood grouped at the foot of the pinnacle, waiting for the clouds to lift.

Twenty minutes later, it was snowing more than ever and we decided to turn back. Visibility was now so poor that we could no longer see more than a few yards ahead. Had we not been following a ridge, we would have had great difficulty in finding the way. Our tracks had been completely blotted out and we made our way down slowly and very cautiously. The exposure was no longer visible but we could not afford to forget the tremendous drop on either side. As time went by, I began to wonder how one would set about bivouacking on such a narrow ridge. We came to a place where it appeared to divide: which way had we come? Miraculously the mist lifted for a second and we just had time to make out our two little tents immediately below. We tumbled into them, glad to be out of the blizzard, which seemed to grow fiercer towards the end of the day. During the night it felt as though we must soon become airborne. We had just emerged from our tents next morning, to see how much snow had fallen, when Dawa appeared, followed by four sherpas with empty pack frames. 'Niche!' he said, grinning, and we all moved down to Base Camp.

The weather didn't improve sufficiently for us to be able to go up again until 10th May. By then, however, Dorothea was in bed with a high temperature and sore throat, and was taking penicillin. The Kaigaon coolies had terrible colds and coughs and it seemed likely that she had caught the infection from them. We left the 'Burra Memsahib' at Base, and made our way back to Camp II. There was a lot of snow everywhere and the weather was still very unsettled. We had to wait two days before we could move up to Camp III. The five of us sat in the Moncler tent, discussing how we were going to climb the mountain. Everyone was most self-effacing. After rejecting the pleasant but fanciful idea that five of us should climb the summit together, we adopted the most sensible solution – that Jo and Barbara, who were better acclimatised than the rest of us, should, with Mingma and Pemba, constitute the first assault party. Pat, Nancy, Ang Pema and I would form the second.

On 13th May, eight of us set out from Camp III. I felt more than usually tired on the ridge above the steep slope. Depressing, I thought, not to be acclimatising more quickly. That evening, as my throat grew ever tighter and my temperature rose, I realised that it was not the altitude but flu. The next day dawned extremely cold and windy and at about 5am we could hear Jo and Barbara cursing outside as they put on their crampons with numb fingers. Feeling ghastly, I dozed off, and woke some time later to hear voices coming back towards camp. 'Can't have had time to do it,' I muttered to Nancy, but they had, and in very good time, reaching the summit at 9.30am. It turned out that it was only another hour and a half beyond the ice pinnacle, and there had been no major difficulties. 'Terrific!' 'What's it like?' 'How high is it?' 'What sort of a top?' We congratulated and plied them with questions, while they ate some food, for their breakfast had been scanty that morning.

After their meal, Jo and Barbara decided to go down, and it

seemed wiser for me to go down as well. We spent the night at Camp II, where Dorothea and Dawa were waiting. The next day was fine and we were able to watch the second party, consisting of Nancy, Pat and Ang Pema, reach the summit at about 9am. Dawa, Mingma, Pemba Norbu and I went down to Base Camp. My legs felt strange and I was relieved when we were able to wrap empty polythene bags around ourselves and glissade down the last few hundred feet. When I took my temperature and found that the thermometer persistently read 105°, even after vigorous shaking, I realised it was time to settle down in bed with Nancy's copy of *Dr Zhivago*.

Now that the mountain had been climbed, Jo and Barbara wanted to take one of the sherpas and spend a week surveying on its west side. This would involve going over the col above Camp I, and steeply down the other side into new country. Meanwhile the rest of us would move down to Lower Base Camp; and, after a few days' rest and recuperation, we would carry a camp up to the Kagmara Lekh. From our previous camp we had a very good view of these mountains, which rise on the south side of the Garpung Khola to form a chain about 10 miles long and about 20,000 feet high. The high peak at the east end of the chain, Kagmara I, looked approachable. Below its impressive north face lay a flattish icefield, which we were able to reach quite easily. From the outset, Mingma and Pemba Norbu had favoured the north face, but Dorothea and I were less enthusiastic about it, on account of various crumbling and unhealthy-looking seracs. The west ridge looked possible but when we reached it we found we could not contour a rocky gendarme. We retreated, determined – now – to try the north face.

Next day, tents and food had to be brought up to its foot, and in the afternoon Mingma and Pemba went off to cut steps and put a length of fixed rope on the first steep section. The weather was poor and it was soon snowing heavily. The seracs rumbled in the night. In the morning, there were several inches of fresh snow, but the weather was clearing. Dorothea and I set off with Mingma and Pemba, while Pat and Nancy went with Ang Pema. The climbing was steep and invigorating, with the odd icy bulge where hand and footholds had to be cut. From below it had looked as though the lower part was the steepest and the angle appeared to ease off higher up; in fact, the slope above the seracs was concave and grew considerably steeper towards the summit ridge. We reached the top at noon and started down slowly, the same way, taking great care, for we felt the slope might avalanche. We were just coming down an awkward corner, where the snow came away in slabs from the ice beneath, when Pemba, who was bringing up the rear, shot past us with a dismal shriek. Dorothea, who was next on the rope, brought him to a stop.

Jo, Barbara and Ang Temba were now back from a successful week of exploration, looking much thinner after long days and hard carrying. They had managed to reach a flat, wedge-shaped piece of ground that Nancy and I had seen at the head of the Jagdula Khola, and they had explored the valley immediately north of our mountain. During our last few climbing days, we put a camp on the col between Kagmara I and II, and from it we climbed Kagmara I and III and a small peak south of the Kagmara Lekh, overlooking the Tibrikot Valley. After this we had to go down to Base Camp, where negotiations with Tibetan yakmen were in progress. We now decided that, instead of returning via Jumla and Dailekh, as originally planned, we would rather go north of Dhaulagiri, following the Thuli Bheri and Barbung Khola, and over the Mukut passes to Tukuche.

While we had been climbing, our liaison officer, whose dislike of snow had prevented him from even venturing up to Base Camp, had been busy in Jumla, making our change of plan known to the authorities in Kathmandu. We now split up again. The main party went down to Kaigaon with the yak caravan, sorted out remaining food and equipment there, and hired yaks to take us on the first stage of the return down the Tibrikot Valley. Meanwhile, Dorothea and Jo, with Pemba Norbu, Kachiri and Pasang Sonar, crossed the so-called Tibetan Col at the head of the Garpung Khola, and made their way eastwards towards Ringmo and Phoksundo Lake, a district which no Europeans had visited since David Snellgrove. They then followed the Suli Ghad river in a southerly direction to Dunei, where we all met on 3rd June.

The valleys of the Thuli Bheri and Barbung Khola are magnificent, but not without hazard. We were obliged to change from yaks to coolies and vice versa at frequent intervals, and each time the loads had to be made up to different weights. There was a disastrous incident at Kakkot, where we almost came to blows with the yakmen and their wives. We were told that the yaks did not like our wooden boxes, and were made to empty their contents into inadequate yakhair bags. These were provided by the yakmen, and had to be sewn up. When we realised that the women were hoping to appropriate the boxes, we lost patience, for we were certain to need them in the monsoon rains. Angry screams went up as the sherpas wrested them from the housewives of Kakkot.

Our difficulties were nothing, however, to those of the Japanese Expedition to Mukut Himal, whom we met there. They had made the mistake of hiring yaks from some Tibetan refugees on one side of the river, and then trying to hire more from the inhabitants of Kakkot on the other side. A bitter and vociferous quarrel ensued, accompanied by a great rushing about and throwing of stones. It was a relief to get away. But we had barely gone a few hundred yards when we were confirmed in our suspicion that yaks do not like memsahibs. The sight of one of us out of the corner of an eye was enough to send them charging wildly about, tossing off their loads, which rolled down into the river. Several kitbags were ripped on sharp stones by charging yaks, and their contents hung out of them like entrails. That evening, we took stock of the damage. A great deal of the medical kit had been smashed, our tins of food were 'yakked' (bent out of all recognition), my possessions were soaked and Dorothea's rucksack had disappeared altogether. The charm of yak travel was fading. Next day, everything went back into boxes.

Laden yaks and coolies travel slowly so we got into the habit of spending the middle of the day swimming and writing our diaries, and catching up with the baggage train in the afternoon. On one occasion we failed to notice that the vibram tracks turned uphill from the Barbung Khola towards the high village of Tarengaon. Nancy and I, who were behind everyone else, were following a path at the bottom of the Barbung Khola. As the evening wore on and no camp came into view, we realised that we would have to bivouac. It was growing dark as we hurried along paths that wound in and out of pinewoods. A snake slid across the track. Presently we saw a fire in the woods beneath us and we could just distinguish the silhouettes of a party of tousled Tibetans in the smoky, flickering light. Cautiously we observed them from behind a boulder. One figure was bending over the fire. 'Looks awfully like Jo,' Nancy whispered after a while. Our shout was met by an answering shout and we stumbled down the slope to find Jo, Pat and Barbara, who – like us – had got lost. It was a cold, wet bivouac but things improved when the sun came up next morning. At 10am Mingma and Pasang Sonar appeared, grinning broadly. They had set off at 5am from Tarengaon to bring us breakfast.

It grew progressively cloudier as we went up the Barbung Khola, but it wasn't until we reached Mukutgaon that we had heavy rain. The monsoon seemed to be held in check by the Dhaulagiri range, which forms a dark and imposing barrier on the south side of the river. From Mukutgaon, or Mu as it is more commonly known, we climbed up over the Mukut passes (at approximately 18,500 feet) and enjoyed wonderful views of Dhaulagiri II. We also met pathetic families of Tibetan refugees in the high, barren hills south of Charkabhot. These were not the only signs of political disturbance. Between Sangda and Tukuche, we noticed a number of military camps. The soldiers, said to be 'Khambas', were handsome men, taller than any of the Tibetans we had seen before, and they appeared to be well-equipped.

As if to prepare us for the sophistication of Tukuche, our yakmen, who until now had accompanied us on foot, suddenly acquired gaily caparisoned horses and galloped past us now and then, smiling loftily. The monsoon was well under way when we reached Tukuche, and we were glad to reach the home of Professor Fürer-Haimendorf and his wife, whom we had met in Sangda a few days earlier, and who had very kindly offered us the use of their house on our way down the Gandhaki Valley.

Although we were still a few days away from Pokhara, our expedition had virtually come to an end. Our return via the Barbung Khola had taken us longer than expected and Nancy and

I were both anxious to get back to Britain quickly by flying home from Pokhara. The others, who were driving overland, had plenty of time and hoped to spend a week in Kathmandu before going back to Delhi. Dorothea decided to hurry down to Pokhara with Nancy and me, to book seats on the plane for the rest of the party. Coolies were difficult to find in these parts but by 23rd June we were able to leave Tukuche with three sherpas and three local lads. With traditional white scarves wound about us, we said goodbye to the others and went on down the Kali Gandaki, with the river in spate.

Greetings from members of the
Jagdula Expedition 1962
(Pinnacle Club)

*Clockwise from top left: Lha Shamma from Camp III; Denise filming during the Expedition; Postcard showing members of the Jagdula Expedition, Barbara and Pemba Norbu returning from the summit of Lha Shamma to Camp III; Pinnacle Club Journal 1962* PHOTO JO SCARR

## CHAPTER 14

# *A Spanish Cruise with Charles, 1964*

After the Jagdula Expedition I did my best to keep up my fitness by hill walking and helping Charles on the boat. He often sailed with other friends as well. The following winter was snowy, with hard frosts, so hard that Llyn Ogwen froze over. Tony Bradshaw, the husband of one of my Bangor University College Wives Club friends, Betty, was able to convert one of the college 'Fireflies' into an ice yacht, which we sailed on the lake, after a fashion. I don't remember what happened when we changed tack, but at least the ice never gave way. Both Tony and Betty came sailing with us on *Triune*. I was once again heavily pregnant that spring, and gave birth to Robin, my second son, on 22nd June 1963. Robin weighed in at close to 10 pounds.

He was a most contented baby and I could take him with me wherever I went. Pushing the pram one day, as I took Chuck to Hillgrove, the little school in Upper Bangor, we met John, one of Chuck's friends, who leant enquiringly over the pram.

'My brother,' Chuck explained.

'What use is he?' John asked.

'He isn't use but we love him,' replied Chuck.

I was even able to take Robin with me on evening visits to Mr B and Mads. We put him in the next room in his basket, where he could be heard happily burbling and laughing to himself. He earned me many 'brownie points'.

After our skiing trip in Zürs, when Charles had experienced problems with his legs, he underwent numerous tests and his symptoms were eventually diagnosed as the early onset of multiple sclerosis. He then made the most of what we both knew would be the last years before his legs gave way, with a wheelchair existence in prospect. He went on sailing *Triune* with family and friends to Ireland and the Scottish west coast. He had planned a cruise to the Faroe Islands and in 1963, with some of our sailing and climbing friends, including my brother Ian, he sailed up to the Outer Hebrides, where bad weather forced them to abandon the attempt. Our cruise to Spain in *Triune*, in late July 1964, was our last significant sailing trip together and came as something of a bonus.

We had made a few shorter cruises earlier that year, and we had also made a trip round the harbour with a compass adjuster, who fixed up his pelorus for us to use as a sundial and was very expeditious. However, it wasn't until 21st July that we were able to get away with Roger Orgill again for our projected cruise to the Azores, via the northwest coast of Spain. We came aboard in the evening, stowed our gear and sealed the drinks locker before tucking into steak and chips.

Next morning we cast off. The shipping forecast predicted northerly winds, force 2-3, a few fog patches and fair to good visibility, but it was slow going. By 4pm we were seeing faint glimpses of the uplands at the end of the Llŷn Peninsula, and off Bardsey, coming and going in the haze; and then we were becalmed for a couple of days. By the morning of 24th July, *Triune* was finally sailing herself in a light northwesterly breeze.

The next afternoon I spotted the Scillies on the port bow. By 6pm we picked up Bishop Rock Lighthouse to the right of the islands, and used a rather faltering engine for half an hour to clear the lighthouse and nearby rocks. By next morning, we were all tired due to lack of sleep, and had made little progress during the night, which was overcast. Later, however, the sun came out and we sailed all afternoon in an easy swell with little waves. We shed our clothes, brought out our cameras, cleared the carburettor jet, and enjoyed our bread and butter and eggs. Charles wrote in the log that he was anxious about clearing the Scillies and expressed his apprehension at heading out at nightfall into the open Atlantic swell.

We were becalmed again during the night, about 100 miles west of Ushant. The prolonged calms and very light following winds, combined with lack of sleep, made us all crotchety. But the next night, we had a lovely, waning moon with a handful of stars, which did not seem so bright in these latitudes. We saw very few boats, apart from an occasional fishing vessel and the infrequent lights of a distant ship. Next day, a fishing boat came alongside and we exchanged cigarettes for fish. At this point Charles noted in the log that the Azores were too far away for the time we had available, and he therefore decided to limit our cruise to the northwest coast of Spain.

That afternoon the sea was a glorious blue in the sunshine, but a big swell had built up and the barometer had risen again. Charles and Roger had scampi and halibut for supper, while I escaped to the bows. Although it was fine, starry and moonlit, we had an unsteady night, with an unhappy roll and the sails slatting. There were storm petrel about, and Charles wondered whether his vivid dreams could be attributed to the scampi.

In the early hours of 31st July, Charles worked out that we were about 65 miles from Cabo Villano. I then took over and had some trouble dodging fishing boats. At 4am we were quite close, west of Villano. We altered course to weather its rocks, and we then beat in a very strong northeasterly wind to anchor at noon in Corcubion, off the town quay. Coming out of a clear, sunny sky, the wind was strong enough to put the lee rail awash, even with reduced sail. The anchor dragged at first so we tried twice more. Charles observed that we were safer at sea, rather than making such good landfalls that it was a struggle not to hit them. With 20 fathoms of chain down, it was time for a whisky.

On 3rd August, we left Corcubion, bound for Ria Muros. We put in a reef, as it was still gusty at times, and sailed down the Corcubion inlet in a calm sea. In the late afternoon we were beating gently up Ria Muros in hot sunshine with a light northeasterly breeze that brought with it the warm, earthy smell of land. The landscape was dotted with houses in pastel shades and dark groves of trees, with green lawns between them, gurgling water and pleasant heat. Charles and I crept into the shade of the mainsail with our cups of tea.

That evening we anchored off the village of Muros, in hot sunshine, feeling tired. I went ashore to shop while Charles and Roger had a drink and peeled off their clothes to cool off. A British yacht, bigger than *Triune*, had anchored there just before us, with a larger complement and a hired crew. It was a rowdy night, with loud radio music emanating from a nightclub. When I went ashore, I found some dirty, foul-smelling shops which I hesitated to enter, except to buy bare essentials. Charles noticed some old, three-masted smacks moored on the north side of the bay and there were some odd, jetty-like structures, which turned out to be rafts for mussel growing.

On 4th August, we were up late and the other yachts had all gone. We motored to nearby Enseada de Bornalle in search of sandy beaches, and anchored in the western part of the bay. It was a jolly spot. There were pines on grassy knolls ashore, half-moon sandy beaches, a calm sea and gentle breezes to keep us cool, but it was quite exposed to the southwest. We were visited by groups of locals, both men and girls, who either swam or rowed out in small boats. Not knowing any Spanish, we found it difficult to talk to them. Charles was happy to listen to the birds on shore and I was happy to find a marvellous little sandy cove for a swim. Roger showed no desire to go ashore. He and Charles had a prolonged siesta, waiting for the cool of evening. Charles felt content here and settled down to read *Seven Pillars of Wisdom*.

In the evening I rowed Charles round the spit to the bay where the village of Bornalle lay. Charles sat in the dinghy in the sand while I went shopping for unleavened bread rolls, wine and tinned tuna. A man came, leading a cow to paddle at the shore, then another man with a sow and two piglets to turn up worms in the sand at the water's edge. We rowed back at sundown with some supplies and dined in the cockpit, with the hot, evening breeze blowing over us. After dark we lay naked on deck with the warm breeze strong off the land.

On 5th August there was an on-shore morning breeze. Roger rigged an awning and went ashore for bread. It was peaceful. The swimmers started to gather on shore at about 11 and we knew that some of them would swim out to us later. At teatime Charles came out to the cove with us, to swim. For him, alas, this proved to be an uncomfortable affair of involuntary spasms, caused by the touch of cool water. But the cove was lovely. The rocks were rough and brown, warm and worn by the sea, the water clear and green, interfused with shafts of sunlight that reached down to the yellow sands. In the evening we were all aboard. It was calm, the dinghy lapping against the wavelets. Curlews' and sandpipers' cries mingled with crowing cockerels and tootings of motor horns, all serving to intensify the sense of peace and silence. There were crickets, and each night a string of small boats, possibly sardine-catchers, would make for Muros.

On 7th August, we left the Enseada de Bornalle on a south-southwesterly course, and anchored in the afternoon in the Enseada Rianja, after a lovely sail down this interesting coast. In Villagarcia, we anchored in a sheltered spot, inside a number of floats, which we now knew were used for mussel breeding. We thought it our nicest village anchorage so far. In the evening, we went ashore for a meal in the fairly clean Bar de Moelle. The wine was like vinegar but the soup was hot, and the fish in batter and veal and chips were very welcome. Along the nearby road, posh Mercedes cars competed for space with horsedrawn carts. We made our way back to the boat after dark, down the malodorous steps, filthy with fish guts, to the sanctuary of our boat. By now there was drizzling rain and a low mist, above which stars could be seen.

On 11th August we left under main, staysail and small jib, then changed to the yankee. We soon rounded Caneiro and wondered if the brownish haze on the western horizon might be smoke from a forest fire on Sierra de Barbanza. At 10.15am we changed course to clear Cape Finisterre, and by noon we were motoring in calm water. We had to use the engine a lot in the blistering calm and saw mirages everywhere. For a few hours, we sailed in light following airs. Making the most of a change of wind to westerly, we made good progress with engine and sail to anchor in Ria de Camarinas at 6pm. I then went ashore for petrol and some steak, while Charles and Roger cooked two huge crabs but could not find any meat (which is found in the claws, and not under the carapace!). We sat in the cockpit for supper in the cool of the evening. There were no crickets here, unlike Muros, and the hills were barer and less inhabited. Drops of rain began to fall with cloud from the west; then a thunderstorm broke, with brilliant lightning.

Early on 13th August we were at Coruna, and a yacht called the *Bella Donna* came in and anchored near us. We had lunch at the Club, where we met the crew of the new arrival, two doctors, Bob and Sheila Fleming, bound for the West Indies. They came over for a drink later and told us about the self-steering device they were using, developed by Hasler, which they recommended. After lunch we moved stern-on to the quay, to take water on board and then anchored further east to make room for a British frigate, which was due in the next day. A chap at the Yacht Club that night, who helped interpret the menu, told us that the coast round Finisterre was known as the Costa del Muerte ('Coast of Death') because it had once been famed for the activities of wreckers with false lights.

A couple of days later, we departed. That afternoon it was pleasant to be going gently in warm sunshine over a calm sea, hearing the chuckle of water along the planks and the slight 'swoosh, swoosh' as she gently pitched, with no ocean swell and the sea not yet blue. We made very little progress, however, and by 5.30pm we were almost becalmed. We also attracted the attention of a shark, which came cruising round us. After a night of almost no movement, with a sea fog, and steamers hooting astern and to port, Roger took over at 6am on 16th August. Dawn came in quietly, in pale shades of blue and grey. A few hours later, the wind freshened rapidly from the southwest, and Roger and I handed the yankee, and hanked the small jib on the stay, though we did not set it, and reefed the main. She was then much easier to steer. It was hazy and sunny but the sea was getting up. By 3pm, Charles thought we were running a bit fast! We got the sails down and lay ahull. Big seas were getting up quickly and gales were forecast for Sole and North Finisterre. We remained hove-to with no sails set for the next 24 hours.

The next afternoon, we set the small jib, which made the motion much less sickening. The wind and seas moderated a bit and Charles wrote that they were fine to look at 'in form'. I might have added that they were not so good 'in feel', as we were both more or less laid out with seasickness. Roger, by contrast, seemed impervious, and steered valiantly for many extra hours. On 18th August it was blowing hard from the west, and the seas were becoming mountainous. A Swedish tanker came circling round us till we waved and signalled that we were OK. After a miserable night of noise and battering, we were damp, dispirited and cross, as well as sick. We had all our lights and radar reflector up as we had various ships around.

By 6pm the next day, there was a light northwest breeze, the seas were abating and the patients recovering. We appeared to have crossed the shipping lanes to westwards. The next day was again grey and cold, mainly raining, and very dreary. The wind eased at about 8pm, and we set the main, expecting it now to blow more gently from the northeast. Instead, there was torrential rain, lightning and a peal of thunder, and the wind blew very strongly from the southeast. We got out of our sleeping bags and put on oilskins to join Roger, who was in some difficulty. All sail was got off and we lay ahull, pointing southeast.

Next morning we changed to the other tack, heading northwest, with the wind still strong from the northeast. I was feeling lousy and Charles wrote in the log to express his gratitude to Roger and me, for agreeing to stand his night watches, as he was now too ill to stand them. In fact Roger did most of the work, as I was also pretty sick by now. At 6am on 22nd August Charles relieved Roger at the helm and they set the full main, staysail and small jib. With the wind backing northwest, he was able to steer north-northeast (by compass). The sun came up, a livid red, at 9am. It was no longer as warm as on the Spanish coast.

By 4pm, we were sailing with a light beam wind in sunshine on calm seas. It was fine, with towers of white cumulus over the horizon. In the mouth of the Channel there wasn't a ship in sight. We had tea in the cockpit, and fruitcake, with lovely Spanish melons. All our wet things were laid out in the sun to dry. I lay asleep on a mattress on a side deck, while Charles and Roger made up for starvation and tiredness on this restful day. 'A calm sea and a light westerly breeze,' Charles wrote, before going on first watch.

On 23rd August, after a marvellous quiet moonlit night, on a calm sea with a moderate west wind, *Triune* was going fast and steady. There was a full moon and little cumulus clouds, with the whole concourse of the stars 'wheeling in immortal flight', as Charles put it, quoting Milton. At 6am, he noted that the wind was freshening and backing, and there was another livid sunrise. By 9am, we were tearing along under staysail and reefed main. There were two seas: a big swell from the west-northwest and a smaller one from south-southwest. The sky was broken, blue here and there with grey horizons.

On 24th August at 9am Charles saw the coast. Half an hour later we were at the Daunt Rock Light Vessel, and at 11.45am we anchored at Crosshaven, after beating up the Channel in fitful airs against the last of the tide. The log read 520 miles. We could rest at last, and we spent an evening at the Yacht Club. We all made phone calls and Charles arranged for my brother Ian and Pat Wood to fly out to join him in a couple of days. The next day Roger and I left by bus for Dublin and a passage back to Holyhead. Meanwhile Charles took a car to the boat yard to organise repairs, before the arrival of his next crew.

CHAPTER 15

## *Buying Ardincaple*

In 1965 our youngest son, Peter, was born on 18th July. Towards the end of the summer I was able to drive Chuck, our eldest, to sail with Charles to Loch Craignish, via the Crinan Canal. The University of Wales had a rotating Vice-Chancellorship, and in September 1965 it was Charles' turn, which meant more journeys by train or car. The following year, 1966, was eventful. That Easter, Charles started flying in a Chipmunk over Central Wales and Snowdonia. This marked the start of air transport for his crucial university meetings. He was able to get a small plane to take him to London and elsewhere from Valley Airport in Anglesey. The College administrators, and the very helpful porters, made a huge difference to Charles' everyday life. I was grateful to them all and to his indefatigable private secretary, Miss Morris-Jones, who typed out his war memoirs.

While Charles was flying in the Chipmunk, I was taking Chuck, now a sturdy six-year-old, skiing at Hochsölden, in Austria with Nea. It was a high resort, accessible from the valley by chairlift, giving access to wide, open slopes with plenty of snow, and ideal for beginners. Playing in the snow one morning with Chuck outside our hotel, I was accosted by a German who started berating me vociferously but unintelligibly. He seemed to take exception to my having anything to do with this blue-eyed, fair-haired, boy, and I wondered if he had mistaken me for a Jewess. There were many Nazis still around. Chuck quickly took to skiing, and eventually became a strong and capable skier.

For some time, Charles and I had been looking for a house of our own somewhere in Snowdonia. When Charlie Brennand, a friend who lived in Capel Curig, where he ran a climbing shop, told us that a house on the outskirts of the village, known as

'Ardincaple' and later 'Glyn Curig', was for sale, we lost no time in viewing it and putting in an offer. It was exactly the sort of house we wanted, in exactly the right place. It was no surprise to hear that others were after it, notably an education committee, who wanted to turn it into a centre for outdoor recreation. I kept nudging Charles to tell the owners that, if the sale fell through for any reason, we were very keen to acquire the house. He did so – and, because some members of the committee were undecided, the sale did fall through.

We purchased Ardincaple that Easter, and decided to keep the

*Ardincaple*

name, which intrigued us. Cruising in Scotland later, we saw that there was a property on Seal Island in the Firth of Lorne called Ardincaple. We wondered if there was any connection, but did not go ashore to investigate. However, we learned more about the house from the deeds. It was built at the turn of the century by a Scottish gentleman, Hector Macaulay, who came down from Scotland to run Garth Farm, in Capel Curig. He started negotiations with the Penrhyn Estate, to whom the land belonged, in 1887, and, having spent £1,000 on building the house, he signed a lease for £6 per annum with George Penrhyn in 1890. Macaulay also built a footbridge over the River Llugwy, on the far side of the main road, to enable him to reach the farm on foot. By the time we purchased the house in 1966, most of the bridge had been swept away by floods.

Ardincaple stood on a levelled terrace on the slopes that ran up towards the Carneddau range, at the northwest end of Capel Curig in a woodland property of some 2.4 acres. It was solidly built of grey granite, like many other houses in the neighbourhood, and had two floors. The main rooms faced south. Over the years, Charles and I made a number of internal changes, with help from the college architects, but the basic shape stayed the same.

Meanwhile other events took precedence. Charles' mother, Edith, and her sister Dora both fell ill in the summer and, sadly, Edith died in July. Any sailing was limited to local areas, and at the end of the season I had to move *Triune* to Dickie's Yard in September. Charles' health was getting worse and in January 1967 I drove him to the Hospital for Nervous Diseases in London, where he was fitted with a wheelchair and elbow crutches. With specially adapted hand controls, he was still able to drive his car for a time, but getting into it from the wheelchair was a problem, which we overcame by using a polished board to slip under him. It was typical of Charles that he should make the most of being in London to take the nurses on an outing to the *Cutty Sark* and the Greenwich meridian.

By the spring we had begun to make some use of Ardincaple, but in June Charles went down with mumps, and went into the

Northern Hospital in Liverpool, where he stayed for a couple of months. Chuck and I, and many friends, were able to visit him there. Very sadly, but faced with the reality of Charles' illness, I managed to sell *Triune* to three enthusiastic young men, who promptly painted her bright yellow. She changed hands a few times after that, but eventually, many years later, we were very kindly invited to *Triune's* 50th anniversary celebrations by Angela and Roger Richards, who owned her at the time.

Charles was brought home by Ken Tarbuck in August 1967 and in December he was elected President of the Alpine Club. To get to the committee meetings in London, he used to drive to his cousin Glyn's in Hitchin for the night, but for this, and the next two years, the summer meetings were held at Ardincaple.

In June 1968, Margery and Stan Palmer stayed at Bryn Haul, to look after Charles and the boys, while Sheila Crispin, a student at Bangor, who was also a member of the Pinnacle Club, came with me to the Shetlands to explore Foula, an outlying island 12 miles west of Scalloway. Leaving the car in Aberdeen, we sailed to Lerwick, where Captain Inkster very kindly contacted Raffy Cummings, who came to take us by car to Walls. We then took a small boat to Vaila, boarded the *Utopian* and sailed across to Foula. At Ham Voe, we met some locals, who offered us the use of a deserted croft a mile or two inland. We walked along a grassy track in a westerly direction to where it stood, empty and desolate, in the middle of Foula. On the way to the croft, we were incessantly bombarded by arctic skuas, which dived down with an eerie cry to within an inch of our scalps, so that we had to carry sticks above our heads for protection.

Our idea had been to explore and, if possible, climb the stupendous sea-cliffs bordering the island, but although we were able to get close enough to prospect, we soon saw that these sandstone cliffs (which resembled the Old Man of Hoy) would be beyond us. After a late breakfast next day, we walked over to Smallie, between the Sneug (at 1,372 feet, the highest point on the island) and Hamnafjeld, trying not to tread on baby bonxies. It was a long slog. We went down the Sneck of the Smallie and along shag-ridden rocks towards Wester Hoevda, but then turned our attention to the Noup, which looked very rotten. On the other side we saw more small cliffs further south.

It was fine on Monday 1st July and we went up Soberlie Hill, looking over the cliff edge at intervals, sometimes roped up with a view to finding ways down, but saw nothing at all promising. After walking over the Kame, a promontory halfway down the west coast, we walked along a path under the upper tier of cliffs between Wester Hoevda and Smallie, where the cliffs looked better, but very loose. A few days later we explored Ruscar Head. We found the garnetiferous schists mentioned in a geological pamphlet, and managed to prise out pale garnets with a piton hammer! Well pleased with our unusual foray, we made our way back to Lerwick, and left for the Scottish mainland on 9th July.

I spent the rest of the summer in our new house with Charles and the boys. Nea joined us in August, and she and I took Chuck over to the Moelwyns to do *Slick*, which Chuck climbed with ease. We moved down to Bangor on 12th September. During this month I was able to join Dennis Davis and his friend Sheila down at Tremadog, where we climbed *Craig Dhu Wall*, *Scratch* and *Olympic Slab*, as well as *Curving Crack* on Clogwyn Du'r Arddu and *Skylon* in the Llanberis Pass.

At this stage Charles was still able to walk up through our mountain gate to the hillside beyond, and also down the drive, over the road and, with help through scrub, to the river bank. However, taking Charles fly-fishing involved pushing him in his wheelchair over rough ground and through running water to reach a point in the river from which he could cast, and eventually helping him to net his catch. Some of the college porters were adept at these tasks. In particular, Leonard Thomas, who lived down at Plas Gwyn, a recently built hall of residence, close to Bryn Haul, was a keen fly-fisherman himself; and he managed to take Charles fishing on the Conway and the Lledr, to special pools and places which would have been inaccessible to him otherwise.

In October a delegation of Russian climbers, including our good friend Eugene Gippenreuter, came to Wales, and we were able to introduce them to our favourite cliffs, including Clogwyn Du'r Arddu, the Llanberis Pass and Tremadog. Unfortunately Eugene sustained an injury after a fall on Cloggy and ended up in hospital. When we invited him to stay with us to recuperate, he seemed much less bothered about his injuries than staying with his Russian team, no doubt for good political reasons. Fortunately he made a quick recovery.

Charles' deteriorating health prompted me to think about taking a job and in January 1969 I began to teach French in the university, under Dr Busst, Professor of French. It was a position for which I was not sufficiently academically qualified, but my facility with the language meant that I was able to help students with their translations. The students were keen to learn but many of them had not had a sufficiently thorough grounding in the rudiments of French grammar at school, so my work was something of a remedial activity – rather like patching a garment that was full of holes!

I was familiar with the problems of translation, as I had witnessed Nea translating French mountaineering books, and I had worked on my own translation of Jean Franco's *Makalu*. I became particularly interested in metaphor, which of course needs some ingenuity when it comes to translation. Having enjoyed *The Meaning of Meaning*, by Ogden, Richards and Malinowski, I should have stuck to a linguistic approach. Instead, I let myself be sidetracked into following a psycho-linguistic approach, which involved an initial apprenticeship in the rudiments of psychology. But I had to tell the Professor, over a cup of coffee, that I could not go on with the course. 'What will you do?' he asked, and I heard myself answering, as if from another world, 'High latitude sailing,' which was what I really wanted to do. For the time being, however, I kept on with the French classes.

In March there was enough snow for me to carry my skis up to the top of Carnedd Dafydd and ski down into the Ogwen Valley. The next month, I took Chuck skiing in Argentière, near Chamonix, where he continued to make good progress. A couple of months later, on 5th June, Barbara Spark and her friend Kate, who had invited us to dinner the night before, had a very nasty accident on Craig yr Ysfa, when they fell while climbing *Great Gully* and ended up in hospital. I spent most of the next day there. Barbara was very uncomfortable when not doped with medication, and Kate was shellshocked. It brought home to us the down-side of mountaineering in general and rock climbing in particular, but it did not remove my desire to climb.

Both girls recovered, and a few weeks later I was climbing with Janet Rogers, who led me up *The Brother*s at Tremadog and *Pedestal Crack* on Cloggy. After another few days, we tackled a harrowing descent to sea level and up *Stochastic Groove*, a fiendish climb on the sea cliffs at South Stack, where the first pitch involved leaping over a wide chasm full of churning seawater, to grab the cliff on the far side. It was wonderful though, to be helped back to this level of climbing by someone so talented, and to banish, if only temporarily, those 'What if?' feelings.

In June Charles was knighted 'for services to mountaineering' and in November Chuck and I went to see him dubbed by Her Majesty at Buckingham Palace. Afterwards we had a celebratory lunch with Nea and my brother Ian, before going to see the *Battle of Britain* film.

Above: Denise and the boys,
left to right: Chuck, Denise,
Robin and Peter.
Right: Robin, Peter and Chuck

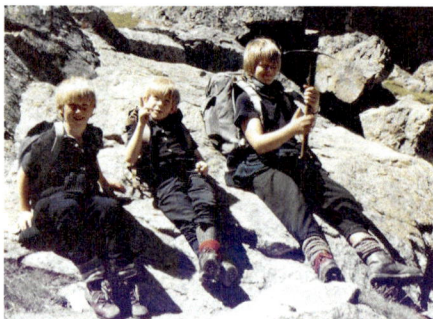

## CHAPTER 16

# Skiing and Sailing with the Boys

At the end of March 1970 I took Chuck to London, where we stayed with Nea at Ian's flat before flying to Geneva and on to Zermatt the next day. We stayed at the comfortable Hotel Flexen, where Ian and his friend John joined us for dinner. They were both staying at the Bahnhof, an excellent base for the less well-off. It was great fun getting to know some of the runs on my first visit to the resort and to be able to ski with Chuck, once we'd got him fitted out with skis and organised lessons for him.

On 7th April, we made an early start in the hope of doing the Breithorn, but the weather was hopeless high up, with strong winds and no visibility. Ian lost a ski screw and I skied down the Mamatt run. The next day we made another early start for the Breithorn and got right up to Testa Grigia in nil visibility. We could see a group of people skiing down; they turned out to be a BBC team who were filming *The Last Blue Mountain*, with John Cleare among them. We went up to a snow hole, then on in wind and snow and mist to a broken lift pylon, dug a hole for lunch, got cold, and skied down.

The day after that, 9th April, dawned fine but cold. Ian and I took Chuck up to the Stockhorn, and skied with him down the big slope to the start of the Stockhorn ski lift, and skied down again. We then took the ski lift up again to the Hotalligrat, on a path where Chuck got very tired going uphill. The next afternoon Ian and I took the Gornergrat train up to Rotenboden with Chuck. We said goodbye to him there and went down a fearful icy slope, sidestepping on skins to the Gornergletscher, before trudging across to the Monte Rosa Hut in fine weather.

The hut was busy, with many skiers bound for Monte Rosa. Ian and I decided instead to make for Castor and Pollux via the

Zwillingsgletscher. The notes in my small diary stop at this point, but the events of the next few hours are firmly fixed in my memory. To reach the Twin Glacier, we covered a mile or so on skis, before putting on our skins. Ian was in the lead, as the more experienced ski mountaineer. My skiing up to now had been almost entirely devoted to pistes.

It was a fine day and all went swimmingly at first, though I found the uphill work quite taxing and must have been a bit of a drag, as I was conspicuously slower. As I plodded up, keeping an eye on Ian's rope, I suddenly became aware that it was no longer snaking out in front of me. Looking up, I could see no sign of Ian, who had simply disappeared. I fabricated a belay with axe and ski poles and hauled on the rope, which did not budge. Minutes passed, but there was no sound and no movement. If Ian could not extricate himself, we were going to need help. We had brought no whistles so I gave six calls in my loudest voice, and repeated them after a few moments. Later I learnt that I was heard by the *gardien* of the Monte Rosa Hut, who had happened to come outside just then.

After what seemed like another age, a head and a hand appeared and I was able to tell Ian that I had called for help. 'Shit!' he said, no doubt worrying about the hefty bill we might have incurred. Luckily Ian had not fallen more than about 30 feet, rattling against the icy walls, on to some kind of ledge, beneath which the crevasse went down further, to darker depths. He was able to remove his skis and eventually to post them up and across the crevasse, and use them to 'mantelshelf' out of it. Apart from straining his left shoulder he was unhurt and we were able to start skiing down, and we hadn't gone very far before a helicopter flew over us. We made vigorous signals to show we were all right, as we skied back to the Monte Rosa Hut, where we spent another night.

Back in Zermatt, we went on skiing with Chuck, who had his last ski lesson on 15th April, which was wonderfully fine and sunny. I went up to Sunnega, Blauherd and Rothorn with Nea and enjoyed superb views. Suddenly Ian turned up. He had spent the night at the top of the Signalkuppe and skied down the same day. The next day Chuck and I went up the Gornergrat. Ian joined us at Riffelberg and we skied up and down together. Later we saw Ian off on his train. By Friday, 17th April, all runs were *abgesperrt* (closed), so we went up lifts to a point near Trockener Steg and messed about looking for garnets on moraines. On Saturday Nea and I went up to Winkelmatten and then up to Trockener Steg. We followed the crest of a moraine up to the Gandegg Hut (3,029 metres) and sat in brilliant sunshine, watching the BBC team high up on the Breithorn.

After our return from Zermatt on 20th April, it was time for Chuck to go back to Heronwater, his prep school, for the summer term. During the next few months, Charles and I spent as much time as possible at Ardincaple. With help from the college and the locals, we made a lawn on the south side of the house (replacing the previous owners' heather garden) and a vegetable patch. It was hard but rewarding work and after a few months we were growing enough vegetables to feed the family during the holidays. Eventually we made an enclosure for raspberries, which did well in our rather wet climate.

There were already a few apple trees, which produced apples suitable for cooking, though they were not as good as Bramleys. I was really more interested in planting a number of colourful dwarf rhododendrons and azaleas to brighten the terrace, as well as enhancing other parts of the garden. There was already a big thuja (evergreen shrub) below the lower terrace, and we planted three more, one for each of the boys, so they could watch them grow as they grew up themselves.

I still found time to explore more remote places, like Cwm Pennant, with Robin and Peter, where they spent happy hours in the stream and also to take Chuck up easy climbs, like *Rowan Route* on Tryfan's Milestone Buttress. I had already taken the boys rowing on the Mymbyr lakes in an old dinghy of ours and now Charles and I decided to get a proper sailing dinghy. We bought a 'Mirror', which I towed back from Leicester on 17th August, and launched it the next day with Chuck. It was a great success and we sailed it from Plas y Brenin up through the narrows to the furthest lake. Towards the end of the month, Chuck and I bivouacked by Llyn Llydaw, and made an early ascent of Lliwedd next day. Meanwhile Charles enjoyed salmon fishing as often as he could find the time. These enjoyable activities did not, however, make up for our great sense of loss on parting with *Triune*. Edwin understood our plight, and very kindly offered to let me sail *Crystal II* with the boys during the next few years, an offer which I accepted gratefully, as I had a lot to learn about managing a yacht. I was glad too that the boys would get some experience of cruising.

In March 1971, after some heavy snow falls, I went with Val Brown and Bridget Marshall, a Bangor friend, up a gully at the top of Nameless Cwm above Idwal, for which we roped up. At the very top there was an accumulation of snow forming a cornice, through which we had to cut our way. It was quite awkward, but good fun. I wondered if Bridget might come sailing with me in June. In the event, she and her husband Donald both came. On 8th June, I drove up to Oban in the Mercedes with Bridget. We reached Oban by teatime, and went for dinner with Edwin, who was staying with Donald Currie, the boatman. I was able to leave the Mercedes in the Curries' garden and conferred with Edwin next morning, while Bridget went ashore to meet Donald's train at about 1pm.

Next morning, the wind seemed rather strong and we all felt apprehensive. By about teatime that afternoon, however, the wind had dropped and we sailed, under double-reefed main, down the Sound of Kerrera, which was sheltered from the northeast. We shot across the Firth of Lorne, which was quite rough, and into Loch Spelve, on the south side of Mull. We were glad of our nice, muddy anchorage off Ardachoil Farm, with the CQR anchor and 'chum' down (a weight that slides down the anchor chain to improve the angle of the chain to the sea bed and improve holding), as the weather was far from pleasant, with rain leaking through the deck. Bridget and Donald went ashore while I listened to forecasts.

On 12th June there were forecasts of strong winds over Malin. We went for a sail in the loch with two reefs in the main, to get the hang of beating, which was very hard work, and anchored again in much the same spot. In the afternoon another yacht came and anchored just inshore of us. We soon made friends with Walter and Peggy Emerson, one of whom was familiar with Harrison's Rocks, and they came over after supper for a chat. The next day, the wind was much lighter; and we sailed out of Loch Spelve at high tide. We then went up the Firth to Duart Point under sail and engine, managing to beat the tide. It was a fine day as we steamed up the Sound of Mull, looked into Tobermory Bay, then went across to Auliston Point where the wind freshened. We put in to Loch Drumbuie, where we filled up with petrol, before running back to Tobermory and anchoring in the Doirlinn Narrows.

On Monday, 14th June, the weather was still propitious as we motored out of the bay and put up the sails. We ran down to Duart Point where we and another yacht were becalmed. The wind came up after a while and we sailed about in the Firth before coming into Oban Bay past Maiden Isle. We gybed off the entrance and again off Dunollie Castle and picked up the mooring under engine. The next morning, we left Oban and, as I drove back to Bangor, I began to realise how much I still had to learn as a skipper.

I had arranged to borrow *Crystal* again at the end of August, this time with Chuck, Robin and Peter, and with Sheila Crispin to help me. After celebrating Chuck's birthday on 24th August, by taking him up the *North Buttress* climb on the east face of Tryfan, I drove the boys back up to Scotland on 28th August. They were so excited they hardly slept the night before. We left at 5am and reached Tighnabruaich in Argyll, where Edwin used to keep *Crystal* over the winter months, by 4pm. Sheila appeared and there was much rowing to and fro. Edwin had already put some food on board, which I was able to cook that evening.

We squeezed into this small cruising boat, which was really only comfortable for two, and somehow we all managed to bed down for the night. The next day, we motored to nearby Glen Caladh, and explored the island, where we found the tomb of a young boy who had sadly drowned there years before. There were a number of motor yachts about and one or two sailing boats. In the middle of the night a yacht came in under engine, moored rather close to us and seemed to drift even closer. We up-anchored first thing in the morning, motored over to the Butt of Bute and looked at the first anchorage, opposite the Burnt Isles. The wind was gusty, and I found the boat awkward to handle, especially compared to *Triune*, which, although much larger, handled like a dinghy.

A couple of days later we moved to a sandy anchorage off Woodpark Farm at the Burnt Isles, and anchored off a buoy, which marked a rock. I was worried about drifting back onto it and the next day I decided to shift to a point south of the buoy. *Crystal's* engine failed to start just as we were about to up-anchor. Sheila thought it had seized up, and we suspected a leak, as we had seen oil in the bilge water. I went ashore with Robin and Peter and walked to the Butt of Bute to see what the wind was doing: it appeared to be coming straight down Loch Riddon. The only solution was to beat back up through the south passage of the Burnt Isle narrows with the tide. This we did, with some trepidation. 'Are we sinking yet?' Robin calmly enquired from below deck, where he was reading about dinosaurs. We sailed back to the mooring, which we just managed to pick up after repeated attempts. I then went to look for Jimmie Smith. On 5th September Jimmie came on board, got the engine going and sailed with us across to Lochranza, where we anchored and went to look at the castle.

Our last few days on *Crystal* were spent back in Glen Caladh, where we went blackberrying, and the boys fished, and went with Sheila to the farm for milk. We made a start at cleaning up *Crystal* before putting her back on her mooring at Tighnabruaich on 8th September for our last night on board. At 7.30am the next day, Chuck rowed Sheila ashore, and after breakfast I drove the boys down to Balquhidder to visit and thank Edwin, who lived in what he called his hut, a cottage in the grounds of Achtubhmore, a big house which had once belonged to his family.

CHAPTER 17

## *Family Matters*

In early 1972 I was following psychology courses on thinking and language, as well as on experimental design. Looking back, I can see that I had taken on more than I could cope with. Meanwhile Charles was busy settling problems in the college as well as hosting various visiting lecturers, including Dorothy Hodgkin (a Nobel Prize-winning chemist), who spent a wet afternoon with us, when she clearly would have preferred a gathering of like-minded intellectuals. Charles was by now having visits from Eleanor, who came weekly to give him physio, to ease his paralysed legs. Fortunately I had secured the services of a really good and trustworthy domestic helper, Sheila Davies, whose husband Owen also helped me in the garden at Ardincaple.

At the beginning of April, Aunt Micheline sent us a telegram saying that she was ill, and I felt sad that I was not in a position to help her. A few days later I took a train to Liverpool and spent a few days at the Northern Hospital, where our friend Dr Thelwall Jones gave me a thorough 'going over', eventually deciding that, though my blood levels were 'rather swingy', everything appeared to be in order. Soon after that, we heard that Micheline had died. Ian rang to say that she had left no will, and I foresaw inheritance problems connected with the Ranelagh flat in Paris. In the end I handed the matter over to a lawyer to sort out, which may have been a mistake.

Chuck, who was now head boy at Heronwater, passed his Common Entrance exam in June. After much deliberation, Charles and I decided to send him to Eton which, surprisingly enough, turned out to be the right school for him, where he was able to make the most of his rowing and sculling prowess. On 3rd August we left for Scotland very early with Chuck and Robin and met

*Top: The family in the late 1960s. Above: Denise sailing, 1973.*

Edwin and Sheila at Oban that afternoon. Next day we mended sails, filled breakers (plastic water containers, typically 25 litres), shopped, got the centrifugal pump mended, and sailed down the Sound of Kerrera until we could see the entrance to Loch Spelve, before returning to the Brandystone. After that, we motored up the Sound of Mull to Tobermory, and sailed into Loch Sunart. We anchored in mud in the southeast corner of Loch Drumbuie (Loch na Droma Buidhe) and then Chuck rowed us out from the east end of the loch and we landed on the island of Eilan Nan Eildean.

After a reasonable forecast a couple of days later, we set off for Ardnamurchan in rain and poor visiblity. The wind was southerly, the sea lumpy, and landmarks were blotted out by intermittent rain squalls. We picked up Eigg Beacon and Bo Faskadale and set a course up the Sound of Sleat. Having picked up the light on Sleat Point, we identified Mallaig through binoculars. We left the boat in Mallaig, to be brought south again, and my diary resumes on 17th August, when we drove to Balquhidder. We spent the evening with Edwin and stayed at the Kingshouse Hotel for the night. A couple of days later I drove to Callander, where I bought two small steel wood axes for Robin and Peter, before starting for home. Edwin seemed shocked at my giving them such lethal presents.

For the second half of August, the weather was fine and we spent a lot of time on the hills and in the swimming pool at Plas y Brenin. We had to water our fruit and vegetables regularly, every day. But we found time for a great family expedition one afternoon to *Rowan Route* on the Milestone Buttress, where Chuck led Nea on one rope and I led Robin and Peter on another. Ian came to stay with Mickie, his girlfriend, and took Chuck up Crib Goch.

Chuck's first 'half' started on 12th September and I drove down to Eton with him and Robin. Towards the end of the month, I drove over to Anglesey to spend some time with Mr B, whose life was coming to an end. He sounded quite lively though at times confused, and I already felt the loss of his very special friendship, and very sorry too for Mads, his constant companion. Charles completed his second term as Vice-Chancellor of the University of Wales in 1973, and we were able to live up at Ardincaple from

May to November. We sowed grass seed on the south side of the house, and made a lawn, which was apt to get rather mossy. We were very glad of our hillside water supply, which never ran out, though Charles worried that it might, and I was able to water our kitchen vegetables regularly every day.

Charles held his last Alpine Club Committee meeting at the house. We also celebrated the 20th Everest Reunion in May, and had many visits from old-timers, notably Noel Odell, who came to dinner, and whose verve as a raconteur seemed undiminished. (Geologist Noel Odell recorded the last sighting of George Mallory and Andrew Irvine before they disappeared on Everest in June 1924.) Meanwhile, our old friend Edwin suffered his first major operation in Glasgow and spent some time in a nursing home, before getting back to his hut at Achtubhmore.

In August I drove the boys to France in the Mercedes, while Charles bought a new Rover, fitted with special hand controls. At this time there was an embargo on anyone spending more than £200 abroad and I envisaged problems feeding my brood as well as buying fuel. I therefore stocked up with as much dried and canned food as possible and stowed it mainly in the ample Mercedes boot. We took the ferry to Calais, where we became aware that the boot had dropped below its normal level and was knocking on the cobblestones. Alarmed, we pulled into a garage where they told us we had broken the hydro-pneumatic compensating spring, and would need a new one, which would have to be sent for from Lille. We found some cheap accommodation, and next morning the new compensating spring was fitted. Paying for it used up all our contingency money in one go. We redistributed the weight further forward in the car before launching down the A16 for the South, somewhat abashed by this early *contretemps*.

Later that evening we pulled off the motorway somewhere beween Tournus and Mâcon, in the heart of Burgundy, and camped in a field for the night. I would have liked to spend more time in this warm, wine-rich zone, but if we were to reach the Hautes Alpes we had to move on in the morning. By the next evening, we had reached Vizille, a little town south of Grenoble, which had an official campsite. As we came out of the malodorous *toilettes*, Robin asked, 'Do we have to use these places?' to which I replied, 'That's the last one.' We were now well on our way to the Bourg d'Oisans, La Grave and the Col du Lautaret, which gave access to Briançon and the Vallouise Valley. As we sped over and down the pass, I was reminded of the many happy family holidays I had enjoyed here over the years, and hoped the boys would have similar experiences.

From the valley floor down below Briançon, we turned right up a small road that led past the Vallon des Étages to the end of the road at Cézanne. We camped on grassy level ground just above the treeline. There were other children nearby, with whom Robin made friends. We soon had our tents up and before going to bed I had recourse to what the boys referred to as 'Mummy's little help-along': a tot of whisky. This became something of a routine.

The next morning we packed our sacks with what we thought we would need for the next few days up on the glacier, which meant ice axes, crampons, ropes, slings for each of us, dark glasses, snack food, anoraks, over-trousers and so on. Wearing our heavy boots, we began the steep trudge towards the Glacier Blanc, several hundred metres above us. It was hard work and we were unaccustomed to the height. Every now and then Peter would fling down his axe in mutinous fashion, but somehow we all reached the foot of the glacier, and energies revived as the boys had their first experience of glacier ice, which was bare of snow at this level. They enjoyed peering down deep crevasses and hearing the gurgling of meltwater far below. Once they'd got them properly strapped on, they quickly adapted to wearing crampons, and became quite nimble.

We followed a well-trodden path, marked at intervals by cairns. The large and well-built Refuge du Glacier Blanc (2,550m) stood on a terrace beneath the Montagne des Agneaux, not far from the old Refuge Tuckett, which preceded it. Les Agneaux had been my first big Alpine peak, when Micheline and her friend Etienne took me up it in the 1950s. The *refuge* was now extremely busy and expensive, but we managed to find space in one of the *dortoirs* for the night.

Next morning, we set off for the upper section of the Glacier Blanc, leading to what was then known as the Refuge Caron (3,170m). After putting on our crampons, we roped up. The art of climbing roped, with coils of rope in one hand and an ice axe in the other, does not come naturally. It has to be learned and needs much patience. All went well until we came to a point where we needed to descend from our branch of the glacier to the main branch, across a bergschrund, where it was important not to slide on down under the ice into the remote depths of the glacier. Once this essential manoeuvre had been completed, and not without some trouble, it was simply a matter of plodding on and on, up the main glacier, stopping often for snacks and drinks as the sun bore down on us, and trying to avoid losing anything down the crevasses we crossed.

Some time later that afternoon we reached the Refuge Caron, and made ourselves known to the *gardien*. I remembered climbing here many years earlier, when Jacques Monod had taken me and his two young sons up the Pic du Glacier Blanc. I wondered if I might be able to repeat the climb with Chuck, who was well up for it, but it would have meant leaving Robin and Peter behind in the hut unsupervised. Understanding my predicament, the *gardien* offered to look after the younger boys while we did the climb, and I accepted gratefully. Chuck and I crept out early next morning, heading for a bergschrund, which proved to be the crux of our climb. After negotiating it successfully, we gained the col, from which an easy ridge led to the summit of the Pic du Glacier Blanc. Well pleased, we carefully negotiated the bergschrund in reverse, and hurried back to the hut, where Robin and Peter were happily playing in the snow. Phew!

We made our way right down to Cézanne the next day and spent a day or two relaxing before deciding to move back to the Lautaret Valley. The heat of the summer sun made us long for high places, so we decided to go above La Grave, towards the Col du Galibier. We thought we would camp in open meadowland there, where we knew it would be much cooler. On the way, however, we stopped at Monêtier-les-Bains, and I decided to take my crew up to the Chalet de l'Alpe hut, which was easily accessible from the village, where we left the car, after some provisioning. My Aunt Micheline had taken me there many years earlier to climb the Tour Carrée de Rocheméane, which I had no thought of climbing with the boys. Just getting to the hut would be entertaining enough, following a track which wound in and out of *couloirs* (rocky side gullies) high above the torrent below. 'I love the coolers, Mum,' said Peter later.

The *gardien* proved most helpful and put us in a small *dortoir* for the night. The next day I felt bold enough to take Chuck, Robin and Peter up to the next hut, named after Adèle Planchard, at over 3,000 metres. The boys coped quite well with the change in height, but they were ravenous and we depended on the *gardien* for extra food, as our supplies were running out. After some fun in the snow, we made our way back to Le Monêtier-les-Bains, where we camped for the night and shopped for provisions before driving back up towards the Col du Lautaret. Leaving the car in a convenient layby, we shouldered our loads and set off up the mountainside to the pastures below the Col de l'Iseran, where Micheline's friend Marcelle Motte kept a gift shop. Sharing these mountain meadows with cows and sheep, we had time and space for rest and recuperation before our return through France and Britain, and finally to Ardincaple, where Ken and Marjorie Pearson were very kindly looking after Charles.

In 1974, Charles collected copies of John Merton's drawing of him, which was also exhibited at the Royal Academy. My own diary records seeing the film *Ring of Bright Water* in the new Arts building at Bangor University, and the first mention of riding lessons down at the riding school near Criccieth, to which I had already been in the war years. Now, partly influenced by Val Brown (who was a keen rider and took her own girls), I returned with the boys. It was good fun and I soon found myself going over small jumps. I was keen, too that the boys should get used to horses.

It was cold and snowy in January, and on the last day of Chuck's Christmas holiday we carried our skis up to the ridge between Carnedd Dafydd and Carnedd Llewelyn, where we found a large snowdrift. We skied there till 4pm, before retreating in wind and rain to Helyg and back to Ardincaple for tea. Later that January I cleared a lot of brambles in the garden and also planted a *picea glaucis* because I liked the blueish tinge of the needles. The blue spruce grew for a few years but then died. I did much better with seedlings from our local thuja, which was already a large tree, if a more ordinary green colour.

In early February, there was a special dinner for Professor J.Z. Young, who gave the annual Ballard Matthews Science Lecture, which was probably one of the best lectures on a scientific subject we ever heard. The following month, Richard Hughes (author of *A High Wind in Jamaica* and friend of Dylan Thomas) gave the annual Rowland Hughes Arts Lecture on 'Wales as the Writer's Habitat'. He claimed that the novel was the only art form where you could get into the mind of another being. What about biography, I wondered, but perhaps that did not qualify as an art form? Around this time, a man from Bang and Olufsen came to Ardincaple to install our new hifi system. Charles and I both enjoyed listening to classical music and were well-pleased with the improved quality of sound. In the garden the yellow crocuses were out and the blue ones just opening. It was heavenly.

I rang Nea to suggest a trip to Chamonix in April, to which she agreed. We both knew she would not be able to ski but we thought she might be able to do walks locally. By taking the lift up to the Col de Balme, she could do more walks up there, and have wonderful views of the Chamonix Valley; and so it proved. After various peregrinations, and a night journey by train from Paris to Chamonix, Nea and I, together with Chuck, Robin and Peter, made our way on 9th April to the head of the Chamonix Valley, to the village of Le Tour. There we hired boots and skis. We then took the small ski lift close by and the boys and I went up and down the easiest runs several times. The next morning we took a cable car up to the Chalets de Charamillon, and the Col de Balme, for the first time, and spent an hour or so identifying the Chamonix Aiguilles, with which Nea was, of course, very familiar. The boys and I turned to point our skis downhill and began to get to know the easier pistes.

A couple of days later, Nea, my brother Ian, the three boys and I met up with Jeanne Franco (who had been on the 1959 all-woman Nepal Expedition) and Marianne Terray (another climbing friend), who took me up to the Grands Montets and down the 'Glacier', an off-piste route. The next day, Ian, Chuck and I met Marianne at Lognan. She and Jeanne took us down the 'Glacier' run, and then the 'Point de Vue'. On that second run, Chuck broke a ski but was able to ski down back to Le Tour, while Ian and I went up again and did the Traversée Bochard. On Easter Day, I went back up to the Col de Balme with Chuck and Peter and we met Ian, who was trying out skins on his new skis. It began to snow and then rain but Peter managed four *descentes* before lunch at the hotel.

Having 'settled u'p in Le Tour, we went down to Jeanne's chalet 'Le Lyrure' with all our bags. Marianne turned up and Jeanne made supper for us, after which we took a taxi to the station, and boarded a night train to Paris. We slept surprisingly well on the *couchettes* and arrived at 7am on 23rd April, the anniversary of Micheline's death. We spent the day in Paris and went to see Colette before taking a night passage to London.

*Denise by Glaslyn, Wales, in the 1970s*

## CHAPTER 18

### *Sailing in the Hebrides*

I was delighted when Nea agreed to come with me and the boys on *Crystal II* in August 1974. It was to be a different kind of holiday from our usual cruising. After picking up the boat from the yard in Mallaig, I planned to sail or motor her round into Loch Nevis and anchor at the southern end of Loch Tarbert, where Donald MacDonald and his sister kindly offered to put Nea up in their lochside croft. The boys and I would live on board and use Crystal and her dinghy to explore the neighbourhood and do some walking in the hinterland.

All went according to plan, though when we picked *Crystal* up in Mallaig she reeked of petrol, as the yard had just refuelled her. Having stowed all our food and gear, we set off for Loch Nevis, which was only about 12 miles to the north. The weather was fine but I thought it wiser to dispense with sails and simply motor to our anchorage. We got into Tarbert at 8pm with the oil pressure on 'red', but we still needed the motor to anchor. Once this had been achieved, we rowed ashore and introduced ourselves to Mr MacDonald and his sister, who welcomed Nea to their cottage. After a good night's sleep, we rowed back to the cottage and in the afternoon we walked over to the next bay north of ours and saw an old boat on shore which had belonged to Tom McClean, whom we met there. He had rowed it single-handed across the Atlantic. Someone else did the same in an even smaller boat, whereupon Tom cut down his boat to make it shorter still, and repeated the feat. It sounded a crazy enterprise.

A few days after our arrival, Robin took Edwin's dinghy for a row, and we suddenly realised that he had somehow lost an oar overboard. Quick as a flash, Chuck said, 'Shall I jump in?' I said, 'Yes', and he swam purposefully to the oar, which was closer to us than the dinghy, in which Robin was now floating away down the loch. Carrying the oar as he swam, Chuck managed to reach Robin, climb into the dinghy and row back. Nea and I both felt that I should have been the one to jump in, but Chuck was probably the stronger swimmer, and had saved his brother.

Not long after this, Chuck sailed the dinghy round to Easter Cottage; and the day after, we rowed to Beith Island and saw seals basking on the rocks. On 9th August we rowed to Stoul in the dinghy and saw some deer. Peter and I peered into an eerie-looking deserted cottage there, which had an unpleasantly musty smell. The next day, Mr MacDonald took us in his boat to Camusrory, from which Chuck and I were able to climb Sgurr na Ciche, which was about the same height as Snowdon. Near the top we felt an earth tremor, which was disquieting.

On Sunday 11th August the mailboat arrived but had no petrol for us, so we made arrangements with Tom McClean to bring some. A couple of days later, the weather was very fine and we washed in the nearby waterfall stream. We were now keen to get back to Mallaig but the weather grew really stormy during the next few days. The forecast on 16th August, the day of our departure, spoke of southwesterly winds, force 6–8, veering northwesterly, force 5. The morning started unpromisingly, with rain and wind and no visibility, but later the weather quietened and lifted. After a couple of hours getting ready and weighing anchors which were not too badly tangled, we got away by about 12.30 and reached Mallaig a couple of hours later, with the engine going steadily, though the oil pressure was low.

The next day, I bought an anchor for Donald MacDonald, by way of a thank-you present, hoping it would reach him by mailboat. Rùm, Eigg and Skye looked lovely as we drove along the coast between Morar and Arisaig. We rang Charles, had supper at the Kingshouse, paid a visit to Edwin, and did the same over the following two days, before heading back to Wales on 20th August.

After our return to Wales, in early September, my old friends, Gaie and Toby, his mother and their son Jonathan came to dinner one evening. Two days later, we went up Cwm Pennant with them and then on to the main ridge above. Mulling over the boys' education, we decided to change Robin and Peter's prep schools. To help Robin pass his entrance exams for public school, we planned to send him to South Lea, on the south coast, for special coaching by a Mr Vibert. Meanwhile, Peter would go to Lockers Park, where the Trower boys all went. Nea left for the south while I began packing for the boys' last term at Heronwater. Charles and I drove them back there on 17th September, and we moved down to Bangor in November.

Later that month, Charles was able to bring Ivor and Dorothy Richards from London back to Bangor by plane for a ten-day visit, which gave us all great pleasure. (Ivor Richards was a noted literary critic and his wife Dorothy, a prominent mountaineer, helped found the Pinnacle Club.) Ivor had been asked to give a lecture on a subject of his choosing. He chose 'The Phoenix and the Turtle', a rather obscure late poem by Shakespeare, for his first talk, and gave us a masterly analysis. He had that rare gift as a speaker of making you feel, while he spoke, that you understood. While they were with us, I drove them to the Idwal Slabs, where Ivor and Dorothy, together with C.F. Holland, had made the first ascent of *Hollytree Wall Original Route* on 22nd May 1918. Ivor also brought a matchbox for Charles containing a holly leaf from the original tree. On the path up to the lake we had to climb over some stiles. As she bestrode one of these, I was amused to hear Dorothy call out imperiously, 'Support me at once, Ivor!'

We stayed at Ardincaple well on into November in 1974, improving the house and garden, and carrying on with riding lessons as well as walking and a little climbing with the boys. Charles had a slight relapse of MS in the autumn and was put on a drug called ACTH. For the next few years, I borrowed *Crystal* in the summer months, often with Sheila Crispin, and we went on exploring the west coast of Scotland and then the east coast of the Outer Hebrides, as we nudged a little further westwards.

Now that I had become increasingly familiar with Scottish waters, I began to think again about getting out to St Kilda. I had been unable to go with Charles when he sailed there in *Triune of*

*Troy* in 1962, as I had just come back from the Jagdula Expedition and was needed at home. Charles' photographs from that trip showed a sinister group of stacks and islets which rose starkly from the sea under a threatening sky. I had read Martin Martin's account, published in 1698, in which he describes this group of islands as 'being well fenced with a raging sea', and was sorry to have missed the experience. Sheila was by now at Cambridge, and was not always available. So, in the summer of 1976, I persuaded two young doctors to sail with me on *Crystal*: Charles Roberts, the son of my husband's cousin, Glyn; and Bertie Bulmer, his friend.

The St Kilda group of islands and stacks lies 40 miles west of Shillay, an island on the east coast of the Outer Hebrides, at the entrance to the Sound of Harris, the main channel from the Minch to the west. The Sound is a maze of islets, reefs and sandbanks, through which there are two passages. The Northern Passage, used by Charles in 1962, involves some tricky navigation, for which good visibility is essential. The southern route, Cope Passage, is used by the army to supply its base on St Kilda, and is well buoyed. I chose the southern route, which presented no difficulty, though any deviation from the buoyed channel could have proved disastrous. The high pressure system lying over the British Isles at the beginning of July 1976 gave us very foggy conditions, and I took the precaution of marking on the chart the precise alterations of course needed to take us from buoy to buoy. (We were very glad of these bearings on the return journey, when we could not see from one buoy to the next.)

Once through the Sound, we set a course for St Kilda, but made very little headway as we were becalmed for a whole night. Nevertheless, we managed to get within 20 miles of the islands, before having to turn back the next morning as we had not brought enough fuel for the double journey under engine (a bad mistake on my part) and the doctors were worried about running out of time. We could not fix our position, as we could see nothing and had to rely entirely on dead reckoning. The return to Shillay, in worsening visibility and rising wind, was daunting. Ironically, the wind sprang up from the northwest as soon as we turned back. The possibility of running into the outlying reefs (if our calculations put us a couple of miles off course) was always in my mind. When Little Shillay loomed out of the mist on the starboard bow there was an exhilarating moment of reprieve. Our dead reckoning had been accurate after all. We dropped anchor on the leeward side of Shillay and waited for conditions to improve on the bar at the west end of the Sound of Harris. For weeks after this episode I had a recurring dream that I was on the wrong side of something, but I was determined to try again.

A chance conversation with Angela Faller (physicist and climber) in November 1976 revealed that her partner, Jack Soper (geologist and climber), had become very interested in boats. I was quick to follow up on this news, for Charles and I had discovered years before that climbers tend to make good sailing companions. Angela, Jack and I sailed to Bardsey in another boat one fine weekend in May, and Jack agreed to sail with me on *Crystal*, bringing another friend of his, Vic Croft. They made an ideal crew. Jack was already planning to buy a boat of his own; and Vic was a resourceful engineer, well able to cope with the vagaries of *Crystal's* engine, and an absolute wizard with her corroded and unreliable electrical system.

Had I known all this before they joined me in Oban, I would have been less depressed by the terrible state of *Crystal* in 1977. Her decks were leaking badly and her bilges were half full of water. The bunks were soaking wet and the mahogany drawers under the chart table had swollen and stuck fast. Things were no better on deck: the running and the standing rigging were rusty and needed replacing, and the rail stanchions were loose and rickety. I closed my eyes, to be roused by the boatman saying in his inimitable dour Scottish voice, 'I wouldnae take her out in a blow if I were you.' However, after a couple of days of hard work, *Crystal* began to look more shipshape. Jack and Vic arrived and we set off.

Miraculously the weather, which until then had been changeable with gales and rain, began to improve, as another high pressure system settled over the British Isles. We had an uneventful passage across the Minch to Lochmaddy (on the east coast of North Uist, a few miles south of the Sound of Harris), and anchored off the pier in the early hours of 6th July. Having slept, we ate and refuelled, taking enough petrol to motor to St Kilda and back, if necessary.

We left Lochmaddy early the next morning in a light northeasterly breeze, with the glass very high, almost 'set fair', and motored once again through Cope Passage. Leaving the bar buoys astern and the island of Pabbay to port, we headed out to the open sea through the Sound of Shillay and set a course for St Kilda. It was fine but very hazy and after the first few miles we were unable to fix our positions by compass bearings as the west coast of the Outer Hebrides faded from view. Once again, we had to rely entirely on dead reckoning. A light north-northwesterly breeze started and we were soon making 3 to 4 knots, close-hauled. I changed course to allow for leeway, hoping it would be enough. When the wind dropped and we had to use the motor, which happened quite a few times, we changed back to the original course. At 1pm I took a sunsight but because the horizon was so misty the result put us about 60 miles north of our real latitude! At least it gave me a chance to use the sextant and practise the method.

There was no sign of St Kilda by 8pm, and visibility was down to about a mile. With the rain came thunder and lightning. We supposed St Kilda to be somewhere in there, though we also feared that we might have missed it altogether. With such poor visibility, it would have been perfectly possible to pass a mile or two to the south and see nothing; perhaps even to slip through between Boreray, the northernmost island, and Hirta, the main island. The thought of heading out into the Atlantic was dispiriting. We wondered if the seabirds might help us find the island and it wasn't until after the voyage, on re-reading Martin's account, that I realised that the seabirds were indeed the islanders' compass. Thunder and lightning had now become dramatic and rain was coming down in torrents. *Crystal's* decks leaked horribly, the chart table was flooded and our charts were getting very soggy.

Suddenly, through the mist, we saw the faint silhouette of a stack on our starboard bow. Altering course towards it, we pored over our damp chart, deciding it must be Levenish, which lies a couple of miles to the southeast of Village Bay. Then, shortly after 9pm, a mist-wreathed volcanic formation unveiled itself, looking indescribably dark and sinister. It was an amazing landfall. As we drew nearer we took photographs of the spectacular bastions of Dùn island, which forms the south side of Village Bay. At 10.15pm we dropped anchor at the head of the bay. After a late and jubilant meal we slept soundly, at once mindful and yet careless of the fact that the bay is exposed to the southeast, and that a shift of wind to any point between south and east would mean having to clear out. Even a temporary anchorage was welcome, like a bivouac ledge high up on a mountain face. I felt proud of *Crystal*, on Edwin's behalf, and determined to send him word as soon as possible.

I was very grateful to our old friend for letting me borrow *Crystal* year after year, but at the same time I was embarrassed that he (now in failing health) was bearing the cost of maintaining the yacht. Charles and I both thought I needed a boat of my own, and we began to look around. Meanwhile we went on with our family activities much as usual. In January and February, Chuck was working on the tubular bridge across the Menai Straits before going to the South of France and then joining Peter and me for skiing at Le Tour, while Nea looked after Charles and Robin in Bangor. Chuck, a schoolfriend of his, Peter and I all skied down the Vallée Blanche together, which was exciting, and a good effort by Peter, who was only 12 years old. The top part of the descent, along a rocky ridge with huge drops on the Chamonix side, was quite frightening.

Towards the end of May, I helped Jack and Angela Soper (recently married) bring a small cruising boat from Dale in Milford Haven to North Wales in misty conditions and a total absence of wind. Fortunately the boat had a good engine. Charles came to meet us in Port Dinorwic. During our summer cruising in Loch Drumbuie over the years, we had made friends with the Thompson family. Their boat, *Starbuck*, was a fair-sized family cruiser with room for six. It seemed to have all mod cons, including a TV for their children and, importantly, a good diesel engine. When Sarah

Thompson offered to lend me their yacht in the summer, I accepted with alacrity, as it was a welcome opportunity for me to handle another boat. They kept *Starbuck* at Kircudbright; and I set off with Peter, the Orgill family and Dave Wilson on 24th July for a cruise to Crinan, Oban, Nevis, Plockton, South Rona and Mull, and back, via the Small Isles, to Kirkcudbright. It was a great success, and I was suitably profuse in my thanks to Sarah.

In 1979 I borrowed the Sopers' new boat, *Alba*, which was berthed at Arisaig. Angela came with us for the first part of the cruise. We drove in my car and stayed at a climbers' hut in the north of England on the way. Robin and Peter were soon exploring the bunks upstairs and Angela, who was unused to the natural exuberance of boys, told them that every sound they made could be heard down below. As we left Arisaig, I tried to memorise the way out through a small channel to the Sound of Sleat for our eventual return. We sailed up the Sound into Loch Nevis and anchored close under Sgurr na Ciche. Angela gave us various directions about *Alba*, we rowed her ashore and watched as she strode purposefully up the mountain, before heading off in the direction of Loch Quoich.

Investigating the contents of various lockers, Robin and Peter soon found the outboard engine, full of fuel and ready to go. Although Angela had explicitly told us not to use it, once she had disappeared over the summit I'm afraid I was guilty of letting the boys lift it out and attach it to the dinghy. Who knew when we might really need it? Eventually they managed to start it, and had endless fun zooming round the loch. For them it was the best form of entertainment. I don't think we committed any other major crimes, as we were careful to keep the boat as clean and shipshape as possible. *Alba* was well-stocked and we made serious inroads into her copious supplies of Chunky Chicken. We had no problems getting back to Arisaig, but as we were coming in we heard news on the radio of the Fastnet disaster, in which several crews were drowned. We were lucky that the bad weather in the south had not reached this far north.

Back at Ardincaple, we celebrated some of the boys' successes.

Robin had passed his Common Entrance exam to Wrekin College, and Chuck rowed in the Eton VIII when they won the British Schools Championship. He had also passed his A-level exams and gained a place at Magdalene College, Cambridge. Chuck and Peter went fishing with Charles, and Charles and Chuck caught a 5-pound salmon from the Tyn y Cae run. This was also the year of the Welsh language troubles, when students raided the university and made off with a mass of papers which they scattered over Snowdonia. Charles had problems, not only with the students but also some of his staff, who were sympathetic to the nationalist cause, and thought sending the culprits down was too harsh.

*Denise in 1979*

CHAPTER 19

# *Adventures and Health Problems*

I had the chance of more sailing experience when I crewed for John Murray, who worked at Plas y Brenin, and was planning to sail his 30-foot steel sloop *Oyo* to the Azores in autumn 1979. John had sailed her, single-handed, down to Plymouth, where he had some very good friends, with whom we stayed before setting out on the last day of September. By 6th October, we heard gale warnings for Biscay and Finisterre, just where we were heading, and for many other places. Charles, who had been following our progress, had an anxious day.

We had, of course, downed all sail in good time, and simply lay ahull for the next five days. I had already experiencd a big gale coming back from Spain with Charles, in *Triune*, but there we had plenty of space in the open ocean, where the seas were regular. Here we were not far from the Channel coasts, where the waves, though smaller, were more chaotic. *Oyo* was rather slow in normal conditions, because she was so heavy. Now in these turbulent winds and waves, her weight became an asset, as she 'lay doggo' in the stormy sea. John and I were on either side of the cabin, in bunks made of steel tubes which had been welded in during her construction. We felt relatively safe, but the seas crashing against her topsides made a tremendous racket. It was like being inside a drum in a wild cacophony; not unlike some modern music, but on a vaster scale.

As the winds moderated John was able to take some sunsights, which I then worked out for him at the chart table. I was hoping we could now press on, but John decided to put back to Plymouth. I was bitterly disappointed but, looking back, it was perhaps the right decision for him. I was surprised, however, when some months later John decided to sail *Oyo* singlehanded across the

Atlantic; and even more surprised to hear that when he reached the coast, instead of going ashore, he sailed all the way back home.

My next opportunity came when Tony Johnson, an old friend of Gaie's, invited me to sail with him and his crew in his 60-foot ketch, *La Brouette*, from Bermuda back to Gibraltar. I flew to Bermuda on 23rd May 1980, and was met by Tony, who took me by car to St George's, where the boat was lying, to meet the crew: Ian, Steve and David. On 30th May, Police and Customs gave us clearance. Tony brought his shotgun on board, which meant we had to leave immediately. We motored through the buoyed passage to the St George's end of the island in lovely weather. On leaving the St George's bar buoys, we hoisted genoa and staysail, main, mizzen and mizzen staysail and I had an exhilarating impression of speed. Later I began to feel queasy, then sick, but I was determined to stand my two-hour watches with the others. I had recourse to Gravol suppositories, which I found much better than trying to swallow pills. (The Scopolamine patches I would later use were not yet on the market.)

We had an uneventful passage down to the Azores, arrived in Horta on 11th June, after a rather misty approach, and spent the night ashore. It was wonderful to have a bath and a bed. Tony and I visited Capelinhos, where the old lighthouse is half buried in the ash from the 1957 volcanic eruption. We also saw a series of photos of the actual event, which must have been very impressive. I posted my second Horta letter to Charles, and we were off by about noon. After giving a tow to a Polish staysail schooner, we sailed along Pico's south shore, most of which was still shrouded in mist, and then along the north coast of San Miguel. We passed Cape St Vincent in very light winds, motoring, as we seemed to have done most of the way. I had the impression that Tony was now impatient to be done with the whole enterprise. Relations between him and Ian, an older man, had not been very good. This did not, however, spoil my enjoyment of the approach to Gibraltar along the Spanish coast.

We berthed in the New Marina for £5 per night. There were good facilities there, with showers and a Lipton supermarket close by, with lovely Moroccan oranges for sale. Electronic equipment seemed cheap. Everywhere, though, I noticed traces of wartime emplacements. Tony took us all out for a farewell meal and I just had time for a deliciously cool swim over at Sandy Beach, on the Mediterranean side, and a scramble up the summit ridge of the Rock itself, before packing up and leaving for the air strip with Ian and co. Our flight to Gatwick left at 6.20pm.

As soon as we landed, I rang Nea, took a taxi to Tunbridge Wells, arrived about 11pm, and rang Charles. Nea had not been so well but was cheerful and we watched tennis together in the afternoon. That evening I took a train back to London and spent the night with my old friend Gaie, happening to arrive in the middle of one of her Gestalt psychology sessions. The next day, 27th June, Chuck was collecting his degree, so Gaie lent me a dress and took me to King's Cross early next morning to catch a train to Cambridge, where I took a taxi first to Madgalene College and then to the Senate House. I had drinks with Chuck and his friends in Pepys Court, where we had a wonderful lunch, after which I made my slightly tipsy way back to Wales.

Back home I drove over to the Wrekin to collect Robin from school and ordered German marks for him. He left for Germany on 13th July. Peter had by now acquired a motorbike, on which he planned to ride up to Scotland. Thankfully wiser counsels prevailed, and he put his energies into VS rock climbing instead, at which he already showed a marked aptitude. I seconded him as often as I could. He liked to drive us down to Tremadog while I cowered beside him with my crash hat already strapped on. We started with *Christmas Curry*, where we met Angela and Brede Arkless, then *One Step in the Clouds,* which was pleasant enough. But two days later I found *Clapton's Crack* very strenuous indeed. The next day he led me up *Craig Dhu Wall* with the VS finish, which I also very much enjoyed. The following day was also fine and Peter drove us to the Llanberis Pass to do the *Nose Direct* on Dinas Mot.

Another memorable climb Peter led me up was *Belle Vue Bastion*, with which I was familiar, having led it years before. Apart from the crux pitch, he found it rather easy. Then came *Curving*

*Denise at Bangor, 1982*

*Crack* on Cloggy's East Buttress, *Longland's* on the West Buttress, and finally *Cenotaph Corner,* on 2nd September, with Barbara James, who met us in the pass. Although the back of the crack was wet, Peter decided to give it a go. Barbara lent him her fifi hook, and he was soon gaining height. Somehow he made the best of inadequate holds on the right and left walls and got to the top. As I followed, with some difficulty, I was full of admiration for Jo Scarr, who had led the climb in 1961.

My gyrations, as I swung about at the end of Peter's rope on climbs that were obviously too hard for me, became something of a family spectator sport for Charles, Nea and Robin, who watched from the car. We climbed day after day until the weather broke, on 7th September. The next day I drove Robin down to his school in Wellington – he was quite looking forward to being in the prefects' study. Meanwhile Peter drove down to Tremadog, where he soloed four climbs, including *Valerie's Rib* and *Merlin*. At the Pinnacle Club weekend in November, I climbed with Angela Soper on the Mot. She wanted to do the *Diagonal*, but I demurred, so we went to Tremadog, where she took me up the *Fang*, which I found desperate.

Later in November I began to experience pain and heavy bleeding, and Mr J.P. Williams persuaded me to have a preliminary investigation under general anaesthetic at Llandudno General Hospital. Mr Williams told me I had a swelling which was probably an ovarian cyst. The anaesthetic made me feel so groggy, it was surprising that I managed to drive myself back home from the hospital. Meanwhile Nea was also seeing a specialist and I was keen for her to come and stay with us for Christmas. Ian drove her to Wales on 12th December, slipping through between heavy, countrywide snowstorms, while trains were disrupted and motorways impassable. Robin and Peter were both home five days later. The next day dawned fine and clear. Peter and I drove to Pen y Pass and made for *Central Trinity Gully* on Snowdon, which frightened us both. The snow was rather floury and insecure, but there was a fair amount of it. It was very cold and we were glad of our down jackets. We came back in the dark along the Miners' Track and were late home.

After spending the night at Capel on 20th December, Peter cycled to Tryfan and went up North Gully in deep snow. It was waist-deep along the Heather Terrace. He got into a spot of bother somewhere and had to leave a sling before coming down the west face. On 22nd December I took the boys to Idwal in the afternoon to practise using crampons on icy bosses. It was very cold and fine, but too late for sunshine. More bad weather was forecast, but it was still fine at noon the next day. As it was very dark and windy round Ogwen, we decided against the Nameless Cwm, and Robin and Peter went to the Carneddau, while I went to Ardincaple to chase out sheep and visit Charlie Brennand (who previously owned a small climbing shop in Capel Curig).

I phoned Charles, who brought Nea in his car, and she came with me to the Brennands. She and Robin and I then went back to Bangor with Charles. However, Nea began to have a stroke just as we got there. Robin somehow carried her into the house and put her down on the settee in Charles' big office downstairs. I held her hand as she began to lose consciousness, and tried to reassure her as best I could. At about midnight she was admitted to St David's Hospital in Bangor and, when I visited her there, she was drifting in and out of consciousness. A few days later, she was eating and drinking better but her speech was rambling and incoherent. It was distressing to see her in so much discomfort. Though she looked better physically, there was no sign of life in her right leg and right arm. After doing some tests, the doctors made it clear that Nea's long-term prospects were pretty poor. We had to get her out of St David's, but where next?

I knew I could not care for her adequately at Bryn Haul, as Charles' needs were gradually increasing. My brother Ian, who was now a lecturer in the Department of Experimental Psychology at London University, came to the rescue. On 5th January, Ian rang to say that she could be admitted to University College Hospital, but then there were blizzards and Nea could not go south. On Wednesday 20th January, I went to St David's to give her lunch and tea, by which time she had forgotten that I had been there earlier. Her speech was improving and her appetite was good, but morale was fluctuating for both of us. Nea was finally sent to London in late January, where Ian found her a suitable care home and I visited as often as I could; but Ian told me that she was very frustrated, and was getting into rages, though she had been visited by our friends Janet, Margaret and Nancy.

Meanwhile, after various interviews and tests by doctors, it was decided that I was going to need a hysterectomy. Charles and Len drove me to the hospital in Llandudno on 23rd February. After the business of signing consent forms, they left, and the day dragged by interminably. I noticed, with some anger, that the hospital seemed more anxious to have my husband's consent than my own. Blood was taken, parts shaved, and the ward felt terribly hot. I was woken at 5am and told to give myself a bath. The bath stood in the centre of a large and otherwise empty ward and I felt I was taking part in some strange ritual. At 7.30 I was given an injection of Largactil, which brought on a horrible feeling of drugged drowsiness. I came to as they were lifting me back into bed, aware of having been 'done over'.

After a very rough night I began to focus on the drip, which made it hard to move about. I was offered a side ward, and had hardly settled in when Charles arrived with Brenda, who was kindly looking after him. Charles and Yvonne brought me home on 6th March, still feeling groggy. I sat on the sofa in Charles' room, thinking of Nea. Nevertheless by Easter 1982 I was back rock-climbing with Robin and Peter.

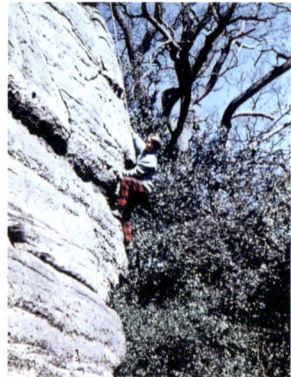

*Above: Denise and Robin
near Capel Curig 1982.
Right: Denise climbing at
Harrison's Rocks, East Sussex,
in her late forties.*

CHAPTER 20

## *Travels in France*

By way of convalescence, I decided to fly from Gatwick to Rhodes with Nancy Smith, changing there for a plane to Karpathos, a lesser-known island, where we planned to enjoy some swimming and sunshine. Back in London, I went shopping for flowers for Nea, and on to her new nursing home in Pimlico. Although she was still confused, she seemed better than when I had last seen her, and clearly enjoyed the strawberries, grapes and goat's cheese I brought. Len met me at Bangor Station and I found Charles in good form at Bryn Haul.

For the next couple of months I made the most of the fine weather to do as much walking and climbing as possible. Peter and I were planning a summer trip to the French Alps, together with Val Brown and Sally Keir, with whom we did some of the harder climbs in the Llanberis Pass and down at Tremadog, by way of training. We took it in turns to lead and all gained in confidence. On 18th July Peter and I drove to London in Charles' old Rover. It was overheating by the time we reached Edgware Road, and then the speedometer packed in. We tried but failed to find anyone to mend it. Val and Sally joined us in London that night, and we all took the ferry from Dover to Calais next morning.

Driving through the *Boulevard Périphérique*, on the outskirts of Paris, the engine overheated to the point where it simply stopped, and we had to wait an hour for it to cool down. We got it to a garage somehow, where they took out the thermostat. Eventually we reached Larchant and set up camp above the Dame Jeanne, a well-known prominent sandstone rock, which we all climbed, although it was really too hot for climbing. We then drove to Bourg-en-Bresse, with the car still overheating. There, we had to buy new tyres, as the garage man noticed they had worn smooth.

Having driven to Le Tour, we met up again with Val and Sally, who had set up camp at Argentière. On 24th July Peter and I made our way over to the Trient Hut via the Col Supérieur du Tour in rapidly worsening weather and roped up on the glacier, where I was very slow. On the col we decided to press on to the Trient Hut, as the Aiguille du Tour had by now completely disappeared and we were in thick mist.

The next day we walked down to Orsières in a blizzard and took a train back to Montroc, happily using French money for the train tickets. The descent was particularly hard on the knees, but Peter and I were both able to run down through the forest until we were given a lift by a Swiss German party in their Mercedes. Two days later Peter led me up the north-northeast ridge of the Aiguille de l'M, which proved a lovely rock climb, once we had located it. We both climbed in our PAs, carrying our boots. Peter led in fine style, finding the crack pitch rather hard. He helped me with a pulley system. We went down by the easy way up, which I remembered climbing *en famille* when I was 15.

John Thompson then joined Peter and me at the Albert Premier Hut for a traverse of the Aiguille du Chardonnet, starting at 2am the next day. The weather was fine and all went well on the traverse itself, which I really enjoyed. However, we were well down the steep chimney that led back to the glacier, when we realised that we had inadvertently left the spare rope somewhere above. Leaving Peter and me sheltering as best we could in the chimney, where we were soon shaking with cold, John climbed back up to find the rope and bring it down. This all took some time. Peter and I were both half-frozen so climbing down the steep névé at the top of the glacier became something of an ordeal. We moved slowly and carefully, but lower down we came to the main bergschrund. To get past this, we had to hurl ourselves bodily, wearing crampons of course, from a position just above the schrund, to land on the snow slope well below. It was a three-dimensional long-jump with a difference. I sensed the boys' apprehension, as well as my own, as I prepared to jump. They fielded me as I landed and we went on down. This little epic lasted 17 hours all told.

On the way down from the Refuge Albert Premier, on 30th July, we stopped for a most enjoyable lunch of steak and chips at the Col de Balme, one of my favourite locations for a complete view of the Chamonix Valley and its aiguilles. The next day, after a terribly wet, thundery night, Peter and I went to see Jeanne Franco in Chamonix. Although the weather forecast was good for the next day or so, another depression was expected and I decided to move on to the Dauphiné. Val and Sally were already on their way there.

Peter and I drove to La Bérarde via the Col du Galibier, where we saw Marcelle Motte and her brother. Marcelle was very depressed to hear bad news of Nea, and generally saddened by deaths among her own generation and people round her. The car, meanwhile, boiled everywhere and we had an epic journey to La Bérarde, with numerous stops to cool the engine. We found Val's car at the Vallon des Étages, though there was no note, and we supposed they had moved up to the Aiguille Dibona. Peter and I surfaced rather late on 2nd August, to find Val and Sally had returned, as the weather didn't seem good. Sally was terribly disappointed to have missed the Dibona so I offered to go back up to it with her the next day. We set out at 6.30am and, although Sally carried everything, it took me three hours to get up to the hut. After a drink we did the *Voie Boell* in doubtful weather. It started to rain and we almost turned back. We were late back at the hut.

On 4th August Peter and I started on the *Voie Berthet* behind two French boys, but it started to rain and eventually we all came down, having moved out of the 'tunnel', which was part of a chimney pitch. The next day Peter led me up the *Berthet* with the Stofer variations, where we both enjoyed the texture of the limestone rock. We came down to our camp in the Vallon des Étages afterwards, to find a note from Val saying she and Sally had gone up to the Chatelleret Hut for a two-day walk. After going to a bank in Bourg d'Oisans, we eventually made our way back up to Cézanne, where we left the car and plodded up to the Glacier Blanc Hut. There, we met Dave Jones and his party from Ogwen Cottage. He was planning to do the *Agneaux* and then move up to the Refuge des Écrins.

We were up at 4am next morning, and reached the Refuge des Écrins in a couple of hours. After a rest and a drink we went up the Pic de Neige Cordier, which I had climbed with Chuck in 1973. It was misty and windy at the Col Émile Pic, but we went on up the ridge in crampons and were down at the Écrins Hut by 12.30. Early next morning, we were off to the Barre des Écrins. We had only one head torch, but the moon was up and the sky fairly clear. In about an hour we reached a point where the north-facing Glacier Blanc steepens into a wall. We hesitated at the Brèche Lory between the rock route up the 'barre' and the ice. Peter chose the latter and was hassled from behind by some Italians. When we reached the summit ridge, we felt so tired that we did not reach the summit itself but decided to turn back – in rising wind and mist. We abseiled down to the Brèche Lory, our rope stretching just far enough. We went right back to the valley, drove back round to La Bérarde and camped at the same place at Les Étages.

The next day, 11th August, the weather was good. We drove up to La Bérarde, left the car, walked up to the Promontoire Hut, and stopped at the Chatelleret for a drink and a rest. At the Promontoire we met some delightful young climbers, some of whom were planning to do the South Face of the Meije and some of the traverse. It was a lovely evening but we had a bad night. After very little sleep, we were disturbed by the early starters, and I had much trouble in waking Peter for breakfast at 4.30am. The weather was really fine but Peter was so tired as to make the traverse out of the question. He simply said it was too big for us, so we went right down and rested in camp. I was disappointed. We drove back to Chamonix on 13th August, and the bad weather hit us while we were on the Lautaret Pass, from which we could see the Meije. Looking through a telescope, we saw climbers making their way along the ridge. We reached Jeanne Franco that evening and spent the night in her chalet, after eating a sustaining *fondue bourguignonne*.

Apart from sickness, due to something we had both eaten further north, we had an uneventful passage back across the Channel. When I rang Charles, he told me that the husband of our faithful retainer, Mrs Pollington, had just died; so, after dropping Peter off, I drove straight to Mrs Pollington's house at Rust Hall. Polly, as we called her, was a splendid character, who had helped us through thick and thin after the war years. When Nea began to go downhill, Polly had removed some of her most treasured possessions from no. 17, and stored them in her own loft. She now wanted me to take them, so we got them down, and I asked her to choose a piece of silverware as a memento, and put the rest in the car. Back at no. 17, there were all Granny Barnard's Corot paintings and drawings, but they would have to wait for another visit. We then made a leisurely start for London, calling on Chuck about noon, and going on to Nea's Pimlico nursing home. Though still confused, she seemed a little better.

Our Alpine summer in 1982 whetted our appetites for more rock climbing, and Peter and I, sometimes with Val and Sally, went on doing what were for me hard rock climbs well into the autumn. We tackled all the old favourites in the Llanberis Pass, on 'Cloggy' and at Tremadog as well as some that were new to me, including *Cemetery Gates* and *Tantalus*, both of which Peter led in fine style.

CHAPTER 21

## *A Boat of My Own*

On 4th December, Peter and I drove down to Tunbridge Wells to meet Ian and Mickie, and decide what to do with Nea's pictures and furniture. After lunch we got down to the business of sorting out her possessions. Peter started loading the car and Mrs Pollington came next morning to pack up more glasses and tableware. We left at 12.30 for Chichester, planning to look at cruising boats in the yards at Birdham Pool, first to Saltern's and then to Williams and Smithells.

At the first yard we saw a Vertue, which was the sort of boat Charles had in mind. Peter and I liked her but thought she was too small. We then went on to the Hamble, where there was nothing to view on the spot but we were given a list of second-hand boats for sale. We then drove to Easton's in Lymington where Commander Easton was most helpful. At one point we gave him a lift in the car and I was amused when he called out to Peter, who was driving: 'Mind that bicycle, boy!'

Early in 1983 the boys and I were once again doing a lot of hill walking and rock climbing. But when I learned from Commander Easton that *Dunlin of Wessex*, a Tradewind 33, was for sale down at Marks Tey, I dropped everything and drove down to view her. Charles did not need much persuasion to have a look at her himself. He was by now driving a new car, with specially adapted hand controls, which made driving a pleasure for him. He drove down to Walton-on-the-Naze with me to admire her lines, as she lay on the hard, all ready to go. She looked in good condition, though we could not tell much about the engine and the electrics.

Back at Marks Tey Hotel, we had another large meal, after which I had to keep very still as we had the unexpected pleasure of listening to Peter Ustinov's rendition of the choral section of

Beethoven's Ninth, sung in Arabic. Charles had already rung Commander Easton, and made an offer of £29,000. We both had misgivings in the early hours, but the die was cast and we drove home with mixed feelings of delight and apprehension, comforted by a distant view of the Welsh hills under snow. Alastair Easton rang again in the morning to say the sale was on, and Charles then sent our deposit.

My next move was to sail the boat up to the Menai Straits with Johnny Jackson, son of John Jackson, who had been with Charles on the first ascent of Kangchenjunga, and Brenda, who was keen to come. I drove down to Walton-on-the-Naze with Brenda in Charles' Rover. We found *Dunlin* in the yacht basin and soon had everything on board. Monday, 20th June, marked the start of a very busy week at Walton, making sure *Dunlin* was ready by Friday evening. While an engineer worked on the engine, Brenda cleaned the boat below decks. The sails all needed checking; some were missing. I chased up the sailmaker. There was a bewildering confusion of jobs to be done and not much time, but after the first 24 hours *Dunlin* began to feel like home. Friday was the most hectic day of all, and we still had no Walker Log. We moved down to the marina at high tide to meet the compass adjuster and engineer, and went down the creek to adjust. The engine trials went OK except for a charging fault. John Jackson Jr arrived, and later Glyn and Margaret Roberts, Charles' cousins, who took Charles' car away.

After phoning Charles, we got away at about midday on 25th June and made good time to the 'Sunk' Lightship, but the tide turned against us as we came to North Foreland. We anchored for a few hours in the 'small downs' to wait for the next favourable tide. Weighing anchor at about 5am, we found little wind and motored down-channel most of the day. Darkness found us off Brighton Pier. We made a fast passage from Land's End to the Smalls, covering the 90 miles in 13 hours, averaging 7 knots, and we soon reached Cardigan Bay. Early morning on 1st July found us nearing Llanddwyn but we were too early for the tide, so we sailed about between Llanddwyn and South Stack till 11am when we crossed the bar, and were in Port Dinorwic dock before midday. John and

Eileen Jackson were there to welcome us, Charles arrived and we all had lunch together before Charles drove us back to Capel.

For the next few days I felt as if the land was swaying. But the sailing bug had not yet ousted the climbing bug, and I was soon doing hard climbs again with Sally, with whom I 'led through' on *Kirkus's Route* on Craig Cwm Silyn with renewed confidence, and back on Dinas Mot, where we led through on *Western Slabs*, where I led the long second pitch and also the hard crack at the top. On 15th July Peter rang from Chamonix to say that he and Sammie had done the *Aiguille du Tour Voie Normale*, the *Dent du Géant Voie Normale* and the *Papillon Arête* on the Aiguille du Peigne.

My brother Ian, and Mark (a friend), joined me on 26th for another cruise up to Scotland. We left the next day and reached Oban on 1st August after days of mixed winds and weather. Ian then took a train south, while Mark and I went on to Ardentraive, where we were able to pick up a mooring, refuel, and get sorted out. We were joined by Tim and Eileen Healey and their son Jamie on 2nd August, sailed up to Loch Aline in the afternoon and anchored in good mud. The next day, we anchored in Loch Drumbuie, and on the 4th we reached Canna and set a course for Barra on 5th.

It was misty as we approached the Outer Hebrides but we identified Eriskay and other islets and, using compass bearings, we made our way into Barra Harbour. After seeing Mark off next morning, we shopped in Barra, where every other house turned out to be some sort of grocery store. Using compass courses and counting islets, we found Pabbay Sound and went through it, keeping clear of growlers off Geo na Gainmhich, then set a course for St Kilda. The Healeys felt a bit queasy because of the Atlantic swell, but we had a quiet night with a gentle southwesterly breeze. Next morning we noticed a gradual increase in bird life. One bird, which we eventually identified as a rock pipit, landed on Eileen's head as she was helming. Suddenly the tunnel under the Dun appeared under the mists. We located Stack Levenish before proceeding into Village Bay, where one other yacht was already anchored.

Leaving Village Bay on the morning of 8th August in dense fog, we set a course to clear the Flannans. We had splendid glimpses of the top of Boreray before the fog closed in for good. We could hear engines in the mist but saw nothing till evening, when we distinguished a small islet off the mainland, just before dark. The next day we took a series of radio bearings. Behind us, the white arch of a mist bow took shape. Eventually we were able to make out the Butt of Lewis. It seemed a long way round the Eye peninsula and we were late into Stornoway, where we anchored at dusk off the castle. It was very crowded and we found ourselves rather too close to the *Aeolian*, a yawl of some age and elegance. Tim and Eileen needed to leave at 4am so we rowed ashore. I then rowed back to the boat for some sleep, but woke again a few hours later to find the rocks, and the *Aeolian*, rather too close. I felt obliged to up-anchor, which I found quite an effort on my own, and came alongside a fishing boat with the help of its skipper.

Sarah arrived at 4pm to help me sail back to Wales, and we had a meal ashore. Next morning Sarah seemed quite keen to leave Stornoway, and I rather less so, but we did get off in a rather strong west-southwesterly wind. Close-reaching and beating with the tide, we were soon past Loch Erisort and decide to go into Loch Ouirn, where we anchored rather close to some fishing buoys. As the wind was still quite strong on 12th August, we decided to spend a second night there. The next day we sailed from Loch Ouirn past Kebock Head early in the morning to catch the tide. Beating to and fro between Usinish and the Shiants, we gradually gained ground. We sailed into Loch Seaforth and up into Loch Maaruig, where we anchored. This turned out to be all to the good as the wind strengthened to gale force from the southwest. I was able to ring Charles from a phonebox on shore, to celebrate our wedding anniversary on the 14th, which I spent doing boat maintenance in Loch Maaruig, a first-rate anchorage, in my view.

Sarah and I also went for long walks ashore, along the Tarbert road. We used the winch to get the anchor up next day before sailing across to Loch Dunvegan. Realising that darkness would overtake us before we could reach harbour, we decided to put into Loch Bay (a northern branch of the loch) which we found in semi-darkness. It provided an easy entry and we followed the coastline to the sheltered head of the loch, where we anchored close inshore. From Loch Bay we sailed to Loch Skiport, and from Loch Skiport to Canna Harbour. From there, we sailed across to the Rùm shore in a rising southeasterly. We sailed down the coast of Rùm till we could lay a course for the west end of Muck, in nil visibility. We were glad to find Muck after a cold and rather miserable passage. Past Ardnamurchan, we set a course for Ardmore Point to anchor at the south end of Tobermory Bay, off Aros House.

Sarah and I were up early to leave Aros House in time to catch the tide down the Sound of Mull. This enabled us to reach Ardentraive by mid-afternoon. We hung about for a mooring and got fuel alongside the jetty. It was sunny and warm enough for shorts, and we had an evening walk ashore, exploring Kerrera, finding litle beaches and bays, and delicious mushrooms. We moved *Dunlin* over to the pontoons for water and shopping before Tim Healey turned up to sail with us back to the Menai Straits.

On 22nd August we caught an early morning tide round the Mull of Kintyre, which we glimpsed momentarily high above the mists, before motoring on down the channel between Northern Ireland and the Galloway coast. We set a course for the 'Chicken Rock', navigating by dead reckoning and radio fixes, eventually closing it in the mists, and from there we sailed to Lynas Point. I decided to anchor for the night off Moelfre, to wait for a tide through the Menai Straits the next day. I rowed ashore in the afternoon to phone Charles, who then drove over and took us all out to dinner at the Bull Bay Hotel, to celebrate my fifty-second birthday. We rowed back to *Dunlin* in the dark and were up in time to catch the tide through the Straits. Tim took a train to Chester and Sarah spent a night with us at Bryn Haul.

In September we had a visit from Ann Sutton, Geoff's wife, with whom Nea and I had climbed in the Lakes, where Ann had previously led some very hard climbs. After a rather protracted shopping expedition to Joe Brown's, Ann and I got off to Pen y Pass, scrambled over Crib Goch in the rain, and came down from Bwlch y Moch. The next day Charles drove us both to Bangor to look at *Dunlin*, where Ann showed a definite interest in my projected cruise to the Azores the following year. We laid *Dunlin* up for the winter at Dickie's Yard on 9th September.

In October Charles and I accepted an invitation to spend a few days with John and Sarah Thompson at Dipton Foot in Northumberland. We both enjoyed driving through the Lake District, and seeing Hadrian's Wall. Sarah and John had gone out of their way to make it possible for Charles, who now used a wheelchair, to stay with them. Although it was wet, we all went for a drive, with Charles at the wheel, through the Northumberland countryside, which we found spacious and windy. We went to Otterburn, then halfway to Alnwick in worsening weather. Charles and I came home in equally wet conditions, and poor visibility, which made motorway driving unpleasant. At one point I noticed that Charles was doing 90 miles per hour.

Now that we had *Dunlin*, I was keen to revisit all the places I had sailed to before in *Crystal* on the Scottish west coast, including our much-loved Summer Isles. I was able to explore Isle Martin, the innermost island, where I first met Sandy Watters and his wife, Barbara, who lived on the mainland close by. They were both amazingly kind and helpful, and I soon got to know their daughter, Charlotte, and her fiancé Dan Johnson. I also met Dan's parents, who lived in Shropshire. Dan's father had built a remarkable, one-off wooden boat, powered by foot pedals, which I was invited to try out with them one day on Bala Lake. The trial was very successful and I saw that Dan's father was no ordinary boatbuilder. Dan had clearly inherited his father's talents as he went on to build his own sea-going yacht, and sail away in it with Charlotte a few years later to West Africa and back.

In October I began doing a Yachtmaster's course at Plas Menai, run by John Mills, whom we already knew. There was a lot to learn but I was keen to navigate under sail to the Azores in *Dunlin*, and had already learnt a lot from Charles, who not only showed me how to take sunsights with a sextant, but also how to work them out afterwards, using sight reduction tables. The little maths I had learnt at school enabled me to follow Charles' explanations of the underlying principles of celestial navigation. Meanwhile Charles, who was familiar with boat maintenace and the importance of attending to the requirements of marine engines, drove me over to Furness Vale, to see Mr Webb, who specialised in Bukh engines. We took *Dunlin's* alternator, which turned out to have a faulty regulator (an expensive item), and Mr Webb gave us good advice. The road conditions were good for Charles, who did so love to drive his splendid new car.

*Charles*

*Denise and Peter*

## CHAPTER 22

# *Sailing* Dunlin *to the Azores*

I was busy with navigation classes at Plas Menai in early 1984, and by the spring I had passed all my Yachtmaster Theory papers. Meanwhile Peter was working at the Climber and Rambler shop at Betws-y-Coed, Chuck had passed his accountancy exams, and Robin was planning to join the army. The gullies were full of snow and at the end of February I went up *Central Trinity Gully* on Snowdon by myself. Conditions were good but I found it rather frightening. From the top I had a lovely view down the Llŷn, the Rivals standing out in white swirling mists against a powder-blue sky, and the sun shining on St Tudwal's Islands: an enchanted landscape.

Down in London, I was able to do some meteorology, before going to see Nea for a few hours, and giving her supper. I then went to meet Sally Humphreys (a classical scholar and experienced sailor). Sally was keen to join John and me for the return trip from the Azores. She was also ready to come for a weekend at the beginning of May for a brief sail on *Dunlin*. I met her train at Bangor; and, picking up John and Sharida en route, we drove to Holyhead. On board I found, to my consternation, that someone had broken in to *Dunlin* and stolen several hundred pounds' worth of instruments and gear. Dumbfounded, I rang the police and phoned Charles.

Nevertheless we pressed on with our plans and took *Dunlin* back to Holyhead: John and Sharida were seasick, but Sally was unaffected. The seas were lumpy till we reached the Anglesey coast and we were back in Holyhead by 8pm. At the weekend Charles and I sat outside at Ardincaple, picnicking and sunbathing and filling in claim forms for the theft from *Dunlin*. Preparations for our departure to the Azores were well under way and we had a lot of help from Gerrard Fraser-Williams, a prominent member of the Holyhead Sailing Club. Charles drove me to Furness Vale for spare parts and tools from Mr Webb. I went on with enough food on board to last the next few months. Happily, *Dunlin* was a very roomy boat and her tanks below deck could take a large supply of drinking water, as well as fuel.

Ann Sutton arrived, and on 10th June 1984 she, John Whitley and I left Port Dinorwic dock, bound for the Azores. We motored in a faint northerly breeze which soon died, along the Llŷn Peninsula, with the tide taking us towards Bardsey, until it turned at 3pm. Charles was planning to drive to the end of the Llŷn to see us off, and I wondered if he would be able to make us out at all. We spent the night drifting about in Cardigan Bay. There was a moon and stars, but we made very little progress. By the early morning on 12th June, the sea was getting ever steeper and lumpier as the wind increased to force 7. We gradually reduced sail to double-reefed main alone, and steering became very hard work. After a night hove-to not far south of Hook Head, whose light, flashing every three seconds, we were able to identify, and with the wind in the southwest, we decided to sail along the south coast of Ireland and put in somewhere for a rest. All three of us were very tired indeed.

At least we were coastal sailing again, with plenty to look at and identify. The weather was fine and we initially made good progress in a westerly direction, but having to tack round headlands added miles to our course. We had already taken a week to reach the latitude of the Scillies, and were still not there. I was disinclined to use the engine, except to get out of the way of fishing boats, as I felt we might need it for further emergencies or doldrums later on. On the 16th, I noted a falling glass and hoped it might provide some wind. Sure enough, a breeze picked up from the north and we were able to maintain a southwesterly course. However, on that quiet, grey afternoon our peace was suddenly shattered by two very loud explosions, as of missiles being fired, for which we could find no explanation. A numbered carrier pigeon landed for rest and recuperation and some food and drink, which we put out for it on the after-deck, where it left a nasty mess, before flying away again.

One or two tankers sailed across our course, indicating that we were in the path of the shipping lanes, and needed to be watchful.

A few days later, the wind picked up from the northeast, and northeasterly gales were forecast for sea area Finisterre, into which we were now moving. John and Ann hoisted the no. 2 genoa and boomed it out, which worked well, and we were able to goosewing for long stretches. The miles were totting up now. That afternoon, the wind strengthened and the sea got up and we had to shorten sail, but even with two reefs we were still moving quite well, though the following seas were harder to contend with. The wind increased to northeasterly 6 in the night, and the following seas were steep and difficult to see, despite the phosphorescence. Nevertheless, we seemed to be well on our way.

There followed another uncomfortable night, with big following seas, but then the wind dropped and we were under-canvassed. After a rather grey start on 21st June, the sun came through and the wind picked up and soon we were batting along, doing a good 5 knots. Mares' tails crossing the sky from the north, a ring round the sun, made us think another depression was in the offing. We reefed the main, and took down the genoa, but the wind then fell almost completely, and there was much slamming and banging. The glass also began to rise again. The next day, it was grey soon after dawn. But by the evening the wind was freshening from the northwest and we were making good speed.

On 23rd June the seas were piling up astern and requiring some concentration, though *Dunlin* had not shipped any water so far. At some point we took off the dodgers, which vastly improved visibility all round. The wind then lessened but the seas were still very big. A depression over Portugal appeared to be more or less stationary, so we expected these winds to persist. The nights were very trying and we tried to avoid sail changes during the hours of darkness, which lasted until 6am in these parts. Although Jupiter was huge, we could never get planets or stars at the same time as a decent horizon. Soon, however, morning and noon sunsights were possible again and we found that Ponta do Arnel was some 90 miles distant.

In the early morning, on 27th June, John saw light flashing dead ahead every five seconds: we appeared to be on target. A few hours later the grey silhouette of San Miguel Island began to emerge. There was sunshine on the lower slopes of Pico da Vara, which was the same height as Snowdon, and the top was wreathed in mist. We slipped along towards it and by 3pm Ponta do Arnel Lighthouse was abeam. The wind then grew fickle and headed us. It was fine and sunny and we enjoyed a scenic view of the lush green fields on the south side of San Miguel. It looked very well cultivated, with vineyards, hedges, woods and vegetable gardens, giving the impression of green plenty.

Putting in to Punta Delgada harbour, we anchored at a secluded distance from the yachts on a nearby pontoon. The Capitania soon made their appearance in the Pilotos boat and there followed a mercifully brief session of form-filling. I found the Portuguese officials helpful and considerate. John and I were both sorry to say goodbye to Ann, who now took a plane back to Switzerland. Before Sally Humphreys arrived (to replace Ann), John and I experienced an odd little interlude, during which we were invited by the Capitania to visit their military headquarters. We both felt distinctly uneasy to start with, as we witnessed a young officer belabouring his unfortunate dog at the entrance. We felt even more uneasy as we walked through gloomy corridors to a distant inner office, where we were questioned as to our reasons for coming to the Azores. We decided to leave the premises as soon as we could – and fled down the dark passages, looking for the way out!

Sally arrived in the evening on 4th July, and the next afternoon we left the Molhe Salazar pier. We sailed first to Angra do Heroismo on Terceira Island, then on to Praia da Vitória, and from there to Velas on San Jorge Island on a lovely day. After a walk up behind Velas, I was able to do a watercolour of Pico.

In the afternoon we sailed across to Madalena but a swell setting across the harbour entrance persuaded us to go on to Horta. Next morning we paid a visit to the Capitania and Guarda Fiscal. John and Sally were both off to Pico in the afternoon on the 12th. Meanwhile I visited Bob Silvermann, the sailmaker, with our big genoa, which he patched. We had a long chat and he kindly drove me back to Horta, after treating me to a glass of Pico Branco, which had quite an effect. I paid him with whisky!

We left Horta on 15th July in a light northeasterly wind, with Castelo Branco abeam. We then moved on past the site of the 1957 eruption and the old lighthouse, which is now inland, of course. At 12 noon the next day, we found Flores, and soon Corvo appeared. Flores was covered in hydrangea hedges as blue as the sky. Large dolphins were disporting themselves nearby and we saw a small turtle. John tried fishing with a mackerel line, as there were a lot of tuna jumping about, but with no weight to keep the line down, he had no luck. We motored on to the large, open bay north of Ponta da Caveira, bounded to the north by the promontory with the Santana Astronomical Observatory. There was a big swell and we were justifiably nervous about going too far in, as the sea was breaking on Baixa Ribeira and other rocks. We anchored in about 11 metres and *Dunlin* rolled horribly all night.

While Sally made a meal on board, John and I rowed ashore with water cans as we could see a stream flowing down to the beach. But we reckoned without the swell, which turned into angry breakers close inshore, where it pounded onto large boulders. We had nearly made it, when up reared a great comber and capsized us into the shallows. Darkness was gathering as we realised we could not carry much water, as we could not get past the surf. It took all our strength to wade out through the undertow, jump into the dinghy and row furiously away from the shore, with the dinghy half-filled with breaking waves. Wet through, but somewhat wiser, we bailed our way back to *Dunlin*, where we were met by a very welcome hot meal. We held an anchor watch that night, with the person on watch curled up in a sleeping bag on the chart table seat, a more comfortable nook than our bunks. Fortunately, the anchor held splendidly and we were able to catch up a little on sleep in the early morning.

On 17th July, a lovely sunny day but with the glass dropping, we got the anchor up and were away under engine, towing the dinghy astern, planning to put in to Santa Cruz to get more water and stores. However, Santa Cruz harbour was already full of yachts, and surf was breaking angrily on the surrounding rocks, so we decided to carry on to the south end of Corvo, Vila Nova. We thought we might find temporary anchorage there, but again there was quite a swell breaking on Vila Nova breakwater and the surrounding rocks.

After the Flores experience, I had some doubts about the wisdom of a shore party, but the crew were keen and the water desirable; I stayed on *Dunlin*, under main and with the engine running, while Sally and John rowed ashore. No sooner were they in the dinghy than my doubts returned. Bothered by a rock two or three cables off the breakwater, I had left them with rather a long way to row, and it took them about 20 minutes. I saw them disappear behind the breakwater, and reappear on shore, parleying with the locals. It was difficult to make much out through the binoculars. I circled back towards the shore, determined to pick them up as close in as I dared. Time passed and nothing much seemed to be happening and I began to feel rather lonely. I thought about how comforting it was to have a crew, and wondered what the hell I would do if the wind and sea got up. Eventually I saw them coming back and we were soon reunited.

Apart from filling a can with water and doing some washing, they had been unable to do anything much on shore, as they had not brought their passports. An officious little man had apparently kept them under surveillance on the pier while he went to confer with his superiors in Flores. He wanted to send John back to the yacht for the passports, while keeping Sally ashore as a hostage. After more parleying, Sally had filled in some forms with an imaginary passport number and they were allowed to leave, with help from a friendly local fisherman who launched them through the surf.

Everyone I had spoken to had said 'go north to get westerlies', and this was what we had been doing, but for the last few days we'd had a preponderance of northwesterly winds. By 19th July, we were heading for the Chaucer Bank, and there were dark clouds bringing rain. We shortened sail, as the seas became lumpy and uncomfortable. We must have gone over part of the Chaucer Bank in the early hours of the next day, as the seas began to improve. I felt queasy but the sun was out and I was determined to get more sights. It turned into a fine day but with the wind unfortunately coming from the northeast. We weren't making much headway and I felt the northeasterly winds were getting more than their fair share of action this summer.

Though we were becalmed all night, we deferred motoring till 9am on the 25th. The sea was glassy and the horizon seemed to melt into the sky in a sunny, grey haze with a ring round the sun, though the glass was still high. As the calms persisted, we decided to have a swim, having set up a rope ladder with the Avon dinghy alongside. The surface water was warm but cooler below and most refreshing. We swam round the boat after diving in. However, later that afternoon we were perturbed to see the two black fins of a shark circling round the boat, and we no longer felt like swimming.

The next morning brought another radiant dawn, after a night spent following the stars through the heavens. Motoring again, we were able to get sunsights with a good horizon. The timer on the sextant was a great help, but we were still unable to get sights in quick succession. We clearly needed more practice. After another long period of calms the next day, we became aware of Morse messages being flashed, perhaps at us.

On 31st July we spotted land to port and thought it might be Cape Clear. We waited for confirmation till we could see the Fastnet Rock Lighthouse in the gathering dark. We were still heading for Kinsale but I decided to press on towards the Tuskar Rock, rather than putting in; and my decision was confirmed by a reasonable forecast for Fastnet and Irish Sea. During John's watch and mine, we had a race with another yacht, which came up astern and overtook us. She was a faster boat and carried more sail. Meanwhile we took in another reef and hoisted the storm jib. The wind was very strong and about as much as we could take without heaving-to, but it seemed important to get east of Tuskar, so we pressed on. Happily the wind then began to moderate.

Despite forecasts of cyclonic winds for many sea areas and a depression over Ireland, the Irish Sea remained strangely benign and sunny. We were now, in fact, heading for the old Head of Kinsale. I warned Sally that we might not actually put in there, and after hearing the latest forecast, which predicted southeasterly winds, force 4–6, I decided to carry on to the Tuskar. We never actually saw the rock itself, but we did see the Rosslare Ferry and also a submarine. We had a lovely sunny sail up the Irish Sea in a moderate southeasterly breeze instead of dire cyclonic winds. John spotted Bardsey and, as we took bearings on the lighthouse, the Llŷn Peninsula gradually emerged. We came up to Bardsey in the late afternoon, and the tide helped us round the Stacks to reach Holyhead by 3.30am. I rang Charles, who drove over to pick us up, and Yvonne came to take John home.

By the beginning of October, Charles had officially retired and we moved for good to Capel Curig on 15th October. Our erstwhile Bangor colleagues very kindly held a dinner for us at Bodysgallen Hall, where I found it rather sad to see our professors and their wives looking as ancient as we felt ourselves. Charles and I were both glad, however, that our Bangor years were now over.

*Pico by Denise*

Sailing the North Atlantic

'Triune of Troy'

'Dunlin of Wessex'

North

Shetland
Bergen
1960
1961
Oban
North Sea
Ireland
Holyhead
UK
NORTH ATLANTIC
OCEAN
France
EUROPE
from Bermuda
1988
1991
1964
Bay of
Biscay
1984
Coruna
Portugal
1985
1990
Azores
1987
Spain
Mediterranean Sea
1988
Madeira
Morocco
to Barbados 1988
Canary Islands
SAHARA DESERT
Cape Verde
Mauritania
AFRICA
Senegal
to Rio 1990

Florida

to Bermuda

The Bahamas

NORTH ATLANTIC
OCEAN

Cuba

Haiti

Jamaica

CARIBBEAN SEA

Cristóbal
(Colón)

Balboa
(Panama City)

Panama

Venezuela

Colombia

Guyana

Suriname

EQUATOR

Ecuador

SOUTH AMERICA

1991

Peru

Bolivia

Brazil

PACIFIC
OCEAN

Rio de Janiro

1990 from
Cape Verde Islands

Chile

Algarrobo

Santiago

Uruguay

Plate Estuary

Humboldt Current

Argentina

Punta del Este

Valdivia

Valdes Peninsula

SOUTH ATLANTIC
OCEAN

Golfo San Jorge

PATAGONIA

Falkland Islands

Punta Arenas

TIERRA DEL FUEGO

DRAKE PASSAGE

Cape Horn

Voyage round South America

178

CHAPTER 23

# *Sailing Round South America*

Up at Capel Curig we had snow in early January 1985, and looked out on a glazed and enchanted kingdom. I went up Snowdon on 11th January, where snow lay deep on the south side of Crib Goch, and the path up the Pyg Track felt soft to the tread. At the top of the zigzags, I had lovely views of Moel Cynghorion, the Rivals, and the sea beyond, to the southwest.

Early in February I went down to Dickie's Yard in Bangor to find that *Dunlin*, along with fourteen other boats, had been vandalised. The miscreants had broken into *Dunlin*'s main hatch, stolen the ship's clock, and turned her cabin upside down. I was met by a scene of devastation, in which glue-sniffing parties had taken place, sailbags had been slashed and drinks spilled everywhere. It brought little comfort to learn later that those responsible had been apprehended.

My plans for the coming sailing season were already under way. Sally Humphreys, Tim and Eileen Healey had agreed to help sail *Dunlin* to the Canaries at the end of June, and Penny Minney and Jim agreed to sail her back home again in August with Peter and me. Before we sailed, Tim came over for some navigation sessions with Charles, who gave us both instruction on the taking of sunsights. I was glad to have someone else on board who could take sunsights, and work them out.

Sadly, we heard from Tony Streather (who had been with Charles on the 1955 Kangchenjunga Expedition) that Dawa Tenzing had died. We were not sure of his age, but thought he might have been seventy. After an accident in a bus in Nepal, Dawa had lost the use of an arm, and life had become very difficult for him. Charles had known him for many years before I ever went to Nepal, but we were both grateful to have known Dawa as a true

179

friend, of the sort that would see one through thick and thin.

A few years later, I was busy planning a much longer voyage. My interest in the Chilean channels had first been aroused by reading Captain Slocum's *Sailing Alone Around the World* and Lucas Bridges' *Uttermost Part of the Earth*, and later by Tilman's account in *Mischief in Patagonia*. Through a chance meeting in 1984 with Ian Keith, an American sailor familiar with South America, I had my first glimpse of the Chilean Hydrographic Atlas. Back home, I bought a copy and began to take in the marvellous complexity of those waters, and to think it might be fun to sail *Dunlin* down there. Evenings were spent by the fireside, learning a little Spanish, poring over charts and pilots, and revelling in such names as Punta Anxious, Fondeadero Spiteful and Isla Deceit.

Much needed doing to *Dunlin*, and we installed a new engine, an MF radio and a satnav. I renewed the standing rigging, ordered a heavy-duty roachless mainsail with three reefs, and generally prepared the boat and myself for the rigours of the South Atlantic. Peter, my youngest son, would be free to sail with me for a year, after taking his finals in June 1990, and could bring his friend Peter Boswell Brown, to be known as Bos. We needed three crew members for insurance purposes. I also needed to be back by July 1991 for Chuck's wedding to Caroline. Could we reasonably expect to circumnavigate South America in a year? Tilman had done so in his much heavier 45-foot Bristol Channel pilot cutter, *Mischief*, and had crossed an ice cap as well. I felt sure we could.

Another question was which way to go. We had a year's grace from the beginning of July 1990. This predisposed me to go clockwise round South America to avoid crossing the Caribbean during the hurricane season. Two major disadvantages were that we would reach the eastern entrance to the Magellan Straits in November, at a time when the winds (almost always contrary) would be strongest; and later that we would be trying to make northing through the Patagonian channels against winds that were invariably northerly! On the other hand, we would enjoy the long hours of sunlight of the southern summer in the Fuegian Channels, and when we came out into the Pacific we would have the benefit of the Humboldt Current and southerly winds almost as far as the Gulf of Panama.

On 8th July 1990 we sailed out of the Menai Straits and over the Caernarfon Bar and enjoyed an uneventful passage to Madeira. The satnav packed in on the first day, but Peter soon learned to take sunsights with the sextant, and to work them out in the traditional way. The new paraffin cooker did nothing but coke up, the Tilley lamp consumed mantles and the new wind generator blew its fuse. More troublesome was the shearing of the fuel inlet pipe several days before reaching Mindelo in the Cape Verde Islands. The hollow bolt through which the fuel passes had been overtightened, and all at once we were deprived of power.

The wind now grew fickle and the days intolerably hot. As we neared the islands, it became increasingly important to hit the right approach between Ilha de São Vincente and Ilha de Santo Antão, so that we should not be set too far westwards by the Canaries Current, which at this point strengthens as it flows west. In the event, a moonsight gave us a position line at the crucial moment and we had no trouble sailing into Mindelo. Here we were able to get a new bolt made in the local engineering workshop.

We left Mindelo on 15th August and, following the directions in *Ocean Passages* fairly closely, persisted on the starboard tack in a southeasterly direction. We were only a few hundred miles from the African continent, which I fancied I could smell, like the hot fumes from a distant furnace. During our few days of waiting in the doldrums, we threw overboard our supply of cabbages, which were already beginning to rot, until we were surrounded by a little flotilla of bobbing cabbages, for which there were no takers. The skies were impressive, with strange complex cloud formations, full of seeming menace but quite harmless. They dispensed gallons of rainwater, which we collected in a bucket on the after end of the boom. The tanks were filled and it was a real pleasure to wash ourselves and our salt-encrusted clothes.

Rio was our next landfall, the most spectacular to date. On 18th September it was fine and sunny, and a brisk following wind enabled us to goosewing into Baia Guanabara. Coastal features gradually grew more conspicuous and resolved themselves into the famous Sugarloaf and other landmarks. We sailed as far as possible into Botafogo Bay before starting the engine. For some time now, we had been worried by a whining sound coming from the gearbox or propeller shaft. It was an ominous, expensive sound – and our worst fears were soon confirmed. The gearbox had not been properly heat-treated in the factory and the output shaft was badly worn. Both the engine and gearbox were still under guarantee and the obvious solution was to have a replacement sent out, but because of import costs and the delays involved, I decided to have the faulty parts replaced locally. This turned out to be a mistake.

While waiting for this repair, we had time to get sails mended and stores shipped, as well as making friends ashore and with our neighbours at the Marina Gloria. From Guido of the *Elena* we bought a new fibreglass dinghy, which came in two halves and stowed neatly on the foredeck. Peter and Bos climbed the Sugarloaf by a rockface, while I was invited to spend a few nights in Buzios. We were so royally entertained that it was with regret that we left Rio on 6th October and made our way to Isla Grande, where we spent a few nights at anchor in the lovely Enseada das Palmas before starting on the next leg to Punta del Este. The gearbox no longer made a whining sound but we had little power in forward gear.

Staying about 120 miles offshore, we sailed down the Brazilian coast till we were level with Arroio Chui on the Uruguayan frontier, where we turned west towards Cabo Polonio. We were now in the mouth of the Plate Estuary, where the sea became very shallow and smelt like the Sole Bank. Here Peter caught his first and last dorado, which was delicious. As we closed the coast near Cabo Santa Maria, we noticed the *baba del diablo* or 'devil's dribble' (described by Tilman as the 'gossamer webs of the aeronaut spider') clinging to the rigging everywhere, even on the Windex at the masthead. They are supposed to herald the approach of a *pampero* (strong southwesterly wind) but by the time the bad weather arrived we were comfortably berthed in the marina at Punta del Este, which we reached on 22nd October. At this time of year Punta del Este was a ghost city, but we were able to stock up again, to check the alignment of the engine, and to get a diver to clean the hull, which had acquired a thick coat of weed and barnacles. We hoped this would improve *Dunlin's* performance but found, to our dismay, that she could still only do 3 knots in forward gear.

As we sailed out across the Plate Estuary five days later, we ran into one of the cold fronts that came through at frequent intervals. Each *frente frio* was heralded by a great roll or archway of cloud, stretching from horizon to horizon, or by a whole series of archways. Passing anxiously beneath them, we began to suffer from a condition best described as 'cloud terror'. Our first big blow came on the night of 3rd November, when we were some 60 miles off the Argentine coast, level with the Golfo San Matias. In a matter of minutes we had reefed right down, then taken down all sail and were soon running northeast under bare poles. In these shallow waters, the waves were very steep and a nasty cross sea got up and filled the cockpit so that *Dunlin* lay over alarmingly. Peter tied our two heaviest and longest warps together, and streamed them in a big bight astern. The effect was miraculous: we took no more water aboard and were able to steer reasonably safely as long as the helmsman faced aft to keep the waves in view. But we still lost 80 miles in 24 hours.

While the gale raged, the sun shone brightly between innocent-looking cumulus clouds, which produced a series of violent squalls, and the decks went white with hail. It was bitterly cold. By midnight on 4th November, the gales had died down and we were about 60 miles east by south of Valdes Peninsula. That afternoon we passed under another bank of cloud and by the next morning there was another full gale with huge seas and breaking crests. Noon on 8th November found us partway across the wide Golfo San Jorge, on November 10th we passed close to Penguin Island, and two days later we sighted San Julian, of evil fame. There was a momentary lull. Rafts of seabirds, albatross, booby and Cape pigeon bobbed around us in the eerie calm. As I shook out the dust from my fibre-pile clothing in the afternoon sunshine, I pondered on the ways of Ferdinand Magellan and Francis Drake, but said nothing to the crew, who seemed unaware of the significance of that place, which

Chile, Patagonia &
Tierra del Fuego

is so well described in Pigafetta's account of sailing through these waters with Magellan.

We were soon running southwest again in strong northwesterly winds. Racing to get shelter under the lee of the land from the next southwest winds, we made the mistake of anchoring in the shallow waters off the coast just south of Rio Coig. The anchor held, but in the rising northwest wind, the chain snubbed badly and we were soon obliged to move on. Later that day the wind backed to the southwest, and the early hours of 15th November found us hove-to on the starboard tack, south of Puerto Gallegos, the last inlet before the Magellan Straits, with the Virgines Lighthouse in sight! We put through a call home via Magellanes Radio on a poor line, which was a great boost to our morale in the midst of violent squalls.

Towards evening the wind dropped, enabling us to run down the coast on a course to clear the dangers lying southeast of Cape Virgines. But in the early hours the wind got up again. With wind against tide, the seas grew to a full, rolling boil and it was obvious that we could make no headway. Storm jib and triple reefed main were too much for the mast, which shook and thrummed madly, even with no sail set. Fearful of losing it, we once again turned tail. How I envied the black and white Commerson's dolphins as they slipped in and out of the wave crests, thoroughly at home. *Dunlin* felt safer now but we were still very anxious, as the shallows of the Sarmiento Bank lay inescapably in our path. Once past the bank, however, we were able to heave-to and get some food and sleep.

Towards evening, the wind moderated and we put up a scrap of sail, only to take it down almost at once. By the early hours of 17th November, we were lying ahull again with the tiller lashed down. *Dunlin* was too broadside on for comfort and, as crests started breaking around us, the movement became ever more violent. There was a peculiar fascination about watching the waves as they surged towards us but, curiously, none of us felt sick. As the glass started to fall, early on 18th November, the wind dropped and went round to the north. Once again, we headed for the Cape, keeping well inshore this time. With an escort of black and white dolphins and penguins, we anchored halfway between the Cape

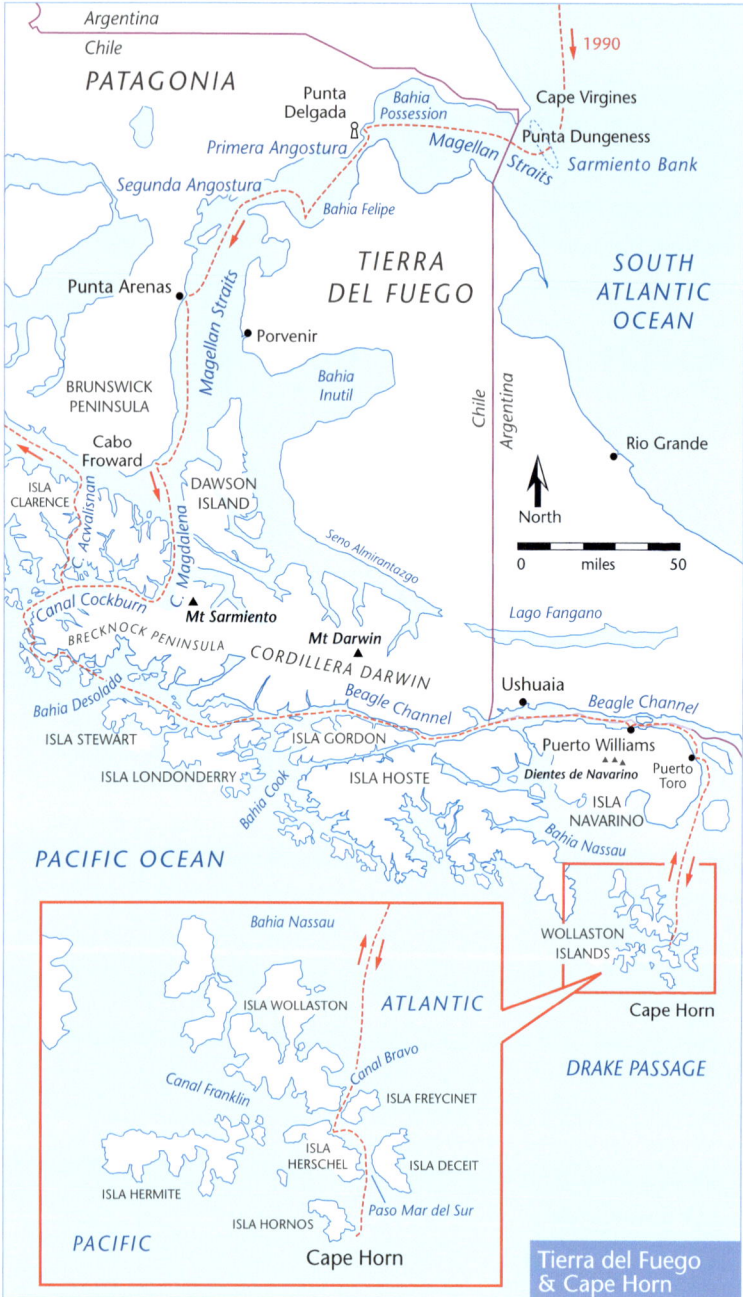

Argentina
Chile
1990
PATAGONIA
Punta Delgada
Bahia Possession
Cape Virgines
Punta Dungeness
Primera Angostura
Magellan Straits
Sarmiento Bank
Segunda Angostura
Bahia Felipe
TIERRA DEL FUEGO
SOUTH ATLANTIC OCEAN
Punta Arenas
Magellan Straits
Porvenir
BRUNSWICK PENINSULA
Bahia Inutil
Chile
Argentina
Rio Grande
Cabo Froward
ISLA CLARENCE
C. Acwalisnan
DAWSON ISLAND
North
0   miles   50
C. Magdalena
Seno Almirantazgo
Canal Cockburn
C.
Mt Sarmiento
Lago Fangano
BRECKNOCK PENINSULA
Mt Darwin
CORDILLERA DARWIN
Bahia Desolada
Beagle Channel
Ushuaia
Beagle Channel
ISLA STEWART
ISLA GORDON
Puerto Williams
ISLA LONDONDERRY
Bahia Cook
ISLA HOSTE
Dientes de Navarino
Puerto Toro
ISLA NAVARINO
PACIFIC OCEAN
Bahia Nassau
WOLLASTON ISLANDS
Bahia Nassau
ATLANTIC
Cape Horn
ISLA WOLLASTON
DRAKE PASSAGE
Canal Bravo
Canal Franklin
ISLA FREYCINET
ISLA HERSCHEL
ISLA DECEIT
ISLA HERMITE
Paso Mar del Sur
ISLA HORNOS
PACIFIC
Cape Horn
Tierra del Fuego & Cape Horn

186

and Punta Dungeness, little realising how well we would get to know this spot. The holding ground of mud and grit was very good, and with two CQR anchors down we never dragged, despite almost constant gale-force winds. Our position was not reassuring, however, for the coastline between the two headlands was barely indented.

Although very close to the border we were in fact in Argentinian waters and in contact on the VHF with Radio Trinidad, the Argentine naval authority. All our comings and goings had to be reported. I did my best to answer their numerous questions about *Dunlin* and her crew, and so became quite friendly with Fernando, the duty officer, and his boss, Tommy. Innocents that we were, we expected to move on up the Straits with the next favourable tide, though it was clear that we also needed a northwesterly wind. By the early hours of 19th November, it had shifted obligingly. We weighed anchor at dawn, cheerfully ran up our brand-new Chilean courtesy flag and headed towards Punta Dungeness. As we passed the Point, the wind backed to the west, rapidly rising to gale force. Disheartened, we turned back to Fondeadero Dungeness and anchored in the same spot, once again hoisting the Argentine flag. It was tempting providence, Boswell observed with gloomy prescience, to fly the Chilean flag.

We made another two attempts, which also failed, obliging us to return to our anchorage. Pretty soon Radio Trinidad began calling us, asking us if we had a problem. 'Yes,' I said, stalling, 'we would soon run out of food.' This was not strictly true, but it soon would be if we had to spend many more weeks at sea. Comestibles were no problem, Fernando told me. They had plenty – the only difficulty was getting them to us. I gave him our shopping list and it was arranged that as soon as the wind dropped, day or night (for the wind tended to drop at dusk), we would go ashore in the dinghy and they would come to meet us.

On the evening of 23rd November, Peter and I put ashore in the new fibreglass dinghy: a remarkably dangerous enterprise. We had become so used to *Dunlin* pitching and rolling that when conditions moderated, even slightly, we tended to think it was calm. Getting and holding the dinghy alongside was a very bumpy business. We also underestimated the surf, but got in well enough. We hauled the boat up the gritty, sandy mud, causing a flock of protesting penguins to waddle away into the hinterland, which was flat and covered with some kind of furze or heather.

Presently, five or six smiling marines appeared, with Fernando in the lead, bearing trays of food. They brought meat, eggs, bread, cheese, vegetables and fruit and would accept no payment for this bounty. We gave them a litre of Grouse and shook hands all round. The food was put into a large polythene bivouac sack and stowed under the thwarts. Our new friends then drew back slightly, saying they must go home as it might rain. Peter and I did our best to launch the dinghy in the surf but we soon capsized. The marines then rushed into the sea to help us right the boat. The food was re-stowed and we were given a good shove which helped Peter row into deeper water, while I bailed. I looked back in the gathering darkness to see Fernando and his men, up to their waists in the water, waving encouragement.

Next morning, 24th November, I spoke to Tommy on the VHF radio and thanked him and the marines for their generous help. With the wind in the northwest and the glass dropping, it seemed reasonable to make another attempt. The tide turned against us before we reached Cabo Possession and we spent six hours stemming it about one and a half miles from the shore, tacking quite often as there was an onshore set. At the turn of the tide, the wind picked up from the west and we hove-to, with three reefs in the main. The prospect was bleak but soon, to our surprise, the wind eased and backed to the southwest, allowing us to sail on a northerly tack.

Darkness found us clawing our way past the northernmost rig, which was brilliantly lit by all manner of coloured lights. By a happy chance, the wind then drew more to the south, allowing us to lay a course for Caleta Municiones at the western end of Bahia Possession. Numb with cold, we reached the anchorage at dawn. It is recommended by the Pilot as suitable for small craft in westerly winds. No sooner had we anchored about half a mile offshore, using both CQRs, than the wind blew furiously from the southwest and we had a very bumpy day of it, with the chain snubbing badly. Caleta Municiones is exposed to a considerable southerly fetch, and for hours on end the wind and sea howled past, drenching the boat and making sleep impossible. At noon on the 26th the wind eased for a few hours, during which we were able to re-anchor a few miles further south and closer inshore, ready for the next onslaught.

By the next morning, conditions had definitely changed. There was a general easterly murk with some drizzle and poor visibility. With the wind in the east and the tide under us, we were able to head south down a narrow 'channel' of slightly deeper water between the shallows of Banco Direccion to the west and those of Banco Plumper to the east. Thus we regained the Straits and laid a course for Punta Delgada on the north shore, just east of Primera Angostura. We anchored three-quarters of a mile northeast of the lighthouse in very tidal waters and an on-shore wind, and called the Chilean authorities to ask for permission to come ashore for water and cigarettes.

Permission was granted and Peter and Boswell lost no time rowing ashore and making their way to the lighthouse. They were soon back in the dinghy, but by now the wind had reached gale force and I was anxious that the boys should wait until it dropped. I communicated my anxiety to the Chileans but they had another plan in mind. Peter came on the VHF and announced that the *Crux Australis*, a drop-bow landing craft, was going to bring them back. This remarkable vessel appeared to scoop up the boys from the beach, dinghy and all. Moments later, some 50 yards up-wind of the yacht, it opened its maw and disgorged them into seas which threatened to sink the dinghy. Peter rowed furiously while the *Crux Australis* stayed to windward to give them some shelter. It was a desperate, foolish manoeuvre, but was somehow accomplished without mishap.

Later that night, the wind went round to the northwest and again the glass dropped, and we left at 2am on 28th November to catch the tide through the Primera Angostura. Conditions seemed unusually propitious. The sea was flat and we made good speed. We were able to lay a course for the west end of Bahia Felipe, on the south side of the Straits just east of the Segunda Angostura, and reached the anchorage at 8am before the tide turned against us. Boswell cooked a delectable lasagne, which we washed down with a bottle of Ring Bo Re before turning in. We weren't too disappointed next morning to find the wind was westerly and unsuitably strong.

Twenty-four hours later we got our next northwester and tacked out of Bahia Felipe to clear Punta San Isidro. Once past the Point, the tide gave us a good lift and by Cabo San Vincente, at the southwest end of the narrows, it fairly spat us out into midstream. The islets of Marta and Magdalena to starboard looked sinister, surrounded by reefs and overfalls. Now, at last, we could head for Punta Arenas, which could be made out some 25 miles away on the starboard bow. Further away, we glimpsed snow peaks under cloud and thought we could see Dawson Island.

With two reefs and a small jib, *Dunlin* went like a train across Paso Ancho: our best sail yet in these waters. Punta Arenas lay spread before us, now in sunshine, now in shadow, as we closed the coast. Although we knew it offered little shelter, being no more than an open roadstead, our hopes rose as we anchored a cable or so west of the Muelle Prat. It had been a daunting passage and we badly needed a rest. However, despite the friendliness of its inhabitants, Punta Arenas is an anxious and frustrating place for yachtsmen. The 400-yard-long Muelle Prat is built on piles, through which the seas sweep to and fro, whipped up by fierce winds. There is a constant coming and going of ships of all sizes, day and night. Mooring alongside can be damaging for larger vessels; for yachts it is potentially fatal.

The anchorage assigned to us, to the west of the pier, was much safer, as the holding ground was good, but it brought other worries. *Dunlin* pitched and rolled wildly in the shallow water and there were days when it was too rough to go ashore. The fibreglass dinghy and the outboard were too heavy and awkward to haul on to the pier. So, on days when this manoeuvre was necessary, we rowed the inflatable dinghy and were always glad to reach the protective calm of the oil slick that extended a couple of hundred yards from the Muelle Prat.

We had barely adjusted to this way of life when Boswell announced that he intended to fly home. Although not altogether unexpected, this was a blow. A minimum of three crew were required for insurance purposes and finding a substitute in this remote spot was going to be difficult. However, there were two other, more urgent problems. The gearbox, which was still giving us only 3 knots in forward gear, needed to come out again. Also, we had recently noticed a certain amount of vertical play in the rudder stock, no doubt due to the pounding poor *Dunlin* had received in the approaches to the Magellan Straits.

Hamilton Carter, the genial Canadian skipper of an American powerboat, very kindly dived down to inspect our rudder. He found some play in the shoe which holds the base of the rudder and offered to dive again on the next fine day and remove the shoe. Our conversations over the VHF on this subject were overheard and reported to the Port Captain, and shortly afterwards Hamilton was expressly forbidden to dive again for us. This was another setback and our first brush with authority. For reasons we never understood, Hamilton seemed to have fallen foul of the Armada (Chilean Navy), whose uniformed presence was apparent everywhere. Freshfaced and smartly dressed young officers thronged the port offices. There was a strangely familiar atmosphere about the place, which Peter was quick to identify as 'public school'.

We enquired about having *Dunlin* lifted out at Asmar, the local dockyard, as on dry land we could attend to both gearbox and rudder. But the price we were quoted was ludicrously high. We then considered the possibility of careening the boat. *Dunlin* drew 5 feet 6 inches and at Punta Arenas the tidal range was insufficient. It was greatest at either end of the Magellan Straits. Careful scrutiny of the Chilean tide tables for 1991 told us that there should be just enough water at Puerto Williams on 2nd and 3rd January. Although there were fewer facilities at Puerto Williams, they were much less busy there and we were more likely to get help. Could we get there in time and would the rudder and the gearbox hold out? It seemed we had no choice but to try.

While we lay at anchor in Punta Arenas, we noticed a couple of American mountaineers, whom we saw rowing past us in a home-made dinghy with sliding seats. They were proposing to row through the channels to mountains of their choice, after first getting a lift with the Chilean Navy. We were impressed by their enterprising spirit, and I kept Dave (one of them) in mind for a possible future cruise. Meanwhile we let it be known that we were looking for crew, and were surprised one evening to find no fewer than four candidates, none of whom had sailed before: an elderly New Zealander, a German, and two very tall, very long-haired Dutch boys who were touring South America together on a shoestring. We rowed them all out together for a drink. *Dunlin* was performing her usual anchor dance and before long two of the applicants were very sick. After some deliberation, Peter and I decided to take the Dutch boys, Herbie and Frank, as far as Puerto Williams on a trial basis. Frank had only one good eye but he had worked on a tugboat back home and we thought they must know something about boats. After all, the Dutch are a seafaring people.

Fuel, water and provisions were taken on board and Peter scoured the town beach for old tyres to use as extra fenders. We collected various items which had been repaired for us by Indu Metal, an obliging and enterprising engineering firm, which also made some new stainless-steel bolts to replace the copper rivets holding the rudder shoe in place. Chilean charts were obtained both for the passage to Puerto Williams and for what we hoped would be our subsequent passage north, through the channels, to Valdivia. This was perhaps tempting fate, but we were unlikely to get charts further on for, as Tilman reminded us, beyond Punta Arenas all was desert.

A minutely detailed itinerary and timetable of our proposed route to Puerto Wlliams was submitted to the Armada, showing every anchorage at which we proposed to stop and on which day, together with the usual information required by officialdom about the boat and her crew. A jaundiced eye was cast over our new recruits, no doubt because of their appearance, but our papers were duly signed and we were able to get away from Punta Arenas at 11.30pm on 18th December.

The wind was very light and we motored slowly through the night in a southerly direction, with Frank at the helm, learning to steer by compass. Herbie retired to the fo'c'sle, blissfully unaware of watch systems, while Peter and I kept an eye on the course. We made slow progress and reached our first anchorage in Bahia de las Aguilas, just past Cabo San Isidro, the following afternoon, after tacking for some hours against a strong headwind. It was an attractive place with wonderfully green, close-cropped meadows running down to the shore, and steep wooded hills rising behind. We sailed as close to the shore as we dared, before anchoring, and Peter and Herbie rowed ashore with two long ropes which they tied to posts planted in the ground for that purpose. A kedge anchor was dropped astern, which saved us from drifting on to the beach the next morning when the wind changed. Variations on this procedure were to become routine over the next fortnight.

It was cold and grey as we crossed over the Straits towards Seno Magdalena, but we had impressive if rather sinister views of Cabo Froward some 10 miles away to starboard, and of the mountains behind and beyond it. Looking south towards Tierra del Fuego 15 miles away, it was disappointing to see only the lower part of Monte Sarmiento, reputed to be the highest mountain in the Cordillera Darwin. There were, however, penguin, seal, orca, dolphin and steamer duck to delight the crew. Soon Punta Anxious was identified to port, while close to starboard lay the entrance to Puerto Hope with its steep backcloth of snowy peaks. It looked dark and squally, a breeding ground for williwaws. A few miles further on, Bahia Morris opened up.

Next morning, as we headed out into Canal Magdalena, the wind became unsteady, and died away altogether when we reached the south end of the Canal, where it turns west into Canal Cockburn. Here, at Cabo Turn, the fjord is only a couple of miles wide, and narrowed further by extensive beds of kelp. It is fed by impressive glaciers that flow down from Monte Sarmiento, but the cloud level was low and once again we were denied a view of the upper slopes. The wind came back from the northwest, bringing heavy sleet showers. Tacking up into the northwest corner of Puerto Soffia, another spectacular anchorage on the north side of Canal Cockburn, was cold, exhausting work. With sails and engine combined, we could barely make headway against increasingly violent gusts.

We left Puerto Soffia early on 23rd December, after noticing with dismay that the gearbox oil needed topping up. The wind in Canal Cockburn was northeasterly force 5 and we enjoyed an exhilarating run for about 25 miles. Out to the southwest, the Pacific was sending in a swell which broke on the Rocas Furias del Oeste and other nearer hazards. Successive *chubascos* (showers) swept over us, blotting out the landmarks, but we were able to lay a course for the entrance to Canal Occasion, which separates Peninsula Brecknock at the western extremity of Tierra del Fuego from Isla Aguirre. The rock-encumbered entrance, where a wind-whipped swell was sending up great plumes of spray, was an awesome sight. Bare, grey glacier-worn peaks rose before us, and as we flew in through the narrow confines of the Canal the scenery grew ever wilder.

We lost the wind for a time but when we turned northeast into Seno Occasion a few miles further on, it came back on the nose. Ahead lay a sombre panorama of grey cliffs, seemingly impenetrable, with a dark headwall looming beyond. Somewhere beneath it lay Caleta Brecknock, remote but secure. Tacking again and again in the constricted space between steep granite walls, we made our way up to narrows leading to an inner basin, over 65 feet deep, with a muddy bottom. It was blowing hard from the northeast, and we made the mistake of anchoring and tying to trees too close to the northeast corner of the cove. We had barely done this when the wind went round to the southwest and blew equally hard from that quarter. With our 60-pound anchor down, it was a tiring business re-anchoring and retying lines from the western shore so that *Dunlin* lay in a more central position, but well worth doing, as the wind and rain kept up from the west and southwest all night and most of the next day.

That day, 24th December, was spent at anchor, baking bread, fetching water and doing our washing in an icy stream that flowed from a hidden lake into the cove through a narrow canyon. Our immediate surroundings were so steep and rocky that it was difficult to explore. It was surprising too that anything could live in this austere and forbidding environment. The Antarctic beech, which is so prolific and adaptable everywhere in southern Chile, clung here, like a giant rock plant, to the cliff face, and we were amazed to see among its sheltering leaves the bright feathers of a jay.

The following day was unusually sunny with a light northwest wind and we made good easting through the intricacies of Caleta Brecknock, which separates the western end of the peninsula from the outer islands. The clouds lifted to reveal a magnificent panorama of snow peaks to the north, on Tierra del Fuego. Out to sea, the view was equally engaging: dozens of small islets in a placid blue Pacific with hardly any breaking surf. It was almost sunbathing weather as we sailed into Canal Ballenero, and the Dutch boys, who were adapting well to life on board, sat on the foredeck and combed their long fair hair. Darkness fell as we moored to the heavy buoy at the head of Puerto Fanny on Isla Stewart.

From there onwards, the Canal became more constricted as it led eastwards into Canal O'Brien, which in turn led into the northwest arm of the Beagle Channel. Lucky at last with the weather, we creamed along this fabulous waterway, enjoying breathtaking views of the icy peaks and snow fields of the Darwin Range high above us, and of the glaciers that tumbled down into the fjord. The most impressive was Ventisquero Italia, which we passed just before turning north into Caleta Olla, a lovely anchorage with a gently shelving sandy beach fringed with trees. While condors wheeled overhead, Herbie and Frank, both keen fishermen, caught an abundance of the much-prized spider king crab, as well as collecting quantities of mussels. These were a welcome addition to our diet but never a substitute for the kilo of dry rice that had to be cooked every evening for a hungry crew.

On 30th December we sailed on eastwards towards the disputed

*Careening Dunlin*

area of the Beagle Channel. Here, the Argentinian authorities, ever watchful for anyone who might stray into their waters, began to ply us with questions on the VHF. They lost interest, however, when they learned that we were not coming to Ushuaia, a large sprawling town, which could be seen on the northern shore beneath a skyline of jagged peaks. Instead, we put into Puerto Navarino on the Chilean shore. We were disturbed in the early hours by the arrival of a French yacht belonging to Alain Caradec, formerly skipper of the *Basile*, of Antarctic fame. Now, like a few other enterprising Frenchmen, he was doing charter work in southern Chile and the Antarctic Peninsula.

On arrival at Puerto Williams, we were directed to moor alongside the *Micalvi*, an old hulk lying in a sheltered inlet in the southwest corner of the harbour. It was a pleasant surprise to find another British yacht here, the diminutive *Xaxero*, skippered by Jonathan Selby, who kindly showed us round. With its dilapidated and rusty superstructure and its tilting decks, the *Micalvi* was not at first a pleasing sight, but it housed a surprisingly well-stocked bar and provided a warm and friendly environment for naval officers, yachtsmen and other visitors to Navarino Island. The panelled bulkheads were covered with relics left by previous sailors, and a well-used logbook showed how popular the Beagle Channel had become as a cruising ground in recent years.

After seeing the New Year in, it was time to think of careening, which made me feel a little nervous. Opposite the *Micalvi*, on the other side of the creek, was a shelving beach of mud and grit with a few loose stones, which the boys soon cleared away. Aware that we were providing onlookers with entertainment, but disregarding their gloomy forecasts that we would never get *Dunlin* afloat again, we put our faith in the tide tables, which predicted that the next two high water and low water springs were the highest and lowest of the year, and went ahead with our plan.

At 4am on 2nd January, the water in the creek was the highest yet and there were still two hours to go. There was no need of the engine. Warps were rowed across the creek and *Dunlin* was hauled into position. Weights were stacked on her starboard side and four tyres suspended from the rail, with a rope running through them to keep them in place. Halyards were run ashore and extended to reach the trees. Gradually *Dunlin* heeled over to an angle of about 60° and settled gently on the beach, her topsides neatly cushioned by the tyres. When the tide had fallen enough, Jonathan came over with his angle grinder and cut off the heads of the three rivets which held the heavy bronze shoe in place. They were badly corroded. Now we got a nasty shock: the new bolts made by Indu Metal were not long enough. We hurried across to the naval dockyard and explained that we needed to get the shoe fixed at the next low water.

The Chileans were very helpful. By 11pm they had made us new bolts out of an odd length of stainless steel; and at nearly 1am on 3rd January Peter and I were struggling by torchlight to knock them back through the shoe. This involved grovelling about in the mud, trying not to lose anything, and it was touch and go whether we could hammer the third bolt home, then fix it with a locking nut, before the seawater – already lapping round Peter's wrists – got too deep. We did it just in time and retired wearily for a few hours' sleep, not to our bunks, which were at a crazy angle, but to the boat's sides and locker fronts. I woke as *Dunlin* began to right herself in the early morning. The keel had dug itself into the mud, but with a kedge out ahead and a halyard to a pontoon in mid-creek, we managed to rock her free.

I had explained to Frank and Herbie before the careening that we could not take them any further, as I did not know how long we might have to stay in Puerto Williams and in the event we were in Chilean waters for 40 days. The boys were naturally upset but were soon consoled when they got an offer of a lift to Ushuaia on a German yacht. From Ushuaia, they would be able to make their way across Argentina to Rio, where they had already booked a flight home.

Meanwhile Peter got down to the hateful job of lifting the gearbox out, not once but several times. The Chilean engineers kindly allowed us to strip it down in their workshops, where we found it had been wrongly reassembled in Rio. A tired bearing was renewed and the whole contraption put together again and lifted back into the boat. By adjusting the selector, we now had more power in forward gear, but almost none in reverse. Thinking we could perhaps live with this, we decided to have a trial run down to Cape Horn and back. Having only two crew members meant that we would be uninsured, but only temporarily, as Charles had managed to find us a replacement, who was due to join us in a week's time.

The cruise from Puerto Williams to Cape Horn, about 80 miles away, had become something of a classic for visiting yachts. When we left on 13th January and made our way past Gable Island and turned south into Paso Picton, the weather was much less settled. After a night in Puerto Toro we left the shelter of Navarino Island and tacked across Bahia Nassau towards the Wollaston Islands which, in outline, looked rather like Skye and Rùm. It was exciting to beat through the narrow and twisting Canal Bravo, which leads southwest into Canal Franklin. Whales were blowing close by, the spume from their lungs hanging for a moment in the wind. We dropped anchor in Caleta Martial on the northeast corner of Herschel Island, and were presently joined by *Torakino* 2, 42 days out from New Zealand and on her way to the Falklands.

By 16th January, the glass was dropping again and the cloud was very low. At 4.30am we headed for the Paso Mar del Sur. With two reefs and a small jib, we sped towards the narrows between the islands of Herschel and Deceit in decreasing visibility and rain. The wind was gusting 7 to 8 and, as we crossed the few miles separating us from Hornos Island, we completely lost sight of the island. At times we could see the vicious-looking stacks on the southeast end of Isla Deceit looming through the mist. Peter spoke on the VHF to an invisible cruise ship, the *Illyria*, some 6 miles away to the east, then Hornos Island loomed up again and we could make out the rocks on its southeast end. We were heading straight for them and steered out to clear them until we could see the outline of the Cape beginning to emerge. Peter took one or two murky photos, and then, disheartened by the lack of visibility and the increasingly violent squalls, we turned back regretfully to Caleta Martial. There we found the gearbox was leaking oil badly, which was even more depressing in view of all the work we had put into it. We had no choice but to make tracks for Puerto Williams and phone home to ask for a new gearbox to be sent out to us from distant Denmark.

Jack, our new crew member, had flown post-haste to join us, so it was embarrassing to have to tell him that we were faced with another long delay. However, he was philosophical and he and I decided to spend the time doing some hillwalking in the Dientes de Navarino. The serrated outline of this small range of snow-capped mountains, about 7 miles southwest of us, looked engaging from our creek. Reaching it was another matter. First came a dense and, in places, impenetrable forest of Antarctic beech that covered several hundred feet of hillside. Large-scale depredations by beavers, particularly near the numerous streams and lakes, meant having to climb over countless fallen tree trunks. I soon tired of this slow-motion hurdling, but Jack, to his credit, reached the top of one of the Dientes. Meanwhile Peter had taken to sailing the fibreglass dinghy in the bay. Shortly after his first sortie, we were startled when a powerful inflatable, manned by two naval ratings, zoomed up and hauled him off to see the Port Captain, who reprimanded him for not asking for permission to sail the dinghy. We had not realised that permission was needed for the movement of any craft, however small, in and around the harbour.

Although spare parts imported off yachts in transit were not dutiable under Chilean law, everyone warned us of how difficult it was to get them, once they were in the hands of the Customs. We were exceptionally lucky in finding two indefatigable helpers. The first was Captain Bollo, head of the engineers at Puerto Williams, who had already given us a great deal of his time when we were trying to mend the old gearbox. The second was Bernardo Matte, a Chilean yachtsman who had put in to Puerto Williams in his elegant Swan. He found out when the new gearbox had arrived in Santiago, and made sure that it reached Punta Arenas. Once it was there, Captain Bollo arranged to have it shipped to Puerto Williams on a naval boat. Incredibly, that boat also developed engine trouble, which meant more delay, but eventually, on 8th February, our new gearbox arrived and the good Captain Bollo brought it to the *Micalvi* (our hulk neighbour) in person.

Adept by now at gearbox installation, Peter connected it up and realigned the engine, and we were ready to leave Puerto Williams by dawn the next day. Having made our way over the Herradura Bank, with the wind coming and going from the northwest and the glass dropping, we saw three torpedo boats: two Chilean and one Argentinian. We were back in Caleta Olla that evening, where Peter took out and replaced the jets on the cooker. Later we were joined by *Scherzo*. Skip Novak had told us that the skipper kept a piano on board, and we could soon hear the strains of Chopin's nocturnes drifting across the anchorage, reminding me, rather sadly, of my father and the past.

We made our way back along the Beagle Channel as quickly as we could, for it was getting late in the season and I was anxious to get north through the channels, past the notorious Golfo de Penas and out into the Pacific before bad weather set in. We caught up with a German sloop, *Koller*, and sailed in company back to Canal Cockburn and through Canal Acwalisnan, which is poorly charted but offers an attractive short cut through to the Magellan Straits. Leaving our new friends in Seno Pedro, we turned northwest into the Straits and pushed on in the same direction for the next 100 miles, sailing or motor sailing by day, for the wind was always heading us, and anchoring at night.

When we drew close to Cape Tamar, however, near the west end of the Magellan Straits, we decided to press on through the darkness, towards the entrance of Canal Smyth. We had an anxious passage: a westerly gale sprang up and with it the sea, which is open here to the Pacific, and the lights of Tamar and Felix were soon obscured in the murk. We had no radar but at least the satnav was working again. It took us many hours to round Tamar Island and to clear the Stragglers, a dangerous group of islets, rocks and wrecks, which lay close to starboard. In the early hours of 20th February we raised the light on Islote Fairway, and dawn found us entering Canal Smyth.

The so-called Patagonian Channels consist of an intricate series of inner leads which enable vessels of all but the largest size to avoid 300 miles of open Pacific, between the Magellan Straits and the Golfo de Penas. For the most part steep-to, these fjords, many of which had still not been sounded, wound through the wildest mountain country imaginable. Apart from the odd settlement, the region was almost wholly uninhabited, and the fear of being stranded through some accident was well-founded, for the only possible communication was with passing ships. However, there was a wealth of wildlife and innumerable sheltered anchorages. Most of these were wooded, making it easier to tie ashore for the night. This was nearly always our practice, for we had atrocious weather for days on end, with gale-force northerly winds, deluges of rain and frequent 'whiteouts'.

On 2nd March we reached Puerto Eden, the most southerly settlement on the main channel, where we bought diesel and some basic food supplies. We were also able to phone Charles on a good line for the first time since leaving the Magellan Straits. In our last anchorage before we emerged from Canal Messier into the Golfo de Penas, we heard reports from a southbound vessel of winds of 70 knots in the Gulf, and it was with some misgivings that we launched into this infamous stretch of water. It soon lived up to its reputation: with the wind in our teeth and heavy seas, it took us 24 hours to gain an offing. Once we were out in the Pacific, however, everything changed and we enjoyed following winds, a favourable current and fine weather almost as far as Panama. Our next port of call was Valdivia, where we tied up at the Yacht Club, downstream from the town centre. Several other yachts were there, including Bernardo's boat *Beagle*, which had left Puerto Williams before us. We decided now to make for Algarrobo, where we were able to get *Dunlin* lifted out in the marina, and could then paint the bottom, as well as having a damaged fuel pipe repaired.

Peter, Jack and I took a bus into Santiago to see Bernardo at his bank in the centre of town. Conscious that we were looking a bit dishevelled, I stopped off in a shop to get Peter a new shirt. Bernardo treated us to a meal in a posh restaurant, where we all had rather too much to drink so that Peter and I found it almost impossible to keep awake and I was dimly aware that my head had dropped down into my plate. Only Jack remained capable of conversation. Afterwards David, who had been with Bernardo on *Beagle*, drove us up to his house in the mountains for the night, where we were able to sleep off our hangovers.

We left Algarrobo on 29th March and motored off to Panama, a 25-day passage. We saw few ships but numerous dolphins and an increasing number of whales. On 10th April, we saw a pair of white-tailed tropicbirds, which showed we were nearing land, and also a frigatebird of sinister aspect. At night we could now see the Plough in the northern sky, which made us feel more at home. When we reached Balboa, we were told to pick up a mooring off the Yacht Club. We spent five days there, getting ready for our passage through the Panama Canal, which involved measurements, form filling and payments, as well as shopping for stores.

The passage through the Canal was 50 miles long and passed through a man-made section before entering Gatun Lake. The regulations stated that each yacht should have four 100-foot lines, four helpers and a pilot, but in the event we were allowed through without extra helpers. Four 100-foot lines were thrown down to us from the high locksides, we made them fast on board, and let out or pulled in as required, to keep the yacht stable and central in the lock. When the sluice gates were opened, the inrush of water was, as expected, very turbulent. We shared the lock with the *Canterbury Star*, a British ship of the Blue Star Line, which was impressively large. Once we were in Gatun Lake, *Dunlin* was able to achieve the recommended speed of 6 knots. We got through the Canal in a day and entered the Atlantic port of Cristobál. Here, we got through formalities amazingly quickly and headed into the Atlantic that same afternoon.

We planned to go home via Bermuda, and decided to leave Cuba to starboard and pass through the Yucatán Passage, as Tilman had done. Beyond the Florida coast we experienced a variety of winds, ranging from complete calm, when we were able to swim, to northeasterly gale-force winds, when we had to reef right down. Our last fix put us nearly level with the Plantagenet Bank, and we spotted land at 9pm. A couple of hours later, we phoned John Fuge, a kind friend who, with his wife Kay, had been helpful to me in the past. They now very kindly helped us to reprovision before we set off on our last leg home. Meanwhile, Peter and Jack went off in the evenings for drinks in town, earning *Dunlin* and her owner a bad reputation.

On 1st June, as we left St George's, John Fuge took pictures of *Dunlin* coming through the Town Cut so we had a record. We spoke to Charles on the radio, and he had already received John's photos of *Dunlin*. Our next bit of excitement came on 11th June, when we saw a sunspot at sunset. Charles warned us when we spoke to him again, that it might cause difficulties in communication. On the 18th, I gybed the main, bending the rail on the damaged side. Three days later, the wind was blowing hard from the west again, as the sun shone through green crests of seawater. We sensed our proximity to the shore somewhere off Ireland. By 23rd June, the sea had died down and we could see the lights of fishing boats, probably off the Sole Bank. Peter recorded seeing the flash of Bardsey Lighthouse at the end of the Llŷn Peninsula on the morning of 26th June, and we rang Charles to tell him we were almost home.

With a following tide, we made a swift passage up the north side of the Llŷn Peninsula on a sunny morning and soon saw the buoys marking the channel over Caernarfon Bar, after which we made our way back into Port Dinorwic and into the same berth we had left a year before. We rang Charles, and the Customs at Holyhead, before going ashore for a fry-up in a nearby restaurant. Holyhead Customs arrived with their entire staff, to check us out for drugs, and spent a happy time taking the headliner out of the forecabin in the course of their search. They took it in turns to come aboard, as there wasn't enough room for all of them at once. Charles arrived a little later, Jack left in the afternoon to catch a train home, and we parted on the best of terms!

## CHAPTER 24

# *A Wedding and a Return to Greenland*

Peter and I were back in good time for Chuck's wedding to Caroline, which took place in Guildford on 20th July 1991. Peter drove Charles and me down to Caroline's home at Hangerfield, along with Margery, who helped to look after Charles. After a most convivial celebration, organised by the Purkhardts (Caroline's family), during which much alcohol was consumed, we drove back to Wales. On 15th September Peter flew out to Bogota, Colombia, to work for Exploration Logistics.

A week later I had to drive to Southport Hospital with Charles who had blood in his urine. There followed several comings and goings to Liverpool as Charles' health deteriorated, with a prostate operation, testicular surgery and a bone scan. On 1st February 1992, I took Charles to hospital in Southport; and in mid-February, we heard news from Chuck and Caroline, of the birth of Natasha, their first child. I drove back to Southport to collect Charles and, in late March, Chuck and Caroline brought their new baby up to Ardincaple for us to celebrate. But by the beginning of April, Charles was in trouble again with a urinary infection.

A few weeks later I took Charles to Holehird, a very comfortable nursing home in Windermere, where he was well looked after. I went to stay with our old friends Sid and Jammie Cross in Langdale, and the three of us were able to take Charles out every day to tour the neighbourhood. In early October, Charles fell ill with a fever; and by the 12th, he was badly dehydrated. I rang his consultant, Krishnan, who arranged an ambulance to take him to Southport Hospital. On 16th October Krishnan was brutally frank about Charles' prospects, which were very poor. I then decided to look for a local nursing home, with the help of cousin Glyn's sister, Margaret. She and I toured the locality and I eventually chose High

Pastures, a nursing home on the outskirts of Llandudno, where there was a south-facing room, with a view of the Conwy Valley and the Carneddau, which I knew would be just right for Charles.

Having got Charles settled, my thoughts turned to sailing again. While taking part in the 1956 expedition to Mount Atter in West Greenland, I had enjoyed breathtaking views of the surrounding peaks and tantalising glimpses of the fjord as it wound between high bastions of rock and ice. I had thought then that it would be good to come back and explore by boat, and it was no surprise to hear that others had had the same idea. Tilman's account of sailing there in *Mischief* in 1962 provided a further stimulus, but it wasn't until 1994 that I was able to sail *Dunlin* into this lovely fjord.

My son Peter and I had by now gained some experience of this kind of sailing in the Chilean channels, but I was apprehensive about taking a fibreglass yacht into ice-encumbered seas, and only partly reassured by (legendary high-latitude sailor) Willy Ker's opinion that a strong fibreglass yacht could be sailed in these waters 'with due seamanlike prudence and work through open pack if need be'. When Willy very kindly lent me a complete set of Danish charts for the west coast of Greenland, I felt we must give it a try. In view of the prevailing westerly winds, Peter and I were aware that it might take a few weeks to sail to Nuuk from Holyhead, and we set about finding two likely lads to share the watch-keeping. Dave, an American climber whom we had first met in Punta Arenas, was keen to come, but the fourth man let us down at the last moment and we took young Arran as a substitute.

Neither Dave nor Arran had made an ocean passage before, which was no great disadvantage. However, the fact that both were vegetarians made me uneasy, as I remembered previous trips with vegetarian crews: the prolonged soaking of black-eyed beans, the hunt for an unspeakable protein substance with the consistency of marshmallow, and the question of whether or not there was pork fat in the baked beans. *Dunlin* had ample stowage space, and wherever possible, we carried plenty of fresh fruit and vegetables, but Peter and I also ate meat, which meant that not all dishes could be shared.

Leaving Holyhead on 10th June, in light, contrary winds, we were obliged to sit out one foul tide and to stem another off the Mull of Oa, before we could lay a course for a waypoint some 200 miles south of Cape Farewell. We had been advised to keep this distance off both by Willy and the sea-ice officer at Bracknell. Though our watches were short and the weather generally good, beating endlessly across the cold, empty wastes of the North Atlantic was dispiriting and made us all seasick at times. Dave was badly affected and lived almost wholly on popcorn, of which he had fortunately brought an ample supply, along with a quantity of vegetarian pills and supplements.

Greenland was eventually sighted on 2nd July, a long, low mountainous frieze to starboard, and we gradually closed the coast through shallowing seas, past grounded bergs and bergy bits. We had been in touch with OXF, the very friendly English-speaking radio station at Qaqortoq (Julianehåb) for some days, but now there were visible signs of life as well and it was cheering to see the bright red colours of the Arctic Line, and to find out from one of their ships that beyond Frederikshaab the coast was clear of ice right up to Nuuk.

*Watercolour painting of Sermitsiaq, near Nuuk, by Denise*

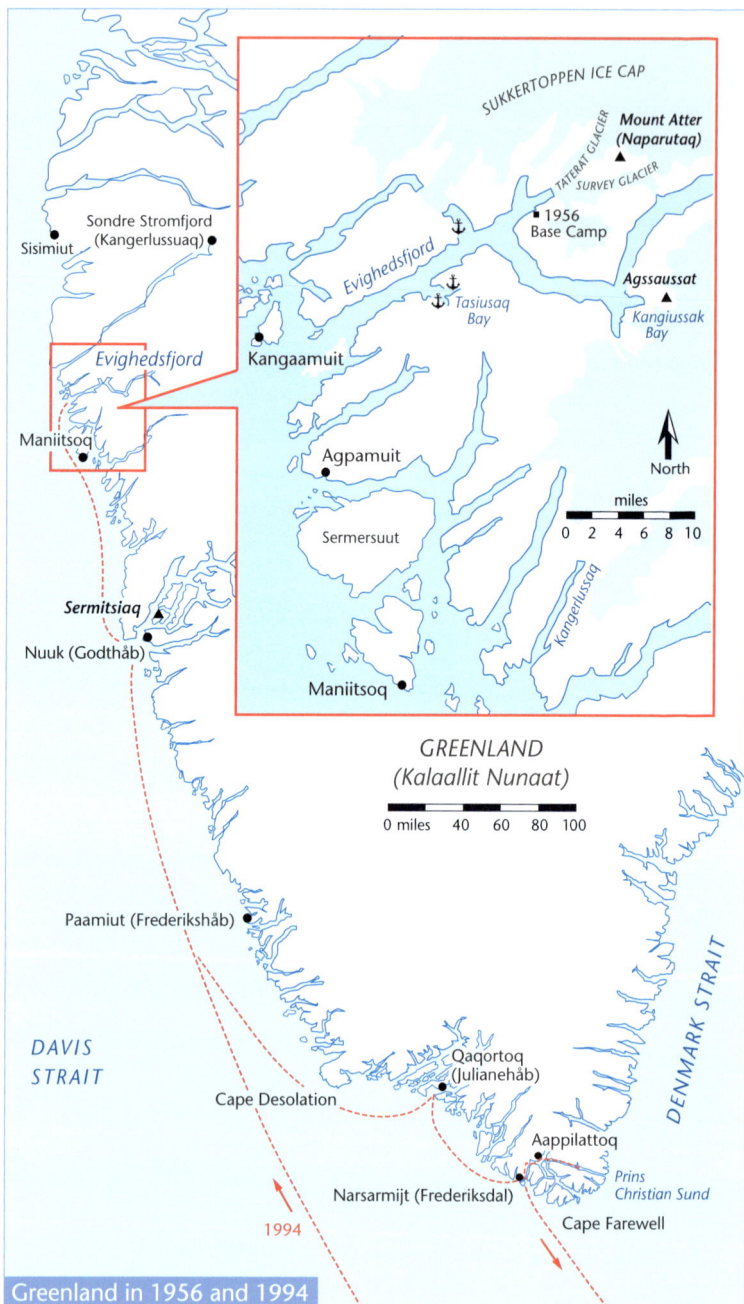

SUKKERTOPPEN ICE CAP

Mount Atter
(Naparutaq)

TATERAT GLACIER

SURVEY GLACIER

1956
Base Camp

Agssaussat

Sondre Stromfjord
(Kangerlussuaq)

Sisimiut

Evighedsfjord

Tasiusaq
Bay

Kangiussak
Bay

Evighedsfjord

Kangaamuit

North

Maniitsoq

miles

0  2  4  6  8  10

Agpamuit

Sermersuut

Kangerlussaq

Sermitsiaq

Nuuk (Godthåb)

Maniitsoq

GREENLAND
(Kalaallit Nunaat)

0 miles   40   60   80  100

Paamiut (Frederikshåb)

DAVIS
STRAIT

Qaqortoq
(Julianehåb)

DENMARK STRAIT

Cape Desolation

Aappilattoq

Prins
Christian Sund

Narsarmijt (Frederiksdal)

1994

Cape Farewell

Greenland in 1956 and 1994

208

The entrance to Godthåb Fjord was guarded by the Kookøerne, a dangerous cluster of low-lying rocks and islets, difficult but important to identify in the prevailing fog. We were extremely glad to have both radar and GPS to guide us. We entered the inner harbour on 5th July. Nuuk had changed out of all recognition since my last visit in 1956. Instead of a one-horse town with a single store, there was a flourishing modern city, complete with hotels, supermarkets and apartment blocks. Instead of fish drying on lines, there were nappies. There were no more Portuguese fishing schooners and certainly no kayaks; instead there were fibreglass motorboats with Yamaha engines. There was even a Spar grocery, where Dave and Arran were soon re-provisioning. Almost anything could be obtained, at a price.

Meanwhile, Peter and I made friends with Erik Moeller, the harbourmaster, a keen sailor with a fund of useful local knowledge. On his advice, we made our way offshore as far as Tovqussaq, and anchored beneath a mountain of the same name, in a pool reminiscent of a Scottish loch and the site of an old whaling station I had visited in 1956. From Tovqussaq to Sukkertoppen, we followed Erik's suggested route through an intricate series of inner leads, which wound between innumerable islets and skerries. The navigation required some care, but it was a pleasant contrast to the fogbound waters out to the west

Our route now took us due north for 20 miles until we could turn west into Hamborgersund. The scenery was no longer Scottish but Alpine and the mountains of Hambogerland and those on the mainland were attractively steep, snowy and glaciated. The weather was fine but as we made our way westwards a sea fog crept in, obscuring the approaches to the Paamiut anchorage used by Willy Ker in 1987. It cleared later to reveal a lovely but rather deserted settlement. Next morning the fog was back again, prompting us to find the easiest way into Evighedsfjord, which we entered on 11th July. As we headed north, the mists parted to reveal a spectacular view, which had not changed over the years. The blue waters of the fjord lay invitingly before us in brilliant sunshine; 20 miles away at its head we could see the impressive calving wall of the Taterat

Glacier, backed by Mount Atter, and behind it the wastes of the Sukkertoppen ice cap. It was an exciting moment and we phoned home to share it with Charles.

As we ran gently northeast, the southwesterly breeze freshened. Knowing there would be no shelter from that direction at the head of the fjord, we anchored for the night close to the south shore of a small subsidiary branch on the north side of the main fjord. Taking a line ashore and sounding from the dinghy, we anchored in 60 metres and then pulled back into a depth of 30 metres, a technique which gave us at least temporary holding in these steep-sided fjords. An anchor watch was kept, for we were close to another glacier and bergy bits had to be fended off. Spirits were high as we hacked off chunks of age-old ice to put in our whisky.

The next day dawned fine and sunny and we motored in flat calm up to the Taterat ice cliff to take photos, before moving back to the site of the 1956 Base Camp. Here, a small spit of land formed a slight bay on the southwest side, giving some shelter from calving bergs, which drifted down from the glacier on tides and currents. Sounding our way in with the dinghy, we adopted the same procedure as before, taking a stern line to a boulder on the moraine, which put us less than 100 metres from the shore. A sudden shift of wind would mean having to get out in a hurry, but for the moment we could relax and turn to fishing in the silty waters beneath the keel, where flatfish were plentiful.

In the afternoon, while Dave and I stayed behind to mind the boat, Peter and Arran set off up the Taterat Glacier, with a view to retracing the 1956 approach to Mount Atter. This involved climbing a tributary of the Taterat, known as Survey Glacier. In 1956 it had been steep but snow-covered; it had now become a distinctly awkward and unpleasant icefall, from which they wisely decided to retreat. The weather was changing, with clouds welling up from the southwest, and Dave and I were becoming apprehensive. The others came back in time, however, and we left on 13th July.

By now it was blowing hard from the southwest and we tacked down the fjord with the engine running. Though it was not dark, visibility was greatly reduced by driving rain. It was difficult, even with radar, to spot the entrance to Tasiusaq (meaning 'lake-like'), a small fjord about 10 miles away, branching off the north shore of Evighedsfjord, where we hoped to find shelter. Tasiusaq, which is uncharted except at the entrance, has two bays, one to the northeast, which is landlocked, and one to the southeast, which we favoured. We had read Tilman's description of anchoring here in *Mischief*, but not carefully enough to avoid some confusion. We sailed too far into our bay and went about only just in time to avoid running into a string of submerged rocks, which became visible at low tide. The anchor held at the second attempt. We kept our eye on a telltale snowpatch on the south shore as *Dunlin*, with her high freeboard, seemed to fly about like a kite. In the evening we had to move from the south side of the bay to a more central position, and re-anchor. The holding was good here and we were able to enjoy 12 hours of sleep.

In spite of this, crew morale was now very low. Some eight months earlier, Arran had been involved in a fatal accident in the Welsh hills and he seemed unable to shake off the memory of this event. We found him weeping on deck, and he declared he wanted to go home. This might have proved awkward, but we were only 12 miles or so from the fishing village of Kangaamiut, where a boat might be found to take him to the big airport at Søndre Strømfjord, further north up the coast. We decided to sail to Kangaamiut forthwith. Dave was not happy either. He had changed from the carefree young man we had encountered in the Magellan Straits, and perhaps we had changed too. He seemed to be pursuing some kind of Utopia, which he could not find with us, and he too now wished to fly home.

Like Sukkertoppen, but on a smaller scale, Kangaamiut was attractively perched on bare, glacier-worn rock. The harbour entrance was made more awkward in the prevailing onshore wind by an unpleasant scend (the push or surge created by a wave). The harbour, a thin strip of water protected by a string of islets to the southwest, gave shelter but little room to manoeuvre. It was raining heavily as we tied up alongside a fishing boat. Arran and Dave soon accepted the offer of a lift to Søndre Strømfjord from a family who were going there to do their weekly shopping. After they had left, *Dunlin* suddenly felt quite spacious.

It was still raining on the morning of 17th July, but flat calm, and Peter and I now decided to motor to the far end of Evighedsfjord. Around 3 miles from the calving wall at the head of the Taterat Glacier, Evighedsfjord ran inland in a northeasterly direction for its last 28 miles, forming a mile-wide canyon between huge almost vertical walls of ice. In places, the numerous hanging glaciers literally seemed to overhang the fjord and shed their surplus ice disconcertingly into its depths. Against a backcloth of black cliffs wreathed in mist, it was an awesome spectacle. We passed Kangiussaq bay, where Tilman had anchored *Mischief*, before climbing Agssaussat. Quantities of floating ice fragments dissuaded us from stopping here and instead we motored straight back to our previous anchorage in Tasiusaq.

By noon the next day, the wind picked up from the northwest and we sheltered in Tilman's land-locked bay. After taking soundings from the dinghy, we motored cautiously over a bar, on a rising tide, through a narrow pass between islet and promontory into a nook at the west end of the bay and took lines ashore. The wind dropped and the sun came out. It was an idyllic spot and we were sleeping peacefully next morning when we were suddenly alerted to an onshore wind. We raised the anchor in double-quick time and recrossed the bar before wind and sea made it impassable. In view of the unstable weather, and the difficulties of anchoring and leaving the boat, now that we were only two, we thought it best to cut our losses to put back to Nuuk, and sail home via Prins Christian Sund if possible.

Back in Nuuk, we renewed our acquaintance with Harry Jensen, a friend we had last seen in the Cape Verde Islands, then set sail for Qaqortoq (previously Julianehåb) on 29th July. The nights were beginning to darken again. Between 11pm and 2am, berg, sea and sky were indistinguishable, even without fog, which soon caught up with us. We had a trying night off Cape Desolation, steering between the bergs entirely by radar, in a world of virtual reality. Next morning, as we entered the Julianehåb Bay, the fog dissipated, and we were gratified to see the icy monsters breaking up. After two nights in Qaqortoq harbour, we made our way southeast through a series of inner leads, hoping they would be less ice-filled than the open sea. We were almost immediately disabused of this idea when, peering through the murk, we saw a barrage of ice blocking the far end of our channel, except for a 30-foot gap on the south side. The water was deep close to the rock, which dropped steeply into the sea, but what about the ram sticking out underwater from the nearest berg?

We squeezed through nervously, as yet unaware that this experience would be repeated many times. Passing through Sardloq harbour, the channel was obstructed by another great mass of ice, but the locals on shore indicated with eloquent gestures a way through on the far side. Visibility was down to 100 metres as we approached Zacharias Havn; and the radar picture, which makes no distinction between rock and ice, was confused by a berg nestling close to the entrance, but all soon became clear and we were glad to get into this protected anchorage.

Our route now took us south of Sydprøven, north of Sermersooq Island and down through the Nanortalik narrows, which in places were alarmingly shallow. Beyond these, a wind sprang up from the west and we sped southeast between gathering bergs towards the south end of the Taterakasik Peninsula. As we raced along its southern shore in rising wind and sea, it was difficult to spot the difference between wave crests and bergy bits. We soon made out the very narrow gap in the cliffs for which we were looking and, with that 'now or never' feeling (for it would have been impossible to turn back), we forged through to what we hoped would be a quiet lagoon. However, a westerly gale was getting up and we anchored as far upwind as we dared.

It blew very hard all night, but next morning was still, and, ever hopeful, we went on naively into the next channel. The bergs had, of course, preceded us, and we soon reached a complete impasse in a narrow gut, where it was difficult even to turn round. There followed an anxious hour as we crept between rocks and skerries in the unsounded waters separating us from the deep-water channel of the Kitsigsut Tunua, where there were few bergs to be seen. Feeling rather foolish, we now made good speed. Picking up two sets of leading lights off Frederiksdal, where a lot of ice was plainly visible, we turned north into Torsukattak Fjord, which eventually gave access to Prins Christian Sund. We now entered a fairytale world of sunlit, red granite spires rising sheer from the blue waters of the fjord. It looked like a rock climber's paradise but anchorages seemed few. About 15 miles in, we passed the attractive Stordalshavn to port. Here a broad green valley ran down to an open, shallow bay, which for the moment was berg-free, but we were not tempted as we were only a few miles from Augpilagtoq (now Aappilattoq), for which we were making.

Inconspicuous between the two rock pinnacles towering above it, this small, picturesque settlement was almost invisible from the fjord. A 60-foot cleft in the rocks led to a minute natural harbour, which was protected from everything except bergs. These not only lingered with intent round the entrance, but drifted in and obstructed our anchor chain with their underwater rams. Undermined by the constant ravages of the sea, bergs become top-heavy and have a frightening tendency to topple over without warning, with gargantuan convulsions and obscene garglings. We could not lie alongside the jetty for there were some half-grounded bergs there too; and the frequent comings and goings of the *Klapmydsoerne*, the strong wooden local boat, which shunted the bergs away each time, made it impractical. We settled for the middle of the pool, where there was just room to swing.

Weekly ice charts produced by 'Ice Central' at Narsarsuaq, with whom we were also in radio contact, made us think it was probably too early in the season to get through Prins Christian Sund, but Erik Moeller's view, that conditions could change very quickly, persuaded us to try. On 5th August, we put through a call to the weather station at the east end of the Sound and were encouraged to learn that they were fairly clear of ice there. Later, however, Ice Central spoke of 4/7 ice in the Sound. Meanwhile the weather took a turn for the worse, and we lay at anchor for the whole of the next day.

By morning it was fine and clear again and we weighed anchor before 5am, determined to go and see for ourselves.

A strong westerly wind carried us through an open stretch of water known as Ilua, where several fjords converged and from which we briefly enjoyed glorious views of jagged peaks before sweeping on past a couple of headlands into the western entrance to Prins Christian Sund. Soon our attention was drawn to an amazingly sheer red granite cliff on the north side of the fjord. At the same time we were overtaking berg after berg, some of them large and tabular, all moving eastwards in stately procession. A few miles further on, at a place labelled Qornoq on the chart, the fjord narrowed to a breadth of less than half a mile, and we could see a barrage of ice stretching right across it. Anxiously scanning ahead for any possible leads, we knew we might soon be in danger of getting hemmed in by the bergs coming up astern. There was no sign of a way through so – without further ado – we went about and beat back to Augpilagtoq.

Hoping for a rest, we re-anchored. It was Sunday and *Dunlin* had by now become a popular attraction. We were on the friendliest terms with the locals, but waiting here we would have no privacy. Regretfully, we decided to sail home and left early on 8th August. It was fine and the wind was still in the west as we headed south for the open sea. Cape Christian and Cape Farewell were clear of ice; leaving them astern, we made our way southeast through widely spread bergs. Apart from a low off Rockall Bank, we had a relatively trouble-free return passage, reaching Holyhead early on my birthday, 23rd August. Charles drove down with Doug and Anne Verity and we all went back to High Pastures (Charles' nursing home), before Peter and I returned to Ardincaple.

Above: Dunlin *in Greenland. Below: Denise in 1994 in Evighedsfjord, Greenland.*

CHAPTER 25

# A Norwegian Cruise and
# Charles' Last Mountain

On 27th August 1994 we heard that Caroline had given birth to Richard Charles (known as Charlie) and a few days later I drove down to Hangerfield to see the 'new boy', a suitably bonny baby. Peter brought Charles home for Christmas lunch, and Chuck, Caroline, Natasha and Charlie, plus their dog, Changtse, stayed with us till New Year's day. Charles had made many visits home in 1994, during which he was taken for local drives, and received numerous visits from his many friends and relatives. However, by late February 1995, he was down with suspected pneumonia and was taken by ambulance to Southport, though he was able to return to High Pastures by 10th March.

Charles and I were able to attend a Kangchenjunga reunion celebration at the Pen y Gwryd Hotel on 27th May 1995, to which Chuck, Caroline and their children also came. A week or so later Peter was home from Chile and *Dunlin* was launched again on 15th June. A fortnight later we started our cruise to the Lofoten Islands with Peter, Jamie Healey and my brother Ian. We cleared customs in Holyhead, where all went smoothly, but the wind was from the northeast and we made rather slow progress. On 4th July we anchored in Loch Drumbuie, where we enjoyed a sunny day ashore, rowing through the Doirlinn Narrows in the dinghy, and remembering old times. The next day, we rounded Ardnamurchan with a westerly wind and picked up a mooring in Armadale Bay, where we waited for a tide to take us through the Kyles.

Jamie left next morning, and Jan Davies came aboard. We were slow till we passed the Crowlin Islands and the Sound of Rona, but thereafter made good time to Stornoway, where we anchored in the harbour. We began to make out North Rona in the early hours. The wind went round to the east, picking up by evening to force 5 or 6. As Cape Wrath disappeared, oil rigs became visible, looking like Christmas trees but not as bright as the Chilean rigs. We made good speed in the lee of the Shetlands and rang Charles on the MF radio, as we did most days. By 1pm, I noted a change in the sea colour, which was now bluer, as we were off the continental shelf. The next day we had the engine on, mainly to recharge; we went through a lot of calms, and even more the following day, when the only event was a plane, which flew low over us. On 14th July the wind was getting up from the northeast and we were passed by a 40-foot German sloop. I saw an arctic skua attacking a gull and making it disgorge its prey, an unpleasant sight.

At about 2.30am next morning, the sun rose on a wild scene as the wind was now blowing force 6–7 from the northeast, veering east, as the glass fell steadily. Two days later, we crossed the Arctic Circle at about 1am. Peter took a moonsight to check that the GPS was accurate! We could now see snowy peaks to starboard on the mainland, while Skomvær became visible to port, marking the entrance to Vestfjorden. There was no wind as we motored into Reine and anchored on a lovely, sunny evening: a marvellous landfall.

There were two other boats in the harbour: one, whose Canadian owner was planning to live in Bodø for the winter; the other, the *Anna*, a very robust, home-made schooner, belonging to Thomas and Anne Berg, who had built her themselves over a period of 12 years – a remarkable achievement. They were a friendly pair and we had a good 'gam' with them, both on their boat and ours. Peter's birthday was on 18th July. We motored up into Kirkefjord in lovely sunshine and took the dinghy ashore, where we celebrated with pork chops and mash, a bottle of wine, and a special chocolate cake made by Jan.

By 20th July we motored into Forsfjorden and anchored just off the power station at the head of the bay. Jan and Ian climbed Hermansdaltinden, while Peter and I stayed on board. I walked up to a waterfall but began to feel unwell with colitis, which continued for a few days. In the evening we returned to Hamnøy, where we anchored in the middle of a most attractive small harbour. We left a couple of days later but lumpy seas and rising wind, combined with poor visibility, prompted us to anchor in Vatterfjord, a bay well sheltered from the southwest, where we spent a quiet night.

On Monday 24th July we motored up Ny Hellesund, taking photos of the peaks to the west. We went into Trollfjord, and tied up alongside a rockface at the far end, but clouds rolling in soon made us leave and we motored 2 or 3 miles further south to Ulvo, between islets, and anchored, as the weather closed in again. A couple of days later, we motored out into Lauksund, down to Digermulen, where we tied up alongside a Norwegian yacht, the *Anaria*, and made friends with her crew, Harald Berg and Turid. I went for a walk up the hill behind Digermulen with Ian, while Peter and Jan looked for some rock-climbing on boiler-plate slabs, without success. Rain drove in while we were on top and we were all back for an early night, as Jan and Ian planned to catch a ferry the next morning. We were all up early to see them off.

We slipped our mooring on 28th July, and entered the Sound, before heading north towards the entrance to Iglesfjord, where we anchored in a sheltered bay off the island of Nesøya. The next day we motored out of Nesøya and made our way westwards along the north shore of Austvågøya. The mountains looked attractive as the clouds lifted. Having moved south into Gimsøystraumen, we waited for the tide and anchored a mile south of Grimsøy. We then motored south through more narrows to Henningsvær, 'the Venice of the Lofoten'. It was just deep enough for us here, but evil-smelling. The night was peaceful, however, and we slept well.

Next day the weather was finer and we moved a few miles up the coast to Kalle, passing beneath some awe-inspiring cliffs and spires of granite. Kalle was a lovely place, where, for the first time, we had both warmth and sunshine. Peter climbed a long ridge while I walked along to Paradiset, a climbers' playground. Here, in spite of my new Pierre Allain footgear, I failed at one point to progress along a 'path', which turned into a VS traverse! On 1st August we went back to Reine, where we anchored.

The next day, we refuelled, watered and provisioned, and up-anchored. However, after an hour or so motoring against a southwest wind and making no headway, we put back to Reine, to wait for more favourable conditions. A low pressure system, centred north of Iceland, was expected to move to Bear Island. The glass fell slowly as the weather deteriorated. Birds were coming inshore and the mountains were blotted out. On 3rd August we motored out of Reine again. The glass was steady and we sailed close-hauled on the starboard tack in a strong west wind. Værøy looked very gloomy, and we made slow progress. By Monday 7th August, the wind was still blowing force 6 or 7 from the northwest but it was a fine day, with sunshine. The Aries (windvane steering system) was broken, and from 8th August onwards we had to hand steer. It was cold, grey and overcast and we had rain and fog as well; I wrote in the log, bemoaning our 'inspissated gloom'.

Three days later, we were off the west side of the Shetlands, passing rigs and fishing boats. There were numerous birds, including great skua (bonxie), and the wind drew to the southeast, making it possible for us to steer southwest but progress was frustratingly slow. By 3am the next morning, we were 10 miles north of Sule Skerry and a few hours later we passed west of it and went through the Nun shallows. As we tacked off Cape Wrath, the tide turned in our favour. We anchored at the southeast end of Loch Inchard, very glad to be back in Scotland, and had supper ashore at the Rhiconich Hotel.

The next day, 14th August, was our wedding anniversary and I rang Charles in the afternoon. I was sad to have to leave *Dunlin* and Peter on 16th August, when I took a bus from Loch Inchard to Inverness, and got a night sleeper to Crewe. I took a very early train from Crewe to Llandudno Junction and had breakfast with Charles an hour later. We had lunch together as well, and he seemed on pretty good form. Two days later, I took him for a drive over the Crimea Pass, stopping in the layby at the top for a picnic, and going home via Rhyd. I didn't realise this would be our last drive together.

On 23rd August, I found Charles not at all well, still not drinking and getting dehydrated, and having difficulty swallowing. I went home thoroughly depressed. The next day he was so dehydrated that he could hardly speak on the phone. I was conscious too that one of his nurses was getting him down. She meant well but somehow could not help patronising him. She had misjudged her man. Saturday 2nd September dawned grey. I drove down to Llanberis and met Peter, his friend Richard and Janet Davies. We set off for Dinas Mot, where we climbed between *Western Rib* and *Western Slab*s. Peter got into an awkward place and was rescued by Richard. I found it all very hard but managed with some tight ropes and some cheating.

Peter and I had been hoping to lay *Dunlin* up for the winter, but it wasn't until 14th October that we were able to bring her round to the Straits in a gentle southeasterly breeze, but the tides were no good for getting her into the yard so we sailed on through the bridges to Port Dinorwic. The Veritys came round on 18th October, bringing champagne and salmon mousse in preparation for Charles' 77th birthday next day, when Chuck rang from Germany and Robin rang from Hong Kong. Ian rang too and Peter and I were present. Alas, Charles' feeding tube had come out in the night and he had refused to let the doctor put it back in. We tried to persuade him, to no avail. But he seemed happy to have us round him, and he ate some birthday cake.

On 21st October my friend Dymmy arrived at Llandudno Junction and I drove her straight round to see Charles, who was well enough to talk to her. The weather was wild on 24th October and Dymmy and I went down to see Charles in the late morning. While we were there, we had a chat with the doctor, who told us what we already knew, that Charles was not getting enough fluid but he could not persuade him to have the tube re-inserted. I felt very sad and tearful. By Monday 30th October, Charles had lost his voice and I had to lip-read, but he was drinking a bit and seemed more cheerful. His cough was much better: I was amazed at his resilience.

Ian's birthday was on 4th November and he met us down at High Pastures just after Charles' lunch. We drove home early, as Charles seemed very sleepy. The next day, Ian went for a walk before driving back to Rydgaled Uchaf, while I did some gardening and lit a bonfire before driving down to see Charles, who seemed much better again. As he seemed more stable, I decided to take the day off on 6th November and walked up Carnedd Llewelyn. The weather was changing and the wind was very strong on the ridge between Carnedd Llewelyn and Carnedd Dafydd. I walked towards yr Elen till I could see my little 'skating lake', Ffynnon Caseg, white with wild horses. On my return I had a call from Henry Anglesey inviting me to Plas Newydd on 18th November at 6pm. He had had my letter about Charles' book and had prodded his editor (Tom Hartman at Leo Cooper's firm Pen and Sword Ltd).

At High Pastures on 8th November, Peter and I found Charles not as bright as the previous day. Charles asked us 'to come closer' so we lay together and hugged. Later he asked me for 'burny mixture' (magnesium trisilicate), but it took him ten minutes to swallow a teaspoonful. The next day, we found him asleep, and came back in the afternoon to find Neil Mather (climber and mountaineer) and his wife Megan sitting with Charles, who looked, and obviously felt, ghastly. We spent some hours there. Megan was not too optimistic and made me tearful, and Charles was too weak to communicate.

Friday 17th November was snowy, and I spent four hours with Charles, who was asleep for a while. Before I left he asked for a hot drink, so I made him a hot chocolate with a dash of brandy. He was drinking much better again, but seemed unable to eat much at all. After a short walk up behind the house, I went back to Charles, who seemed slightly better in the afternoon. At 5pm I drove to Plas Newydd, where Henry and Shirley had good news about Charles' book from Henry's editor, Tom Hartman, who had agreed to publish it. I went down with flu the next day, and Peter too. There was no question of visiting Charles and when I rang him he seemed to understand.

On 25th November, I found Charles quite sleepy, as he had just had some morphine. He took a little lemonade but kept drifting off. Although there wasn't much light in the darkened room, I was able to read the first few chapters of his book, but by about 4.30pm I felt rather desperate. On Sunday 3rd December, the High

Pastures staff rang to tell us that Charles was dying. We drove down independently and found him very dozy, but still taking sips of lemonade. The Cheyne Stokes breathing was very distressing. I wished he could just sleep, but the breathing difficulty brought him round every few minutes. It was as if he were climbing some impossibly high mountain. Not much morphine was getting down his throat, so the doctor prescribed slow-release morphine under the skin. When we next drove down, he seemed really peaceful; his breathing was very subdued and his eyes were closed all the time. We went out for a quick lunch, then sat with him till about 3.15pm, when we slipped out to get some shopping. We came back at about 4.45pm, to find that Charles had died 10 minutes before our return. We were told his breathing had simply stopped. He was still warm.

There was a dusting of snow on the hills on 6th December, when we went down to High Pastures to clear out Charles' room. It felt very strange without him. Everyone was very kind. Peter drove me in his car. We also left Charles' book at Print Place, to be copied. The day of Charles' funeral, 11th December 1995, dawned fine and cold. Our family and close friends all came. Instead of a service, Ian played us tapes of the Adagio from Schubert's late C Major Quintet: some of the most haunting elegiac music ever written. We all went back to Ardincaple afterwards for coffee. Chuck and Caroline, Robin, Peter and I went up Lliwedd in the afternoon. Glyn and Margaret also went for a walk. Chuck and Caroline drove home in the evening and Ian and Mickie drove to Harlech.

The *Times* obituary of Charles next morning was not to our liking, and Jim Perrin came to see me on 13th December to let me know that he would be writing an obituary of Charles for the *Guardian*.

CHAPTER 26

# Skiing, Climbing and Sailing

In late December 1995 Peter and I decided to go skiing in France, and left Capel in snow turning to slush on the 21st. Montgenèvre, which is on the way to Italy, was very busy, and wet, but there was snow on the slopes. Peter found a room for us at the Hôtel des Sports, and we spent the 27th skiing on the Rocher de l'Aigle piste, which ran down a little valley which Micheline had taken me up on skins some 40 years earlier. It was a lovely piste and from the top we had marvellous views of the Pelvoux and the Écrins and towards Rochebrune, which looked most impressive.

It was fine on 1st January 1996 and we went over to Les Deux Alpes where the skiing was lovely and easy with pistes nicely flattened. On the way back we saw lights high up on the mountainside above Alpe d'Huez – and learned later that some skiers had been carried away by an avalanche. Next morning it was misty, warm and wet, so we drove to Bourg d'Oisans and on to Vaujany. There was thick mist here too. We poked about Bourg d'Oisans and got a newspaper telling of the previous day's avalanche. We also saw the mountain rescue team who were looking, or rather sounding, for a young man caught in another avalanche at Vaujany.

The following day was very fine and cold and we went back to Les Deux Alpes, where we were able to ski all day long and right down into the valley. The smooth, easy pistes really made me feel I could still ski. Our only day on the La Grave pistes was 4th January. Peter and I both went down the big slope, which felt more like a wall, down to the in-between station, below the halfway. It took me a very long time. I went up again but did not ski down, as I found turning difficult in deep and crusty snow.

When we got back, the house seemed in one piece, although

there had been a small flood in the guest bedroom. Towards the end of the month, I began to feel really ill. I collected pills from the surgery, and retired to bed on 26th January. A week later, I was feeling better and walked up to Llyn Cwmffynnon for a skating session on the lake. The near end of the lake was smooth and I was able to describe what I thought were smooth arabesques, though my feet hurt and the exertion made my cough worse. On 14th February I ordered booze to be sent to the Alpine Club, in preparation for a Memorial Party for Charles, which was to be held there in early March.

My brother Ian drove up a week later, and we walked up to Glaslyn. There was snow in the gullies and the waterfalls were frozen, but the lakes were clear of ice. Mists descended as we came down and it was snowing gently. I felt very tired. At the end of February, I went up Snowdon by the zigzags and back over the bluffs: a lovely day, with brilliant sunshine and masses of snow. The wind was light and it was warm on the summit. The gullies looked magnificent.

I went to the Alpine Club in Charlotte Street on 5th March, and met some old-timers. I soon saw there were very few facilities there, so I went to a hardware store and bought a dustbin large enough to accomodate 24 bottles of champagne and four bags of ice. I rang round various delicatessens and supermarkets and got 3 pounds of smoked salmon. I also trailed out to Liverpool Street Station to a cheese shop. Ian arrived with bread and he, Mickie, Chuck and I prepared quantities of smoked salmon sandwiches. We had a very successful reunion on 6th March, though very tiring, and my sore throat came back.

The next day, Ann Sutton and I caught the Gatwick Express and we were in Pisa by about 2pm, local time, and then a train to Florence. We went for a short walk round the Duomo, which seemed to be done out in green 'fair-isle' marble. The Campanile had been cleaned and looked superb. We spent several days sightseeing and I very much enjoyed the Michelangelo sculptures and also some of the fourteenth – and fifteenth-century paintings. I particularly liked Botticelli's *Virgin of the Sea* and also his *Madonna and Child with St John and Two Angels*.

On 14th March we had a rather hectic morning and early afternoon, fitting in Casa Buonarotti, where I saw Michelangelo's *Madonna of the Steps* (his earliest known sculpture), the Museo del Duomo and the Museo di San Marco. Chuck met our plane at Gatwick and drove me back to Hangerfield in the Mercedes. Next morning I played with Chuck's children for a while before driving back to Wales. I was still not feeling too well. Peter was already there when I arrived, and Chuck and Caroline arived later. We had a pleasant family evening, almost like old times but for the absence of Charles. Over the weekend, Chuck and Caroline walked in the hills while Peter was busy with the Mountain Rescue team.

The next day, I started abridging Charles' book for the publishers, who wanted me to cut down the original text considerably. However, I found it difficult to précis the text without losing the individual quality of Charles' writing. (A heavily edited version was published in 1997 by Pen and Sword, called *A Doctor in the XIVth Army*. In 2020 Charles' complete book including his mountain treks was compiled by Cathy Woodhead and posted on the Alpine Club website. Entitled *Mandalay and Beyond*, this book is still available online for anyone to read.)

A couple of days later, I spoke to our doctor on the phone and he arranged an appointment to investigate my colon. Meanwhile my Royal Cruising Club papers had arrived and I hoped it had been a good idea to join this august club, to which Tilman had belonged. I went to Llandudno the next day and the dentist confirmed that I had an incipient abcess in a left, lower tooth, and told me that the problem would not go away and it was a volcano waiting to erupt. 'What a bore,' I said, feeling that too many things were conspiring against me.

Peter led me up *Marble Slab* on Bochlwyd Buttress on 5th April. Crowds were gathering elsewhere but we had our cliff to ourselves. It was very cold in the shade, and windy; but I was pleased to find I could still climb, and wanted to do more. However, I felt I should really find myself another climbing companion as I could not expect Peter to take me out all the time. We spent the next day in the garden, clearing the back wall and painting the garage. Peter then went off round the hills. In the evening we both had long conversations with Chuck and Caroline in France. They were very happy in their new place. Caroline said Chuck looked years younger.

Jan Davies came up for the day on 20th April and we did the *North Ridge* of Tryfan together and the *Bristly Ridge* and went down the Gribin. It was a damp day and Jan was wearing a short pair of galoshes, which were no good on wet rock. At the end of April, Peter drove me to Tremadog, where we climbed *Striptease* and part of *Venom*, which I could not properly claim to have climbed, though I did take out the 'runners'. Meanwhile I had decided to go ahead with a root filling for my tooth and was waiting for my dentist to fix an appointment with the specialist.

Later I went with Peter to Tremadog and followed him up *Meshach*, with some help. Peter left early on 7th May. I went first to the surgery and then to Ysbyty Gwynedd, where I saw a very nice doctor, who thoroughly examined my heart, lungs, spleen and thyroid, and took my blood pressure. He passed an unpleasantly large instrument up my colon, but apart from diverticuli he could find nothing abnormal. He told me to take Ciproxin with me to Nepal, which I was planning to visit with members of the Alpine Club.

The next day, I went round the Snowdon Horseshoe with Ian, after which I felt unaccountably tired. Sally Keir arrived on 11th May and we went for a scramble up *Cneifion Arête*, which was longer and not quite as easy as I had remembered. The next day Sally led me up *Belle View Bastion* in fine style. I did not find it hard as a second but was glad not to be leading.

A couple of days later, Roger Higgins, who used to work with me at my uncles' shop in London, came over for coffee. I was able to print out my shortened version of the first four chapters of Charles' book. I also wrote to Willy Ker, who was planning to take his boat, *Assent*, up the east coast of Greenland, a typically bold enterprise. The next day was very fine and a bit warmer, and we had lunch outside. Mike Ward's obituary of Charles arrived. I drove to Llandudno and sat on the seafront near the Little Orme. 'How I do miss him,' I wrote in my diary.

The dentist was most unsatisfactory. He drilled down to what felt like Australia but then stopped suddenly, as if unsure of where he was, and put in some cottonwool and said he would refer me to a dental hospital. On 15th May I went to Bodysgallen, where I met Henry Anglesey and his editor Tom Hartman, who looked much younger than I expected, a tubby man with dark hair. We were a bit wary of each other at first. Henry had been ill but looked better than I was expecting and ate a hearty lunch. Afterwards I handed over my shortened version of the first four chapters of Charles' memoirs, and felt like I used to feel as an Oxford undergraduate: 'Shall I get a Beta– or a Gamma +?'

A few days later, Peter and I went to the boat yard where we anti-fouled *Dunlin* and Peter overhauled the Aries gear. Although we launched *Dunlin* on 5th June, I was unable to put to sea until 21st June. I met Ian at Betws-y-Coed and Peter drove us both to the Holyhead Yacht Club, where we waited for Jan to join us. After a meal we got a launch out to the boat, and so to bed. We were up early to get ready, left under engine, and motored and sailed across to Port St Mary on the Isle of Man.

The next day the wind was still northwesterly. Nevertheless we decided to go through the Calf of Man Sound with the last of the northgoing tide. Rough sea made our progress pretty slow, and we stayed close to the west shore of Man to escape the contrary tide for the next six hours. We sailed up the Galloway shore as far as Port Patrick, where we motored in to wait for the next favourable tide, and lay alongside.

On 25th June we were off with the tide round the Mull of Kintyre and across to Islay, where we anchored off a sandy beach in Craggan Bay, which was open but sheltered from the northwest wind. After going through the Sound of Islay under engine, we were able to sail past the north end of Colonsay and across to the south side of Mull, making our way past the Torran Rocks and, greatly daring in view of the swell, into Tinker's Hole. We anchored in the shallow pool, which was calm and sheltered. Two other yachts came in, and Ian and Jan went ashore in a lovely sunset.

We went north the following day, through the Sound of Iona, past Staffa, across to Coll and up its east shore to the Cairns of

Coll. We were then able to lay a course for Canna. The weather gradually deteriorated, becoming grey and overcast, with mist and rain in the offing. Finding a mainsail tear above the reefing point, Ian took the sail down. The seas were lumpy off Rùm; and we put into Canna Harbour, where four other yachts were sheltering from the predicted gale from the northwest.

The wind got up to force 7–8, and more in the gusts. A handsome ketch sailed in, anchored with great difficulty, and soon dragged. It then circled, menacingly close, and we got the fenders out. Soon, however, we noticed that we were dragging ourselves, though not quite out of the harbour. Efforts to get the anchor up, and re-anchor, having proved hopeless, we let out more chain and eventually put out a kedge anchor, using the engine. Then Ian began clawing back some of the chain, while Jan hauled in on the kedge. After a rest, we started mending the mainsail. Jan noted, 'Denise and I started off enthusiastically, but Ian definitely had the staying power with the needle.' We had virtually finished mending by that evening.

Sunday 30th June was another day of rain and low cloud as we set off for Lochboisdale, tacking for 10 hours against a northwesterly wind. We got in just before the ferry, which brought Pete Davies to join us. The next day, we left for Loch Skiport in the afternoon, for six hours of motoring with no sails as the wind was northerly. On 3rd July, we decided to have a look at the Sound of Harris and went first to Hermetray, to wait for the tide. We walked on the island, which was lovely, leaving at 4pm to catch the tide over the bar. The tide was against us when we set off and the southeasterly wind very strong. As the sea behind also seemed very big, we turned back. We finally anchored for the night at Loch Beacravik, via a narrow entrance.

We motor-sailed towards Toe Head on 6th July, reached Lochmaddy by 2pm, picked up a mooring nearest to the jetty, and all went ashore to phone. Peter and Jan took the ferry to Uig, while Ian stayed with me and we had dinner at the Lochmaddy Hotel. The next day Ian caught the morning ferry to Uig, and I went aboard the French boat in the afternoon. They were a jolly crowd from St Malo, who gave me coffee and Armagnac and we shared some good jokes. They were on their way back to Oban and planning to go to Dunvegan. Afterwards I rowed up to the old wreck (the *Burnside*, a steamship, which caught fire and sank off Lochmaddy Harbour in 1933). It was very quiet there in the evening, apart from the arrival of a small cruise launch.

On 8th July I took the Post Bus to Solles, where there was a good Co-op and had a lift back with the lady who delivered newspapers. I was conscious that *Dunlin* was in a depth of 2.5 metres at low water tide and rather too close to shore in the gusty prevailing wind. I went up to the garage with my diesel cans, though at 65.4p a litre it seemed very expensive! At least they brought it down to the pier for us. I then went aboard the *Ufanova* for coffee with the skipper, John Revie, and heard about their trip to St Kilda, which sounded quite exciting. Another French boat came in, the *Lagon Bleu* from Brest, with nine on board.

Both the *Ufanova* and *Lagon Bleu* left in heavy rain and low mist on 10th July. I then made friends with Graham and Fay Cattell of *Tam o' Shanter* and went on board for a drink. When I motored out of Lochmaddy, the wind was astern. I was wondering how I was going to pick up a mooring in Loch Dunvegan (on the west coast of Skye), if one was available, and began fiddling with the wire strops to make some sort of lassoo. Fortunately it was a quiet afternoon in the Minch, grey with sunlight, a gentle wind and no rain. I lassooed the buoy with a rope weighted by a wire strop. It seemed a good system for loners.

On 14th July I phoned Peter's contact Mike, who put me in touch with a girl called Ruth, who seemed keen to join me on *Dunlin*. She asked if she could bring her friend Paul. They arrived about 6pm and I took them out for a meal to the Tables Hotel, which did vegetarian meals (as they were both 'veggies'). We then went on board and I explained a bit about the boat before it was time for bed. The night was windy but it was calm by morning and we were up early to catch a northgoing tide.

We motored round the north end of Skye and across to the Gare Loch, anchoring at Badachro. The next day, 16th July, we motor-sailed up to the Summer Isles, anchoring off Eilean Ristol, in a small bay. It was a lovely place. My crew went ashore and did not return until 4am. We all slept late, then up-anchored and moved across to the Tanera Beg anchorage, which was as magical as ever. We spent the day exploring, and I went up to the small loch where Charles and I had swum and washed on our way north to the Shetlands. The weather was good and we had wonderful, if hazy, distant views. I was very pleased to have come back.

On 20th July, I spent the day cleaning *Dunlin*. I did all the chores on board, both on deck and below, then rowed ashore at 6pm and had supper in the pub. On 21st July I rowed to the slip where a gentleman helped me carry the dinghy to his garden. He then very kindly gave me a lift to the station. The sleeper got into Crewe at 5.30am, where I caught a train to Llandudno Junction, followed by a train to Betws-y-Coed at 8am. A Sherpa bus then took me to Capel Curig. I felt it was a minor triumph to get all the way home by public transport. Having left my bags at Capel Curig Post Office, I walked up to the house. It was wonderful to be home.

## CHAPTER 27

# *A Return to West Greenland*

My last cruise to Evighedsfjord began on 10th June 1998, with a young crew: Zoe Brown and Jerry Clelford from Llanberis, and Nick Blandy, who had been recommended to me by John Ridgway. I also planned to take on extra crew, once we reached Nuuk and had arranged for Celia Bull, Sally Westmacott's niece, to join us there. We slipped our mooring in Holyhead in a moderate westerly and by 11am we had the Isle of Man in sight. The wind then blew from the northwest, increasing to 6–7 in the early evening, as we drew over to the Irish coast to find shelter. That evening we found petrol in the bilges and Zoe discovered the drinking water had been contaminated. She was very sick and soon Nick also had his first-ever bout of seasickness.

We experimented with the cruising chute, which helped us along, and spent some time admiring seabirds and the school of pilot whales that played round our bows. The whales made a small high-pitched sound like a digital alarm clock. I decided to put in to Port Patrick to pump out the tank and take in more fresh water and after a good night's sleep we left the harbour and headed out for the North Channel.

By the next day we were getting intimations of a Low 50 miles west of South Rockall. Meanwhile we had some good sailing and a great moon in the early hours of 14th June, followed by a sunny morning with fluffy clouds and new seabirds to identify. We were pleased to find we had sailed 140 miles the day before, but the next few days brought nothing more than a light northeasterly. On the evening of the 18th, the galley came adrift, and was adroitly lifted back into place by Nick and Zoe. Meanwhile the southeasterly wind drew more to the east and strengthened. By mid-afternoon, we had taken in our last reef and were running under bare pole, having got the mainsail down altogether. The increase in wind strength seemed to act like an intoxicant on the crew, who began to write strange things in the log about 'Merlin the magician' and 'chaos' and 'Nirvana'.

By the evening of the 20th, both wind and sea had picked up. It must have been Zoe who wrote that 'the nest of hellspawn' was full of diesel fumes again. We all noticed that it was getting much colder and were glad, now that we were over the fold in the chart, that Cape Farewell was the next land mass. The Aries rudder was temporarily removed, as it had taken a bashing, and the cogs had mislocated. On 25th June we had a rare day of dry weather, calm sea and agreeable sailing. In very light easterly winds we used the cruising chute to take us west. On 28th June we spoke to a woman in Greenland. We were all excited about being close to Greenland at last, but we also had a gale warning for the Cape Farewell region.

The next afternoon, the gale began to materialise. We handed the sails and were soon running downwind under bare pole once again. By midnight we had lashed the tiller over and had all retreated below, closing the hatch behind us. That night we changed to Greenlandic time, i.e. back three hours, so that today became yesterday, or yesterday became tomorrow. We were still lying a-hull by 6am the next morning. Though the glass was rising it felt horrible: like Llanberis in November, the crew suggested. There was cause to celebrate, however, as we had moved on to a new page on the chart, and were no longer 'lost in space-time'.

We saw our first icebergs early on 4th July and were soon avoiding more of them on Fiskenæs Bank. The wind rose from force 6 to 7 and we decided to heave-to and wait for it to calm down. We lashed the tiller under double-reefed main in steep, shallow seas. I spent the day making for the Kookøerne islets on 4th July, with Jerry steering while I continuously updated the course. With the wind a good force 7, we were being carried north at a rate of knots. Off the entrance to Nuuk, we spoke to Nuuk Radio on the VHF and got a friendly reception. At 2am we went into the harbour but there was no room in Vester Vig, so we went into the marina where, with some difficulty, we moored bow on to the pontoon. And so to bed.

At 11am the marina man came round, along with Anderes Nilson, Chairman of the Marina Committee, who was also a member of the Home Rule Parliament. Celia Bull had already arrived in Nuuk and we welcomed her aboard. Later, we met up with the crew of *Dodo's Delight*, which had arrived on the same night. Reading letters from home made me really homesick, not for the place but the boys, who were all such good companions to each other and to me. Peter wrote, about leaving Charles on our earlier trips: 'We must have been in his thoughts every day, as you are in mine when I see the sea, and also when I hear the wind in the trees or see the clouds moving overhead.'

There was work to be done, however, to get *Dunlin* ready for the next leg to Evighedsfjord, and we were not ready to leave till the morning of 12th July, when we moved to the filling platform to get Gazoil and Benzin on our way out of Godthåb. It was fine and sunny as we left the harbour, passing through mats of weed. We did a lot of motoring, as the wind had dropped altogether by 8pm. Soon after midnight, Tovqussaq was clearly visible by moonrise. And 2 miles off, we could make out a large iceberg masquerading as an island, while a large fogbank lay to the west. Early on 13th July we made a blind entry into Tovqussaq and the next day, after visiting the old whaling station on a sunny, clear morning, we moved on to Paamiut.

We reached Evighedsfjord two days later; at the entrance we had a spectacular view of whales disporting themselves, and Nick had his first view of a glacier. We decided to try Tilman's anchorage at Timerdlit, behind Maniitsoq, and nosed cautiously into the northeast entrance. As the depths gradually lessened, we looked for an islet which did not seem to exist, and anchored close to the mainland shore at half tide. Jerry caught a large cod here, which made a welcome addition to our supper.

The next day, we motored right up to the innermost part of Evighedsfjord, which Peter and I had hoped to reach a few years earlier. When we reached Kangerlussuaq, the farthest, innermost settlement, we tied lines ashore after Nick and Celia had sounded the way in. It was the most isolated, desolate and beautiful of all the anchorages I had ever visited, tucked away in the heart of a mountain mass, and it made a deep impression on us all. We could only wonder at the courage and fortitude of the Inuit as they eked out a life on these shores. What must it have been like in winter? Did they perhaps canoe back to larger settlements on the coast? We decided not to burn any rubbish on this hallowed ground, but to take it away on board and dispose of it later. I listened to my tapes of late Beethoven and Schubert string quartets while we were there, where their spiritual quality seemed particularly fitting, and shed a few tears for the Inuit.

On 17th July, we went back down the fjord in continuing fine, sunny weather. We went back to the Tasiusaq anchorage that Peter and I had previously used and spent the next two days there. It was very fine and sunny with little wind. However, our expeditions on shore were made unpleasant by vicious mosquitoes. We then ran up Evighedsfjord under jib till we found a small inlet on the south shore, about a mile from the 1956 Base Camp anchorage. This inlet, not immediately apparent behind a slight promontory, gave us some shelter from the southwesterly wind. We motored in and Nick took two lines ashore in a V-pattern, which held us off while Jerry and Zoe prepared for a possible ascent of Mount Atter. Nick took them ashore in the dinghy and left them at the 1956 Base Camp site, from which the Taterat Glacier could be seen and heard calving noisily! Nick and Celia took in our lines and we motored down the fjord. By 11.40pm Niaqornat was abeam, and it was clouding over, with a low mist creeping in from the west.

The repeat ascent of Mount Atter by Jerry and Zoe proved abortive, due to lack of time, and we picked them up at midday on 24th July. The next morning, with the mists lifting, Jerry ferried Celia, Nick and me ashore for an equally unsuccessful attempt on the 1,290 metre Qínguata Qáqai. After a hideous trog through tussocks and swarms of mosquitoes, we reached the foot of a rocky band and followed it for a couple of hours until the rain turned us back. Two days later, Jerry and Nick, who was wearing crampons for the first time, managed to reach the summit of Agssaussat, a peak previously climbed by Tilman, before glissading down a gully, and making another long trog back to the shore.

As we left Evighedsfjord for Kangaamiut on 27th July, we saw another yacht, the *Toswa* from Canada, which had been at sea since May, heading into the fjord. After chatting with them on the VHF, we were soon moored in Kangaamiut harbour, where we made a successful stop for gas, diesel and food. The temperature that night dropped as we got further away from land, and those at the helm enjoyed a peaceful night in a light northerly breeze. Snaggy mountains could be seen rising from the mists.

On 1st August we anchored in the sandy Baadelob anchorage on Kronprinsen Ejland and took lines ashore. We left the island the next day and headed north to Fortune Bay, close-hauled under sail, to anchor in 16 metres. This was our northernmost point so far. It was time, however, to head south, and we left Fortune Bay in the afternoon on 3rd August, with the wind now heading us all the way and icebergs surrounding us. One of them, looking like a ruined cathedral, was breathtakingly beautiful. Another large berg cracked and boomed and started to turn over. The helmsman called for a harness but the berg just pivoted threateningly, before disappearing, shrouded in mist.

Motoring through a calm in the early hours of 5th August, we saw a frighteningly large (possibly 60-foot) whale close to, before it moved away. After a protracted period of quiet, and calm sea, the Evighedsfjord mountains came into view again to port, looking pearly pink in the evening afterglow. By midday on 6th August the wind went round to west-northwest, and with the engine helping, we sailed through confused seas, making good progress in a southerly direction. Early on 7th August we were running off the Sukkertoppen Bank in a northwesterly wind force 6–7, increasing later that night to 7–8. In the evening we heard (on the VHF) about an imminent gale for this sea area. We furled the jib and lashed the tiller over once more. But the next day brought a glorious morning of sunshine and blue sky, with icebergs on the horizon. We had some great sailing, doing 6–7 knots all the way down to Nuuk, where we entered the marina.

Celia now decided to fly home, and Zoe would also have liked to leave, but was persuaded to stay on board with the boys and me, to sail back to Wales. On 9th August we attended to the boat, which involved changing the engine oil, oil and fuel filters, cooling anode, impeller gasket and gearbox oil. After these chores, we re-provisioned and were able to leave Nuuk on the evening of 12th August. We decided to sail south down the Narsaq Lob, a passage with good leading lights, easily identifiable in the strong tidal currents.

On 14th August the Hellefiskeoer were in sight, and we tied alongside in Fiskenaesset harbour. The next day we mended the jib, found the source of water in the bilge to be a leaking exhaust in the after-locker, and made ingenious repairs. We left Fiskenaesset early on 16th August; and that evening we had a large, wet electrical storm, followed by wind and rain. Conditions changed from calm to southeasterly force 7–8 in a matter of moments. The sea built up and we lashed the tiller at 8pm. We remained hove-to until 1.40am, when we were able to motor with three reefs and no jib. The sea was better but still lumpy, and a radar watch became necessary. It grew foggy, and 18th August found us picking our way through fragments of iceberg. By 7.30pm we had a fair wind at last. However, our progress was halted the next day by poor visibility and the need to avoid bergs, and we were soon weaving in and out of ice, with the engine on, using radar. At 6.15pm we spotted a large whale straight ahead; and by the evening, we were enjoying an amazing scenic tour of Nanortalik Bank and watching, awestruck, as a mountainous berg heeled over.

On the morning of the 20th we put up the jib and sailed fast downwind; by 11am, still sailing fast, we were approaching Frederiksdal and its magnificent scenery in hot sunshine. At 5.30pm we were anchored in Aapilattoq, which I remembered very well after my previous visit with Peter. We had a day's rest there on 21st August and left early next morning under dark blue-grey skies, heading down Prins Christian Sund. We were soon nearing Kangerdluk, an arm on the north shore of the Sound, and by 3.30pm we reached the weather station, where we had a warm welcome from the station crew, who came on board. They gave us lunch and we were able to have showers, for which we were hugely grateful. We made friends with Mike Stender, who also had a Tradewind 33, which was in fact the first one of that kind to be produced.

The sea was calm on 23rd August (my sixty-seventh birthday) when we left the weather station on a glorious, sunny morning under engine, and there were few bergs off the entrance. By midday we were level with a large band of ice and steered north to avoid hundreds of seals and a stunning ice palace. We scanned for bears but saw none. By the evening, although we were being taken slowly southwest by a current, we were virtually becalmed until noon on the 25th, when we had a good wind from the south-southwest. It was exhilarating, but with the wind now force 6–7, we were obliged to put in two reefs in the early hours of 26th August.

We had a fine evening, and enjoyed a calm sea and a quiet night on 27th, but the weather had not finished with us yet. The next day we were obliged to take in two reefs and reduce the jib in thick weather and driving rain but we were able to make good easting in a flat sea. The sea became lumpier as we headed purposefully towards Rockall Bank. Somebody noted that we could now hear the cricket commentary on Radio 4. But at 5.50pm the forecast spoke of high pressure over England and a Low 400 miles west of Shannon. At 1pm on 30th August, clocks were put forward by three hours, which meant it was now 4pm and made for some confusion with our timekeeping!

On the morning of 31st August we were becalmed again, west of Rockall Bank, as we headed into the Rockall Trough. We changed course at just after 9pm but we were still close-hauled, with the tiller lashed on the port side, and we were still being pushed northwest. It was lovely that night, and above the mists we enjoyed a 'planet-powdered sky' as our reward. *Dunlin* was going well in spite of a lumpy sea and gusty northeasterly wind, which rose to easterly 7 on 4th September. For lunch that day Nick produced Beaufort Force 7 pancakes, which was a triumph in the circumstances.

The choppy seas made us all ill. Zoe and Jerry threw up, while Nick and I were reported to be lost to the world! As the southeast winds abated, we shook out the reefs and went on the starboard tack again. By 9pm, someone wrote 'Whoops' in the log as the wind veered from easterly to south-southwesterly force 5. It swung back to southeasterly a few times until it finally went round to the southwest that evening.

Rathlin Island came in sight at 2am on 9th September. At first it was fine and sunny as we sailed down the Irish Sea, and we were able to enjoy our last few cans of beer on deck. Southwesterly and west-southwesterly winds, force 6–7, gave us a very swift, if hectic, beat back from the Chicken Rock, and as we drew closer to Holyhead we ran into thick weather and rough seas again. We needed radar to locate the breakwater. The crew spotted an empty canoe off the Langdon buoy, which we reported to the coastguard as we came in to the harbour at 5pm and picked up *Dunlin's* mooring, at the end of our summer cruise to West Greenland.

## CHAPTER 28

# *Last Trip to the Himalayas*

The year 1998 was busy. After laying up *Dunlin* in early October, I went on an autumn trip to the Kanchenjunga region of the Himalayas with a group of Alpine Club friends. We arrived in Kathmandu on 15th October, got our visas and moved to the Marshyangdi Hotel in the evening, and met Ram Tapa, our sirdar. The next day we went to a hotel at Biratnagar to wait for our flight to Suketar.

On the 18th, we had an exciting 20-minute flight, landing on a shelf on the edge of a precipice. We met up with our sherpas and coolies and had lunch near the air strip. A two-and-a-half-hour walk took us along a winding jungle track to a terrace at Lali Kharkha in a lovely forest, but with no views as yet of 'Kanch'. On 19th October (Charles' birthday) we moved down over steep ground to a suspension bridge over the Phawa Khola. After lunch came a steep climb to Bhanjyang and a camp on a pass. The views were obscured by cloud but I took photos of local children.

We crossed the Kasuwa Khola river on 21st October, and contoured the hillside, in and out of tributary valleys and streams, some of which were 'hairy' to cross on slippery tree trunks. We then went down to Khabeli Khola and camped by the river at Yamphudin. It was a very long, hot day but I was at this stage relatively fit. The next day, we climbed steeply through forest for an hour or two to Chitre. Here we camped on a grassy ridge, above amazing forest-clad hillsides between huge, V-shaped valleys. The sherpas did a marvellous job hacking out tent sites. It rained heavily in the night, clearing a bit by dawn.

The tents were still wet when it was time to move on up to Lamite Bhanjyang the next morning. There was a big landslide below, which we crossed, then dropped down to the Simbuwa Khola and camped on the right bank of the river at Torontan. It rained on and off for most of the day and we had no views as it was misty. We reached another very muddy, wet campsite with more leeches, a pest we had had to contend with for days, but the Simbuwa Khola river was very impressive. By 24th October, I had developed a nasty sore throat, and I was finding walking uphill a trial.

I had a long lie-in the next day and rested in the sunshine. While the others went uphill to acclimatise, Jan and I washed our clothes in a stream. I had started to take Diamox that morning and could feel slight tingles in my legs. On 26th October, we went up to Ramche, and camped on a wide yak pasture, with marvellous views of the Kabru and Rathong peaks. After lunch I went up alongside the moraine to get pictures of Kanch and was disappointed not to get a full view of the Yalung face.

The next day, we all followed along up on to the moraine to get photos. It was very fine with sunshine and a blue sky but once again we were disappointed not to see more of the Yalung face or the 1955 Base Camp, which was a long way down, beyond a rocky ridge which ran down from one of the nearer peaks. A couple of days later, we made our way down to a clearing above Tseram, then contoured the hillside pleasantly between rocks and junipers before climbing up steeply to a camp on a high perch by a small lake. It was very picturesque but there wasn't much level ground.

I was still feeling ill: the infection was in my bronchial tubes, and it hurt to cough. We went steeply up again the next day, in a series of zigzags. We crossed three cols: the Mirgin La, the Sinion La, and finally the Sele La, from which we enjoyed stupendous views of Jannu. We could see Makalu, perhaps 80 kilometres away, from the first col. We were now at about 4,000 metres, on a level campsite, by a flowing river. On 30th October we dropped right down to Ghunsa, which lay at the bottom of a V-shaped valley. There we camped in an enclosure next to the head lama's house. We were able to get showers from a vat of hot water with a tap for 50 rupees in the local boarding house. Ghunsa was quite a big place, and boasted a gompa, which we visited in the afternoon. The next day we went up to the village of Kambachen, which lay on the far side of another rubble-strewn landslide. We came across numerous children living up here with their families, along with their yak herds.

From Kambachen, we went on up the valley which drains the Kanchenjunga Glacier to Lhonak, another summer pasture on an alluvial plain. The next day we went across boulder fields to the region known as Pangpema, under a rubbly summit of that name. All this took place on the true right bank of the Kanch Glacier, which was almost completely hidden by moraine debris. After lunch we walked on along our 'shelf' to get a marvellous view of Kanch's north face: a staggering wall of ice-fields and glaciers.

After a lousy night, when I had to get up four times, coughing constantly, I felt too ill to eat breakfast. The fit members of the party set off for Pangpema, while I and several others stayed behind to rest. In the afternoon of 3rd November, we walked back up to the Pangpema Base Camp to take photos and sketch. I felt grim but the summit party came back well-pleased with their rapid ascent and the stunning views they'd had. Mike Westmacott and I, the two oldest members, were the last to be taken up Pangpema, which I found particularly taxing, simply because of the height.

It was soon time to head back to Kathmandu, but instead of repeating our outward itinerary our leader persuaded us to try a different route by crossing a high col immediately south of our highest camp. He no doubt thought that we were all acclimatised by now, and we would somehow be able to make our way to Suketar and fly back to Kathmandu. However, the way back involved crossing completely unknown mountain terrain for which we had no reliable maps, and our delight soon turned to worry over which way to go next. The truth was that we were lost – and we would be lucky to get back to Suketar for our flight.

As I was so much slower than everyone else, I was left behind with our sherpa Pasang and a porter, to follow more slowly, while the main party left on 4th November, heading for Ghunsa, which for them would only constitute a lunch halt. Meanwhile I spent the day trying to rest and get rid of my bronchial infection by taking Cyproxin. I was getting rigors in my legs, which seemed to have developed strange contusions. I disappointed Pasang by being unable to stomach much food, though drinks went down well. A couple of days later, I tried to go uphill a little way to do some sketching but had to stop to get my breath every 50 metres or so. Our Tamang porter smiled gently but said nothing. I found it hard to sketch while being overlooked and soon packed it in and went back to camp, where Pasang could now see that I was really ill.

I felt ghastly again on 7th November but decided to try to get back to Ghunsa. After shepherding me along tracks which Pasang described as flat, he decided we should camp halfway down the valley near a small mountain village. This was a sensible decision and gave me a chance to rest. Back in Ghunsa the next day, I sat by the yak herdsman's fire and watched his wife suckle her baby son. Her husband meanwhile appeared to be taking the roof off the kharka. A hen and goat completed the picture. The goat was trying to swallow a piece of wood in an aggressive way, as though saying 'If you won't give me your socks, see if I don't eat this!'

We spent a second day in Ghunsa, where I watched the head lama intoning his holy book, seated on the wall of his compound. Meanwhile Pasang and the porter relieved the boredom by playing frisbee. It was desperately cold on the morning of 10th November and I went into the lama's house to keep warm by the fire. While his wife made a meal, the lama mended clothes and his son worked out a complicated bill for us. All this was done in semi-darkness and I felt almost frozen before starting down the valley. My leg was painful and the yaks were annoying.

The next day, after much upping and downing, we camped in a meadow for two nights, and met three French-speaking Swiss, one of whom knew Jeanne Franco. They told us that she was still going strong, which I was very glad to hear. They also gave me some more antibiotics in case I needed them. On 12th November we made an endless and very trying descent, interspersed with many 'ups'. Eventually we spotted three houses on a spur of hillside, and put up our tents on a small patch of terraced field. We made friends with the locals in an attractive Sherpa house, in a corner of which stood a great vat of chang (a local brew), over which Pasang seemed to enjoy telling 'tiger stories'.

By 14th November the throng of visitors had left and I was able to have a rest day, and wash my hair and my underwear. My appetite was slowly coming back, though the veins in my legs were still hurting. We were up very early the next day to beat the sun, but the path always seemed to be in the shade and was pleasantly wooded. We camped at Tapethok, where the police officer at the checkpost was a friend of Pasang's. They were all most friendly and helpful, and offered me some mandarin oranges. My tent was pitched in a little wood, quite an original sort of campsite, but best of all was that my appetite had come back.

We left Tapethok early on 16th November and were soon in Chirwa, a village of some size, where I took more paracetamol, as my leg was hurting badly. After Pasang had bought some rice, we had our lunch stop by a stream with a rickety bridge. We then went uphill along a good track, in and out of nullahs, to a small village. Rain set in and two remarkable geese gave voice. It rained that night and was still pattering on our tents the next morning. We made a damp getaway, stopping for lunch very early, and sat under a rock in the prevailing drizzle. My appetite was improving and I managed to eat two boiled eggs with Tibetan bread, and more bread with marmalade, washed down with milky coffee. Afterwards we moved on to a school campsite at Phurumba, high above the Tamur River, where there were bevies of inquisitive children.

A party of British and New Zealand trekkers joined us for the night, and all were heading for Suketar, which we reached after three or four hours' walk on 18th November. The place was a hive of trekking activity, where we were still surrounded by last night's large group. They were planning to fly out on the 19th, and we on the 20th. When we got back to Kathmandu, there was nobody much about and I had a strangely detached feeling. I spent my time in the Pilgrim Bookshop, which was amazingly well-stocked, and found Charles' book *On Climbing* in the antiquarian section! I also found Lucas Bridges' *The Uttermost Part of the Earth*. After leaving Kathmandu on 27th November, I spent the night at the Royal Thames Yacht Club, and took a train back to Wales, at the end of my last visit to the Indian subcontinent.

CHAPTER 29

## *An Irish Cruise*

At some stage during the last few years, my brother Ian had sailed his own small yacht *Chinook* up the spectacular west coast of Ireland with his partner, Mickie, an experience which they both greatly enjoyed. He suggested I should take *Dunlin* there, and agreed to come with me at the end of June 1999, along with Alan and Jonathan Armstrong. We left Holyhead on 29th June in fine weather with light winds.

On 4th July, we sailed from Dunmore East to Crosshaven. We just had time to get some very substandard fish and chips in the village before getting a launch back to *Dunlin*, but our mooring up-river, not far from Drake's Pool, was very peaceful. We could hear curlews calling. We had a pleasant, short passage from Crosshaven to Oysterhaven. It was foggy at first but we could make out Big Sovereign and Little Sovereign, where we turned into Oysterhaven and anchored just beyond Ferry Point in Murray's Creek, where *Spirit of Oysterhaven*, a big schooner, was also moored.

Two days later, we sailed from Oysterhaven to Glandore, past Seven Heads, Galley Head and Goat's Head, identifying Adam and Eve and strange topmarks on beacons, and on the 7th we sailed to Baltimore, where we had some difficulty in finding a deep enough anchorage. It was foggy off the Stags, which looked eerie in the mist. We took a middle path between them and Toe Head. The Armstrongs left us the next day, and Ian and I sailed round to look at North Harbour on Cape Clear Island. It was very foggy as we left Crookhaven on 9th July, and we could only dimly make out Mizzen Head. We sailed past Sheep's Head and Dunmore Bay, across Bantry Bay to Dursey Sound, across Kenmare River to Derrynane, an intricate approach, lining up beacons on shore and a narrow gateway, made more awkward by the swell. The next day, we sailed out to take pictures from a point between the Skelligs, then tacked to clear Lemon Rock and Puffin Island, to get the shelter of Bray Head. From Port Magee we sailed out round Bray Head and out to the Blasket Islands. We tacked near Foze Rocks and back along the south shore of the Big Blasket, and sailed, in clearing weather to Ventry.

On 12th July, we left Ventry and made our way through Blasket Sound in steep seas, till we could clear Sybil Point and head along the north shore of the Dingle Peninsula, past the Three Sisters. We then put in to Smerwick Harbour. We left Smerwick on 13th July for the 66-mile passage to the Aran Islands. We almost decided to go into the Shannon Estuary, but thought better of it, and battled on through rough seas. The engine ran out of oil but Ian managed to put more in just before we entered Gregory Sound, to take us through to the Kilronan anchorage. There were no moorings, but two or three French yachts were already anchored here.

We left Kilronan on 16th, sailed across to the mainland and got a bit lost on the way to Inishmore. We looked at Crognut, Ian's anchorage at the inner end of the bay, but were frightened of not being able to get out. We anchored on the south shore for a few hours before moving on into Cloonile Bay, up a narrow, twisting and tide-ridden backwater, then anchored in a peaceful sheltered nook. The wind blew up in the night, as expected, but the anchor held, though the ICC guide claimed that the holding was poor.

Next day, Ian suddenly felt very sick but we made our way down the narrow, twisting channel. The wind was quite moderate, but we motored across to Gorteen Bay and anchored off a curving, white sandy beach, nicely protected from the southwest. After a very peaceful night, Ian was much better, though still uncomfortable. On the way from Gorteen Bay to Inishbofin, we mistook the Murray Rocks for the Caulty Rock: a near disaster, but we turned away in time! Thence, rather shaken, to Slyne Head and on through the High Island Sound in decreasing to nil visibility to find the entrance, with the help of radar, and anchored in a shallow bay off the pier.

We had a bad night and were up at 2 am to find we were in

a depth of less than 2 metres! We took in a few metres of chain and did not bump, then moved to a fishing boat mooring. It was time to go ashore for showers in Day's Hotel, and afternoon tea. We were glad to be on a mooring as the wind got up. Another boat, a Moody from Belfast, very new and well-appointed, came in and anchored just ahead of us, giving us cause for concern as she ranged about. Happily her anchor held, as the gale-force winds drove straight into the harbour.

We motored out and across to Little Killary, a lovely fjord-like bay, ensconced ouselves in the far end and enjoyed a peaceful evening and night. We were able to get more fresh water from a well. On 22nd July, we sailed outside the Belmullet Peninsula in a strong following wind, and used a 'preventer' to stop the boom swinging across. We almost overshot Frenchport, which looked rather bleak, but it was sheltered from the southwest wind, which was strong to gale force, with rain and mist.

Having made an early departure, it took us a long time to get past the 'Stags' and cross Donegal Bay, but we had a lovely sail on a broad reach, speeding up as we got near Slieve League. On 24th July, Ian and I went ashore to make enquiries and met Jack Gallagher, of Gallagher Brothers, mentioned in the ICC pilot, and he suggested we leave *Dunlin* there, rather than at Killibegs. He promised to keep an eye on the boat, and I decided to leave the keys with him. Ian and I were both very tired, and it seemed a long walk to the pier from the shop in Teelin.

We did our washing on the pier, there being no other facilities. On 26th July, Ian and I embarked on a very long walk along the tops of Slieve League, with spectacular views. The path turned into a knife-edge, which Ian climbed, while I found an easy way round. We went down a cwm and eventually made our way back to Teelin, weary and footsore. On 28th July, we had to be ashore at 7am for Ian's taxi. We said goodbye and I did some boat chores, feeling very tired and glad of a chance to rest during the next few days

By 3rd August, the weather had changed. There was no wind but it was drizzling. I put my bags in the dinghy and rowed to the slip, where the taximan gave me a hand with the dinghy. I then took the bus to Dublin and made my weary way to the Dart station to go to Dun Laoghaire. I had a very quiet crossing, and was met by Peter. On 20th August, Peter and I made our way over to Dublin and back to Teelin by car. Peter did most of the driving. As he was now a serving police officer, he was reluctant to go through Northern Ireland, and we took the road to Sligo, and reached Teelin in time to collect the dinghy. We were both very tired.

Peter was ready to leave by lunchtime on 21st August. I went up the hillside to take pictures as he sailed towards the pier, before running off downwind towards Rathlin 0'Byrne, and vanishing. I felt a little sad and despondent. Next day I headed off to Achill and climbed the ridge leading up to Achill Head along the 'backbone' of the promontory. Though the cliffs were not sheer, the views were impressive, and the grass slippery in the rain.

The weather was disappointing on August 23rd, and I spent the day touring in the Killary region. I found Wittgenstein's residence by the quay at Little Killary pier before going on round Connemara National Park. After a night near Kylemor Lough, I headed for Dublin and booked a ferry to Holyhead on August 26th. There was still time to look at the Burran and the cliffs of Moher, which were spectacular. The Aran Islands looked pretty bleak viewed from the mainland. I went through Limerick and took the N7 to Dublin. After finding somewhere to stay near Ferry Point, I went into Dublin for an evening meal and a stroll round Trinity College.

Back at Ardincaple I found a card from Robin to say he had been promoted to Sergeant and would be coming home next Tuesday. On 27th August, I learned that Chuck and Caroline had very much enjoyed doing the *Traverse of the Meije* together with their guide friend, Anthony. I was impressed that instead of driving round to La Bérarde they first went over the Brèche de la Meije as a way of reaching the Promontoire Hut, from which the traverse usually starts.

Andrew Roberts rang on 10th September: his mother, Janet (Adam Smith) had had a massive stroke, from which she never recovered. He rang again two days later with news of her death. I felt both sadness and gratitude as I thought of her very great friendship and kindness to Nea. Early in December I attended Janet's Memorial Service, which was held at St Columba's Church in Pont Street. Afterwards we repaired to the RGS for a very copious and well-attended party, where I met relatives of Jacques Teissier du Croz.

On 7th December, I took a train from Waterloo to Paris and arrived at Villennes-sur-Seine half-an-hour before Natasha and Charlie came out of school, so I walked to their house until they came home. I met their new dog, Shambala, another Tibetan terrier, which was very frisky, but good-natured. The children were very bouncy. Chuck came home from Nice, where he had been working. I spent most of the 8th with the children, lunching with them at home and attending their school plays in the afternoon. I found these mini-musical pantomimes rather wearing.

I ventured into Paris again on 10th December, this time to the Salon Nautique, the French equivalent to the Boat Show and just as tiring. As expected, there was a rather disappointing collection of the usual snazzy fibreglass yachts, all 'fin and skeg' with drop keels, but no long-keeled boats. Peter returned from police college on 17th December and he and his girlfriend, Non, came with presents at the weekend.

On 28th December, I went for a walk towards Craig yr Ysfa in snow, which was unpleasant and I lost the path. It was snowy again when I went up Y Garn two days later, and came down wearing crampons. On New Year's Eve, I started on a supplement to Janet's obituary. At a party that evening at the Pen y Gwryd, I met John Blacker, a member of both the Alpine Club and the Royal Cruising Club, who kept his boat in Dubrovnik. I was to see more of him later. Robin rang: he hoped to come home in mid-January.

Dunlin *in Spitsbergen, 2001*

## CHAPTER 30

# A Kaleidoscope of Arctic Memories

I was very keen to do more high-latitude sailing, and Spitsbergen seemed an obvious next step. I hurried to make *Dunlin* ready to sail north in early June with two young dreadlocks, Jerry and Quentin. Jerry had been with me on my last cruise to Greenland in 1998; and I had met Quentin the previous year when sailing to Antarctica on the *Europa*, where he struck me as being a very useful hand. Jerry lived in Llanberis, and Quentin arrived by train from London. However, I soon realised that Quentin had been hoping to skipper my cruise and had swiftly to disabuse him of this idea. Although strong and capable, and innovative with the sails, he became increasingly truculent over the next few weeks.

Cruising to the Lofoten Islands six years earlier, I had taken eight or nine days to reach Reine in Vestfjord, sailing directly from Stornoway. This year I planned to take the same route to Norway, but to leave from Lochinver, after collecting some bonded stores. While waiting there for a front to pass through, we made friends with the crew of the 36-foot Bowman ketch, *Artemis of Meon*, which blew in out of the gale. To our pleasant surprise, she was also bound for Spitsbergen, and we drank a toast to our next encounter.

As we left Scottish waters on 22nd June 2001, an extensive high-pressure system settled over the British Isles, and an almost complete absence of wind meant a good deal of motoring, which was worrying, although *Dunlin's* engine was relatively economical. We experimented with every sail combination we could think of, and even rigged up the spare boom as a bowsprit. Whenever possible, we made use of a versatile cruising chute, which, in those glassy seas could give us a couple of knots in the faintest of breezes. Frustration at our slow progress was partly relieved when, some 40 miles west of Foula, we were boarded by a number of crossbilled, vagrant or migrating finches. We put out water for them and muesli, which they clearly enjoyed, but soon the decks were strewn with debris and there were finches everywhere underfoot. The birds stayed with us until 28th June, when we were a good 130 miles from the Halten Bank off the Norwegian coast. By now a cold east wind was rising and we began to make good speed.

However, two days later, in confused seas at the entrance to Vestfjord, we found the starboard lower chainplate had lifted. The main was hurriedly lowered, a rope was made fast under the radar and taken back to the starboard sheet winch, to secure the mast. We were then obliged to motor 27 miles to Bodo, the likeliest place to get a repair. We had no large-scale chart of the approaches, which were cloaked in thick fog, so we made a very cautious entry into this busy port. We berthed alongside the outer pontoon, where there were already a large number of yachts of different nationalities. On removing the chain-plate, we found it had sheared below the deck. Luckily the local yard, Molo Mekaniske, were able to make us a new one, which Jerry and Quentin bolted and sealed into position, despite heavy rain. By 4th July, we had also refuelled and reprovisioned, as well as paying a visit to the very friendly and helpful Bodo Radio Station. They gave us the encouraging news that the west coast of Spitsbergen was ice-free, though there was still fast ice in the inner reaches and in the Hinlopen Strait.

Motoring north across Vestfjord to Lofoten in poor visibility, we anchored first in Ørsvåg, not far west of Svolvær, then caught the tides through Oihellesundet and Raftsundet, making a brief diversion into Trollfjord, before anchoring in Neso. More motoring next day brought us to the Sortland and Risøy bridges and the very secluded anchorage in the southwest corner of Helløy. As we passed the kittiwake cliff on the way out, there was a great commotion and we saw no fewer than four marauding eagles being mobbed by angry swarms of kittiwakes. We moved on across to Senja and Tranøyfjorden, up Solbergfjorden, under the bridge at Finnsnesrenna, past Gibostad, to anchor in rural surroundings in Grunnvåg Haugen. With the tide but with very little wind we were trying to make our way up to the bridge under sail when we saw a yacht coming towards us. It was Inge Eliassen's *Timmi*. Inge was head of Customs in Tromsø. He and his wife had sailed out to meet us and guide us into the inner harbour, a kindness for which I was very grateful.

We tied up alongside in a convenient position off the Rica Ishavshotel in the city for a couple of nights only, as I was anxious to reach Spitsbergen by the middle of July. There were two other British yachts there, both of which we were to see again: *Caelan*, a ketch from Belfast, and *Efyzhea*, a powerful motor cruiser, whose skipper politely pointed out that we were flying an Icelandic courtesy flag, a deplorable breach of etiquette. When I apologised to Inge, he said with a gentle smile that Norwegians were not much bothered by that sort of thing. While we were in Tromsø, Inge very kindly took me to a gunsmith, where I was able to hire a suitable rifle and ammunition to ward off polar bears.

We had barely got an offing from Torsvåg harbour on 10th July than a northeast wind began to make itself felt and increased steadily, while the glass hovered round the 1008 mark. As the wind reached force 7–8, we took a third reef in the main, hoisted the storm jib, and beat uncomfortably to windward for the next eighteen hours. After a lull, the wind picked up again and it grew foggy. To my relief, the radar showed no icebergs, but we were not far from land, on a course parallel to the west coast of Spitsbergen.

In the early hours of Sunday 15th July, as the fog cleared, we were rewarded with a spectacular, if distant, view of Hornsundtind, the highest mountain on south Spitsbergen. Six hours later we entered Hornsund in a light easterly, and began to look for an anchorage that would shelter us from the calving ice that drifted down from the glaciers. Passing the Polish research station at Isbjørnhamna, on the north side of the entrance, we noticed some bergy bits had already gathered in that bay. We dropped anchor a mile further east, in Hansbukta, under the Hansbreen, where a spit of land gave shelter from the head of the fjord. The Hansbreen itself was quiet and there was no ice about. It was time to celebrate our arrival.

I was happy to mind the boat next morning, while the crew climbed Wienertinden, the 925-metre mountain glimpsed

## Voyage to Spitsbergen 2001

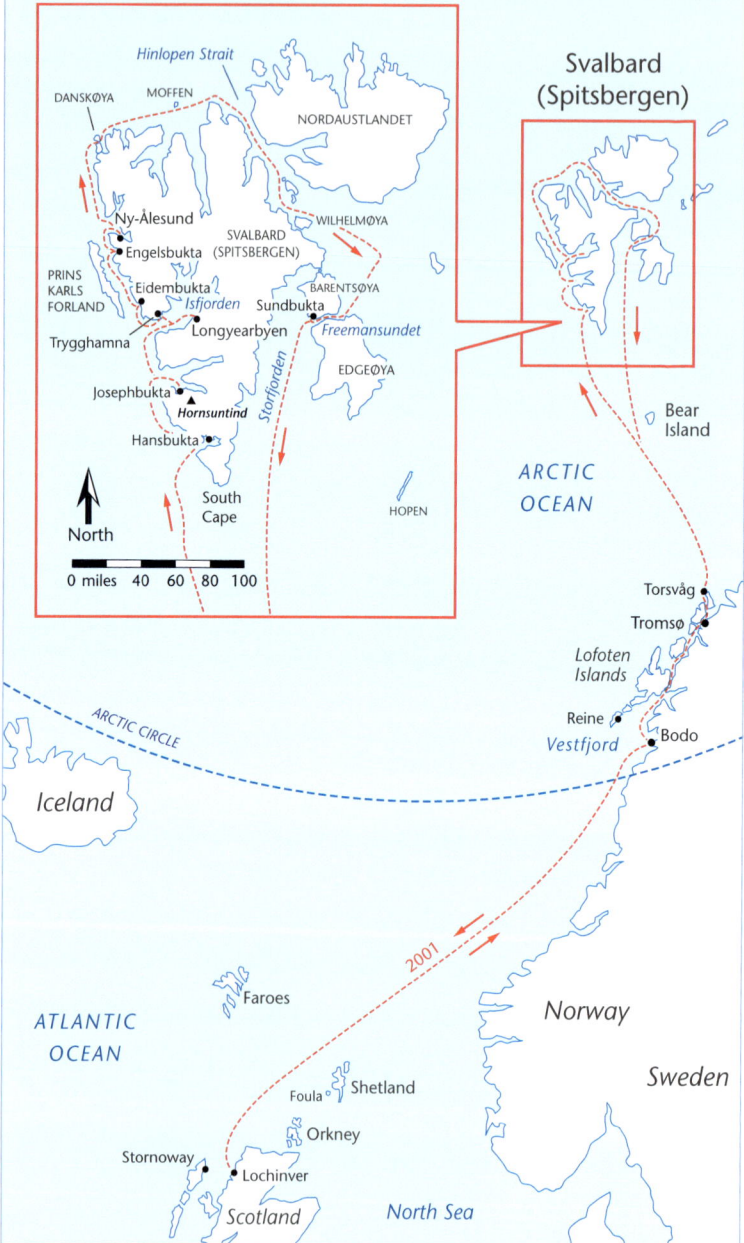

*Hinlopen Strait*

DANSKØYA

MOFFEN

NORDAUSTLANDET

Svalbard
(Spitsbergen)

Ny-Ålesund

Engelsbukta

SVALBARD
(SPITSBERGEN)

WILHELMØYA

PRINS
KARLS
FORLAND

Eidembukta

*Isfjorden*

BARENTSØYA

Sundbukta

Trygghamna

Longyearbyen

*Freemansundet*

*Storfjorden*

EDGEØYA

Josephbukta

▲

*Hornsuntind*

Hansbukta

North

South
Cape

HOPEN

0 miles 40 60 80 100

Bear
Island

ARCTIC
OCEAN

Torsvåg

Tromsø

*Lofoten
Islands*

Reine

Bodo

*Vestfjord*

ARCTIC CIRCLE

*Iceland*

2001

*Faroes*

ATLANTIC
OCEAN

Foula

Shetland

*Norway*

*Sweden*

Orkney

Stornoway

Lochinver

*Scotland*

*North Sea*

through clouds at the back of the Hansbreen. A mass of climbing equipment was loaded into the Avon, including crampons and axes and Jerry's snowboard, which he had managed to conceal hitherto. Finally, the gun had to be taken but was obviously going to be a nuisance, especially on steep ground. While the crew sorted themselves out on the foreshore, I had a brief stroll on the glacier, where the ice looked the same off-white colour as a polar bear. When I rowed ashore in the evening to collect them, I found the crew lying, exhausted, on the beach, but glad to have reached the summit. Jerry had also managed to snowboard down Sofiebreen, a small glacier on the southern flank of the mountain. During the night the cloud base was so low we could see nothing of the spectacular scenery and we decided to push on up the coast to Bellsund. At the entrance to Isfjorden the fog lifted, the sun came out, and our hearts rose at the sight of the mountainous prospect to the north.

Days and nights tend to get confused when there is no darkness but at 3am on 19th July we drew alongside the single pontoon that constitutes the 'marina' in Longyearbyen. Our berth was very shallow, with less than 2 metres at low water springs, which was just coming up. Quentin now deserted us, and flew home at my expense; and Jerry and I made the boat ready for the next leg, for which Jessica Abbot, a young ecology student at Edinburgh University, flew out to join us on 23rd July.

Jessica's arrival coincided with some fine, sunny weather, which prompted us to leave Longyearbyen quickly and gave us some of the most enjoyable cruising of the summer, despite an absence of wind. The ice-chart was encouraging and showed 'very open drift', along the north coast of Spitsbergen, and through most of the Hinlopen Strait, while the west coast of Spitsbergen was completely clear. This meant that we would be able to go north through Forlandsundet, the 50-mile long sound separating Spitsbergen from Prins Karls Forland, a narrow mountainous island to the west.

First we made for Trygghamna, on the north side of Isfjord, at its west end. On the way in we passed close to an arresting horn-shaped pinnacle, Alkhornet, which was swarming with birds. On the beach below we could see a party of canoeists and their tents. Motoring to the head of the fjord we anchored off the stream and enjoyed a peaceful, sunny night. Another short day on July 24th took us round the low-lying headland of Daudmannsodden and into Forlandsundet to Eidembukta, where we anchored at the north end of the bay, off the glacial moraine, behind which the Eidembreen had retreated. We had time here to go ashore for a walk and some gun practice, for none of us had shouldered the rifle till now, and hoped never to have to in earnest.

We left Eidembukta in hazy sunshine next morning in time to get the tide through the sound and enjoyed a fabulous view of Prins Karls Forland and its glaciated peaks. Repeating, like some mantra, 'Jessiefoten in line with Aurtangen' on the bearing given in the pilot, we passed through Forlandsrevet between Murraypynten to the west and Sarstangen to the east. The bottom looked very close through crystal-clear water, but the echo sounder never read less than 4 metres. A slight breeze allowed us to sail across the shallows to Engelsbukta, so-called because it was allotted to the English in whaling days. Passing a bearded seal sunning itself on a small floe, we anchored off the north shore. Too open to give much shelter, it was a perfect place in the prevailing calm. There were family flotillas of geese and duck here, constantly passing to and fro.

We motored round the headland next morning and turned into Kongsfjorden, where there were a few melting bergs drifting about. We needed to put in to Ny-Ålesund as this was the last place where we could top up with diesel. Once we had filled our cans, and paid our respects to Amundsen, there was little incentive to dally so we motored through brash ice to Peirsonhamna and anchored in the middle of the bay. Anticipating an east wind, we put out a kedge before going ashore to explore the tiny settlement, called London, and the old marble quarry. It was an attractive spot, with tiny wild flowers growing on the headland and even a few puff balls. Jessica, a keen botanist, examined the plants with great enthusiasm, marvelling at their hold on life in so precarious an environment.

It was still sunny when we motored past the entrance to Krossfjorden on our way to Kapp Mitra, but between it and Magdalenehuken, we ran into a thick and persistent bank of fog. Relying on GPS, radar and echo sounder, and keeping well into the south side of the fjord, we nearly jumped out of our skins when a shattering blast revealed the presence of a large cruise liner. Moments later, the faint silhouette of a monstrous prow glided past us to port on its way out. My faith in our ability to interpret the radar somewhat shaken, I opted to go outside the islets of Graveneset rather than between them and the spit forming the south shore of Trinityhamna. We could see nothing as we nosed in on the echo sounder, but simply dropped anchor when we reached the 10-metre contour. A little later the fog suddenly cleared to give a breathaking view of all the surrounding peaks and glaciers, and revealed *Artemis of Meon*, anchored a cable or so further inshore.

Late that evening we rowed over for an exchange of past adventures and future plans. The *Artemis* skipper Martin intended to take *Artemis* along the Russian coast later in the summer. Passage through the Hinlopen would offer the most direct route, as it would for us on our way south to Norway. However, Artemis had a powerful and thirsty engine and Martin was clearly uneasy about having enough fuel for prolonged motoring, a worry I shared. We might end up having to motor all the way back if the southern end of the strait was blocked. Jerry was more optimistic and we both knew that with her low fuel consumption *Dunlin* could motor for about 150 hours. Ice and weather were our main concern. A deep depression was expected north of Scotland in a day or two and seemed likely to track our way, but exactly where and when we did not yet know. Martin had no updated information as his Navtex was not working – a not uncommon predicament in these waters. We parted, agreeing to keep in touch.

After a closer look at the famous Waggonwaybreen, at the head of the fjord, we motored out in the morning to catch the tide through Sorgattet, the strait between the mainland and Danskøya to the north. We were soon level with the north end of Danskøya, and could see into Virgohamna. It seemed too early to stop and we decided to go on to the Nordvestøyane, and perhaps anchor in Fairhaven, where Nelson had once anchored as a young midshipman. When we reached Fairhaven we found it too open for comfort and decided instead to put in to Holmiabukta, a mile to the south, where a small inlet provided snug seclusion in lovely surroundings. Martin had warned us that the glacier might be troublesome, but there was no calving in progress. We anchored in a small bay behind the spit on the west side of the entrance. Jerry and Jessica set off at once across the fjord, to climb the mountain on the east side, taking with them gun, snowboard and axes. I was able to follow their route through binoculars, and to see Jerry describing graceful arabesques down a snow slope, while Jessica walked down with the gun.

We left Holmiabukta reluctantly on Sunday, 29th July, not realising that it would be our last anchorage for nearly five days. On our way northeast through Svenskegattet, the small sound between Indre Norskøya and the mainland, we spoke to a research boat coming the other way. They had no weather information but confirmed the absence of ice on the north coast. As we motor-sailed in light winds a few miles offshore, we wondered how far away the pack was. Six hours later, I put through a call via Svalbard Radio to the weather men in Tromsø. They did not think the depression would bring winds of more than force 6 to these waters. We decided we might do better to go straight to Heclahamna, in Sorgfjord, at the entrance to the Hinlopen Strait.

I felt rather wistful as we passed the entrance to Raudfjorden, Woodfjorden and Wijdefjorden, wishing we had time to explore them. Instead, we rounded bleak Verlegenhuken, Spitsbergen's most northerly point, in the early hours of 30th July. We could now see down into Sorgfjord, where I looked forward to anchoring in Heclahamna. Just then, however, a converted fishing boat hove into sight from the direction of the Hinlopen Strait. We immediately called them on the VHF to ask about ice conditions. They had been through twice recently. The first time, a week ago, it had been clear but this time there was a lot of ice in the southern part. We might be able to find a way through, they said. The moment of decision had come.

Though the cloud level was low on either side, what we could see of the strait itself looked perfectly innocuous, the water flat, calm, ice-free. The barometer had levelled off, and if we went on now we might get through the strait and into open water before the weather broke. If we anchored in Heclahamna we might be too late and lose the opportunity. On the other hand, we knew there was a vigorous low in the offing, and that we needed to cover 120 miles before we could reach the entrance to Freemansundet. I worried that a combination of bad weather and ice might catch us out at the southern end of the strait or in the sound.

All three of us felt, however, that it was too good a chance to miss and we decided to press on. Keeping in mid-channel, we motored south-south-east for the next six hours in flat calm, disturbing great numbers of guillemots, auks and puffins. Low mist and cloud obscured the landscape on either side but to starboard we could see the edge of the extensive Valhallfonna Glacier stretching away. By 1pm, we were off the entrance to Lomfjord and altered course to pass east of the Fosterøyane, which lie in mid-sound. It was raining by now. Rounding the islands, we headed southwest into the west channel to avoid ice between Nordaustlandet and Wahlbergøya. Switching the engine off at 5pm, we were able to sail for the next three hours until we reached the Wijkanderøyane, two islets on the west side of the group. Here we motored again. At 11pm, we headed southeast, on a course to clear Wilhelmøya, the largest island in the Hinlopen Strait. Tilman had anchored here in 1974, rowing ashore to get a view to the south from high ground. For us there were no views and we were lucky if we could see the next islet.

In the early hours of 31st July, we motored on towards Sørporten, the southern 'exit' from the strait. A few miles north of the Bastianøyane, a series of islets stretching southeastwards from Wilhelmøya, we ran into ice and began to understand the meaning of 'very open drift' as we made our way through it. Giving us a reproachful look, a large walrus slid from its floe as we came by, leaving an unpleasant brown stain – it may have been moulting. Fog then came down, compounding our difficulties. By

2pm, we were technically in the Olgastretet, the name given by the ornithologist, van Heuglin, to the 60-mile-wide passage between Barentsøya to the west and Svenskøya, one of the Kong Karls Land group, to the east. Who, I wondered, might Olga have been?

The entrance to Freemansundet was only about 20 miles away. Speaking to the weather station in Tromsø on the MF, via Svalbard radio, we were disturbed, but not surprised, to get a gale warning of northeasterly, force 8–9 by midnight. There were no new ice reports, the state of Freemansundet was still unknown and, with a gale coming on, my instinct was to head for open water, if it could be found. The last ice-charts we had seen had shown close drift-ice in Freemansundet, round the northeast corner of Edgeøya and down the east coast of that island, so that was clearly an area to be avoided. During the afternoon and evening the wind picked up steadily. Reefing down in good time, we were able to keep on an easterly course through very open drift. Visibility improved for a while, allowing us to spot three polar bears, probably a mother with two cubs, huddled together on a small floe, looking decidedly dejected. We were none too happy ourselves as the space betwen floes diminished.

Jerry climbed to the cross trees to look for a way through the pack to the south, but the ice was thicker there. By 7.15pm, we had reached a position 20 miles east by north of Kapp Heuglin, the northeast corner of Edgeøya. Taking in a third reef as the wind reached gale force, we went about. The best thing to do, it seemed, was to tack to and fro in the Olgastretet until the gale abated or the visibility improved. In that way we could explore the limits of our confinement but stay in relatively open water in the middle of the strait, without getting carried downwind into the pack. *Dunlin* could beat into force 8, but no more, and we were fortunate that our gale never reached force 9. After about two hours on the port tack we would come up against a barrage of ice, looming white through the fog, and go about. It was like a sinister game of Blind Man's Bluff, and we covered many extra miles.

Taking two-hour spells each at the helm, we kept up our tacking strategy for the rest of the night and the whole of the next day, snatching what sleep we could, fully dressed. It was miserably cold on deck in the sleet and snow, which quickly clung to the rigging and formed slabs on the mainsail, only to be shaken down over the helmsman at every gust. Handling wet, icy sheets made our fingers numb and useless in a matter of moments. I could imagine what it must have been like for the early navigators, having to winter in some icy fastness, hemmed in by the pack. Down below chaos reigned. The cabin was a soggy jumble of fruit teabags and firelighters, socks and cereals and sopping cloths. Needing hot food, I put on some leek and potato soup to heat, carefully holding the pan. Soon leeky vapours were mingling with the all-pervading diesel smells, tinged with garlic and blackcurrant, and I was promptly sick. 'You chose the wrong soup,' said Jerry.

By 1st August, the wind dropped briefly and the fog lifted to reveal the lower part of Barentsøya and Edgeøya, lightly dusted with fresh snow. The entrance to Freemansundet looked clear of ice. We immediately laid a course for Kapp Waldburg, the southeast corner of Barentsøya, and ran down towards it. As we closed the Cape, the shallowing seas grew steeper and *Dunlin* fairly flew over the crests. It was exhilarating, but the tide was against us. We could see no ice at the west end of the sound and were hopeful of getting through into Storfjord. Mindful of Tilman's misadventure in *Baroque*, when he ran aground on the Zeiløyane (low-lying islets in the middle of the eastern entrance), we gave them a wide berth. With the echo sounder on all the time, we paid particular attention to the soundings on the chart. Once in the lee of Barentsøya, the sea was flatter but the wind had backed to the north and was still a good force 7-8. Williwaws came howling down from Freemansbreen, the glacier on Barentsøya, making *Dunlin* difficult to handle as she lay right over in the squalls, and I was reminded of similar conditions in the Magellan Straits, ten years earlier.

We had been on the go now for about five days, the last three without proper food or sleep and I, for one, badly needed a rest and was determined to anchor if it was at all possible. The 60-pound Fisherman anchor was made ready on the foredeck and the chart

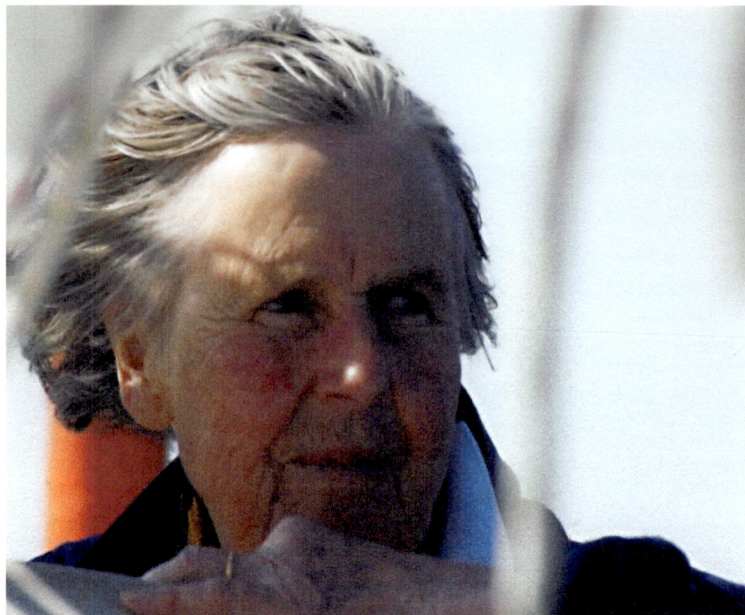

*Above: Denise at sea, in her latter years*
*Below and opposite: Denise aboard* Dunlin of Wessex

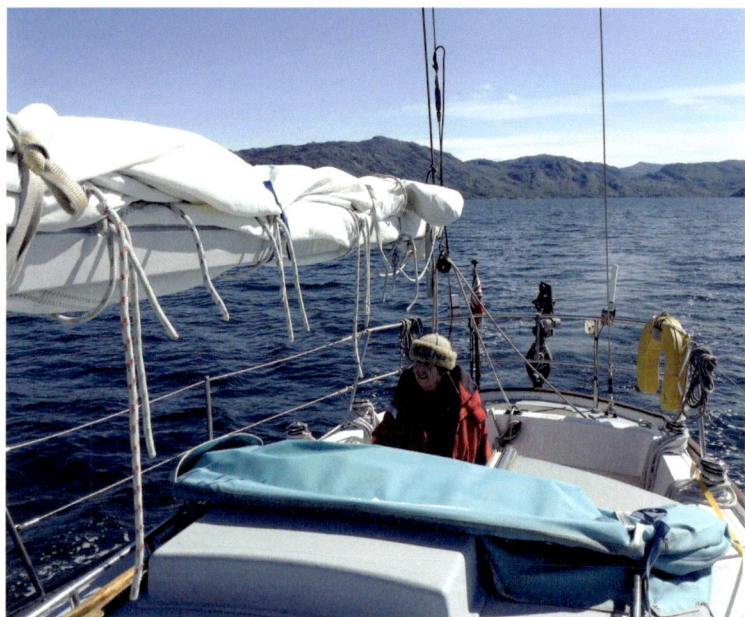

was subjected to careful scrutiny. Motor-sailing at full throttle, we had considerable difficulty in making headway past Sundneset and into Sundbukta. The west side, bounded by a J-shaped island, seemed to offer the smoothest water, which suggested the wind was beginning to back northwest. On 3rd August we anchored at last, half a mile from the island and a mile from the north shore. There was no ice to be seen. Celebrating our good fortune with a stiff whisky, we lit the heater and fell into our bunks. Waking several hours later to blue sky and sunshine, we set about clearing up. While Jerry and Jessica mended sails on deck, I prepared a large meal.

Regretful to be leaving Spitsbergen, but grateful to have come through Hinlopen and and Freemansundet without mishap, we weighed anchor at 4pm and began to tack down Storfjord on the long passage south towards Bear Island, Northern Norway, back to Scotland and home, with a kaleidoscope of Arctic memories.

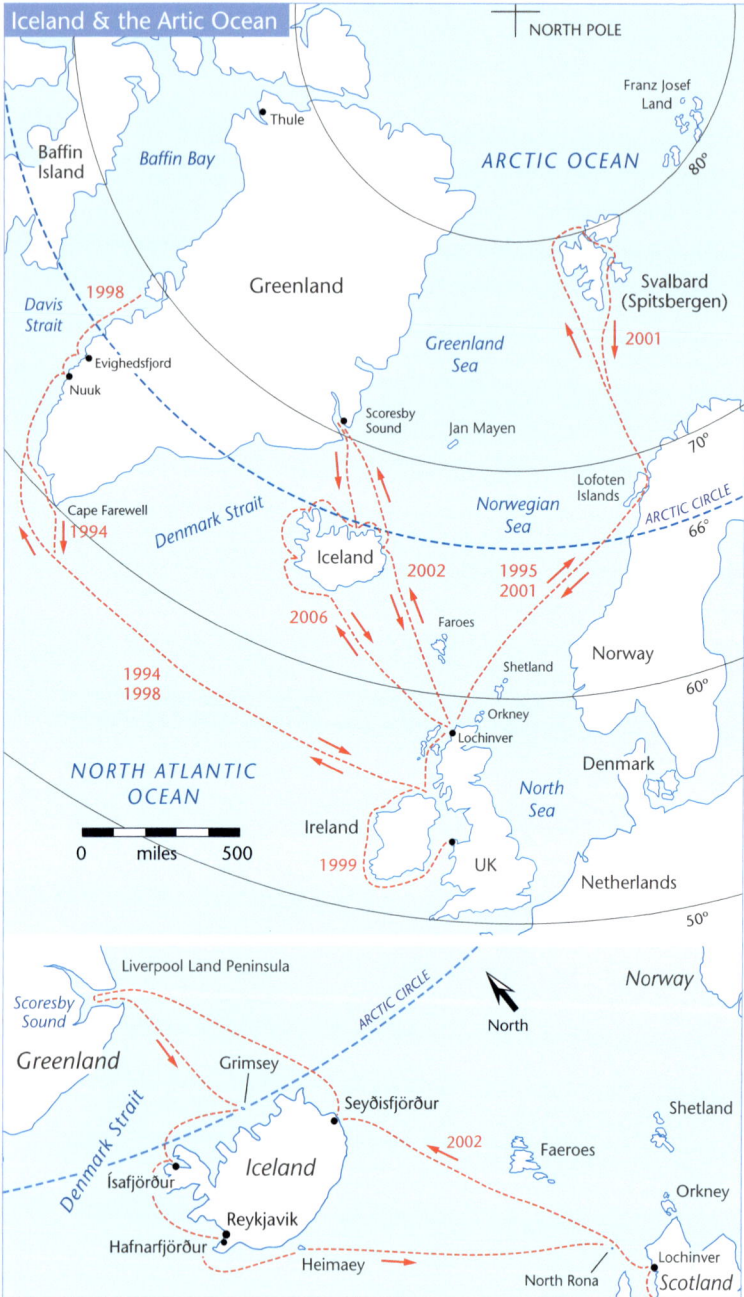

Iceland & the Artic Ocean

NORTH POLE

Franz Josef
Land

Baffin
Island

Baffin Bay

Thule

ARCTIC OCEAN

80°

Davis
Strait

1998

Greenland

Svalbard
(Spitsbergen)

2001

Evighedsfjord

Nuuk

Greenland
Sea

Scoresby
Sound

Jan Mayen

70°

Cape Farewell

1994

Denmark Strait

Iceland

Lofoten
Islands

Norwegian
Sea

ARCTIC CIRCLE

66°

2002

1995
2001

2006

Faroes

1994
1998

Shetland

Norway

60°

NORTH ATLANTIC
OCEAN

Orkney

Lochinver

North
Sea

Denmark

0    miles    500

Ireland

1999

UK

Netherlands

50°

Liverpool Land Peninsula

Scoresby
Sound

ARCTIC CIRCLE

Norway

North

Greenland

Grimsey

Denmark Strait

Ísafjörður

Iceland

Seyðisfjörður

2002

Faeroes

Shetland

Orkney

Reykjavik

Hafnarfjörður

Heimaey

North Rona

Lochinver

Scotland

CHAPTER 31

# *Sailing Round Iceland*

By 2002 I realised that if I was to go on sailing *Dunlin* in Arctic waters, I needed to make some expensive renovations. Like some other Tradewind owners, I thought *Dunlin* might sail better rigged as a cutter, and so had a stainless steel bowsprit or 'bow' made to take an outer forestay. She also needed a new mast, with mast steps, and new standing rigging, including twin backstays. Selden insisted on 10mm stainless steel for the shrouds and inner forestay, with correspondingly beefed-up chainplates all round. The teak deck veneer had worn down over the years, and had to be stripped off, along with all the fixtures. The cockpit combing needed to be rebuilt to include extra winches. I knew all this would be take time, but rather assumed that, once all the changes had been made, our problems would be over.

I soon realised they were not, when my brother Ian and I hit a rock in Sanda Sound off the Mull of Kintyre, on our way north. Things might have been worse, for the resulting leak through a crack in the forefoot was a slow one. After an alarming tow by the lifeboat, which happened to be close by, we were able to make our own way via the Crinan Canal to Ardfern, where help was at hand. It was no consolation to learn that several other yachts had just run into rocks off the Garvellochs – at least we were first in the queue.

News of our misadventure soon reached Jim Pitts, who very kindly suggested I might like to live on board his yacht *Ceres* while *Dunlin* was lifted out for repair, an offer I gratefully accepted. Robert, a skilled worker, was the only man available to mend the keel, but he was laid off for a week with gastric flu. I made some new friends while waiting, including the crew of *Ocean Grace*, who were about to set off for Iceland and the east coast of Greenland. They promised to pass on news of my plight to Willy Ker, whom I had hoped to meet in Kevlavik.

*Dunlin* was ready for relaunching by 20th July, but when I switched on the engine the starter motor jammed. Nothing would induce it to start again. It was removed and hit with hammers, all to no avail. An enthusiastic expert came by and offered to take it to pieces. As he struggled with the finicky little screws, I could see the man was plainly ill, and I had a flashback to the time in Puerto Williams when the Chilean Navy had helped to 'mend' our gearbox in their workshop, where minute parts had dropped irretrievably through the floorboards.

Presently our expert declared that the motor needed rewinding, which could not be done immediately. David Wilkie remembered that somewhere in the yard there was another old Bukh engine, with a starter motor attached. It was found, removed and given the hammer treatment which, to my surprise, brought it to life. However, I took the precaution of asking Peter to bring a new starter motor with him when he came up to Scotland. He had sailed extensively with me in the past but now he could only take a certain number of weeks off work. Tim, who also came out to Iceland with us, was not short of time. Peter was keen to head straight for Scoresby Sound, via the east coast of Iceland, which looked the shortest route.

We reached Seyðisfjörður, halfway up the east coast in about five days, including three of continuous motoring, and ran into dense fog as we closed the land in the early morning. It was a spectacular landfall. As the sun rose, the mists cleared to reveal high mountains on either side. We tied up alongside the wharf, oblivious of everything except the need to sleep. On waking, I became aware of a terrible smell and thought it really was time the boys changed their socks, but soon realised the fish factory was to blame. In all other respects, Seyðisfjörður was everything that could be desired. Everyone we met was very friendly, and food, fuel and water were all readily available. Although it was sad to leave Tim behind, because of sea-sickness, this port was a good place from which to leave, as it enabled him to see something of Iceland before flying home.

The glass was high as Peter and I left on 2nd August, and a brisk southeasterly gave us a good lift towards Langanes. By noon next day though, the wind had dropped and we were obliged to motor once again on our northwesterly course towards Scoresby Sound, some 300 nautical miles away. The latest ice chart showed no ice south of 75° north. Registering with Greenland Command on the new satellite phone, one of my rare concessions to modern technology, we learned that a Norwegian yacht was already in the sound, and there was no ice anywhere. This was almost literally true, although we did see a large chunk of 'pack' a couple of miles to starboard. Progress was slow as we chuntered on through a grey world where sea and sky seemed to merge. But the monotony was relieved by dolphin and whale, the antics of skuas and many little auks. One day I spotted a head in the water belonging to a seal pup, tangled in a fishnet and almost garotted. Peter hauled it out and cut the net free before sliding the pup back into the sea.

By 5th August, we were already close enough to the coast to make out mountains to starboard, which we took to be those of Liverpool Land. In the early hours of the 6th, we ran into thick fog and the wind got up very suddenly from the southwest. We were now a few miles offshore and could plainly see the entrance to Scoresby Sound on the radar, and bergs within it. We didn't fancy running the gauntlet of ice in an effort to get into Andrup Havn, a small harbour tucked into the north shore, and the only likely shelter. We went about, hoping for a lull, but instead the wind increased to force 7. After much hesitation and a keen sense of failure, we decided to retreat and make our way back to Iceland. We had seen very little of it so far; and if we were to complete our circumnavigation and get back to Scotland before the end of August, we needed to press on.

The combined effect of the southwest wind and a clockwise current pushed us too far east, to Sandvik on the small island of Grimsey. A northerly then helped us towards Horn, over 100 miles away to the west. Passing the austere northern cliffs and bays of the Vestfirðir, we turned into Ísafjarðardjúp and made our way to a remote anchorage at the head of Veiðileysufjörður, where the damp and sombre grandeur reminded us of Scotland. Motoring across to Ísafjörður, we prepared for the passage south down the west coast of Iceland. Running past the panoramic splendour of

*Denise in her element*

the seven headlands in evening sunlight, with a good following wind, gave us the most enjoyable sailing so far. I did have a pang of regret though, when we were overtaken by a Danish supply ship in the familiar red livery heading for Greenland.

Our next port of call was Hafnarfjörður, where we were greeted by Geir Giflason, to whom the Lomaxes had given me an introduction. He let us use his berth, drove us into Reykjavik to look for charts, and showed us every kindness, but the possibility of being held up by bad weather was always in our minds. We left for the Vestmannaeyjar on 15th August. A strong northerly enabled us to make good speed past the Reykjanes Peninsula and next morning we rounded Surtsey and turned northeastwards towards Heimaey, past a string of jagged pinnacles and bird-covered islets. Impressed by the narrow entrance to Heimaey harbour and the vertical red cliffs looming over it, we passed close by the pen where 'Keiko' the killer whale had been kept before she was freed, when she swam across to Norway.

Armed with a weather forecast printed in lurid shades of red and green, we left Heimaey on 17th August, on the wings of a passing low. It gave us strong northerlies, which never went above force 8, though the seas were big and confused, and some were breaking. As we drew near North Rona, there followed a period of gentler winds, calm seas and balmy nights, lit by the moon and the aurora borealis.We entered the still, dark waters of Loch Laxford in the early hours of 22nd August. Using radar to pick our way between lobster pots and sleeping gulls, we anchored once again behind Eilean a' Chad-fi.

*Watercolour of Ama Dablam by Denise*

# *Home*

So we've returned and the boat is back.
We live in the house again,
the beds rock
and bergs drift across the lawn.

At night I hear the anchor dragging
on the hard rock of the drive.
In the morning of course
we wake to find the house still here.

The garden – taking advantage of our absence –
has gone berserk,
thigh-deep grass throttling the trees
and hiding the paths as though ashamed.

As the wind shifts I look up
in case we need to reduce sail or alter the sheets
but only driven rain drifts through the trees
and the trunks sway like masts in the wind.

No sun so no sights today,
we must estimate our position.
But below the drive the tarmac ribbon of the road
reminds us always that we rest on land.

Would it were not so,
sigh the mountains,
and the wave-humped bulk of Siabod
rolls towards us through the mist.

PETER EVANS

Denise with her original book Waypoints to Eternity

Peter and Denise

Denise with Robin

Natasha and Charlie

Kai and Freya

Denise and Freya

Denise and Kai

Charlie Evans at his wedding to Anna Jackson

Natasha Evans at her wedding to Richard Longstreet

# Afterword

In 1986 Denise had become the first female president of the Alpine Club, after her predecessor, Anthony Rawlinson, died on Crib Goch. Charles Evans had been president before her, in 1967–1970, and had been knighted in 1969, making her Lady Denise Evans, though she seldom used her formal title.

She continued her sailing adventures, as well as occasional climbing and skiing, into her eighties, despite ongoing health problems. In 2003, she sailed in the Hebrides and the Summer Isles, as well as the Badcall Islands; her son Peter married Sara Burson at the end of August. In 2004, Denise cruised in the Faroes, the Hebrides and Northern Ireland; and Peter's wife Sara gave birth to their daughter Freya in late September.

Denise also continued to get great pleasure from music, theatre and art. In 2004, she mentioned going to the Alpine Club in London to see Julian Cooper's paintings, and then to see more of his work at the Art Space Gallery. She commented, 'There were impressive views of the Eiger, and in particular a very large painting of the exit chimneys on the North Face: a truly daunting place.'

In early June 2005, there were celebrations to mark the 50-year anniversary of the 1955 Kanchenjunga Expedition. These were held at the Pen y Gwryd Hotel and at the Alpine Club; and at the Royal Geographical Society in London, hosted by David Attenborough. Denise went on further cruises to the Faroes, the Summer Isles and western Scotland. For some of her later voyages, she was accompanied by her son Peter, Erle Randall and his wife Carloe, Ian Smith and Eddie Birch. In early November, she went to Plas y Brenin's 50th Anniversary Lunch. After Christmas at Ardincaple, she skied in the French Alps with Chuck and his family in February 2006, followed by a summer cruise to Iceland; and Sara gave birth to a little boy, Kai, on 19th July. In early December, Dennis Davies visited Denise, bringing a CD of Charles' film of the Annapurna IV ascent in 1957.

The following year, 2007, started with a Boat Show Dinner on 4th January. On 12th May there were celebrations for the 150th Anniversary of the Alpine Club at the Pen y Gwryd, and in June a Scottish cruise on *Dunlin* with Denise's grandson Charlie as a crew member, followed by more sailing in the Summer Isles and the Hebrides. In August, Caroline and Chuck's marriage came to an end, and Denise spent some time with Chuck and his children in France.

In January 2008, Denise was informed that all the remaining 'Everesters' were being flown out to New Zealand for Sir Edmund Hillary's state funeral, which took place on 22nd January in Auckland. In March, she was skiing in the French Alps, despite being in need of hip surgery. On 2nd April, there was a memorial service for Edmund Hillary in St George's Chapel in Windsor, which Robin attended. Denise went sailing in Scotland in the summer and in October had surgery on her left hip, before spending Christmas with her family in France, including Chuck's new partner Martine.

In June 2009, Denise undertook another cruise to the Azores shortly before turning 78. Summer 2010 saw her cruising in the Shetlands and Scotland, having had surgery for a couple of small skin cancers. In January 2011 she was skiing at Les Arcs, followed by the usual summer sailing in Scotland and Northern Ireland, and New Year celebrations in France. While she was in Paris in early 2012, she went to an exhibition of de Gaulle's wartime correspondence and found a very complimentary reference to her father, Lieutenant Colonel Jean Morin, as an 'officier de haute valeur'. After a spring break in Sicily, she sailed to the Orkneys, Fairisle and the Shetlands in June, and the Summer Isles in August. That autumn, Chuck was diagnosed with cancer and had surgery, before starting chemotherapy.

In March 2013, Denise met Stephanie Connor, a young woman whose husband had died unexpectedly from a heart attack. Stephanie, a keen skier, climber, canoeist and sailor, had recently sailed the North-West Passage with Bill Shepton in *Dodo's Delight*. They soon made friends and Stephanie, Erle Randall and Ian Smith accompanied Denise on a cruise to western Scotland and the Hebrides in June. The following month, Chuck and Martine joined Denise on *Dunlin* to sail along Ireland's southeast shore.

Denise struggled with diverticulitis in 2014 but managed an autumn cruise to Porthdinllaen. In October she visited Chuck and Martine in France, with her brother Ian. Early in January 2015, Denise and Stephanie went skiing in the French Alps. Chuck went into hospital in April and Denise went to France to spend some time with him when he came home. By January 2016, Chuck was back in hospital. Then, in March, Peter and Denise went to France to be with Chuck, who was on increasing doses of morphine. He died at 5am on 15th March 2016, aged 57. He was cremated in France and his ashes were later scattered on the hillside behind Ardincaple.

In May 2016, Peter, Denise and Stephanie had a Scottish cruise – and Ian Smith and Stephanie helped Denise make her final voyage back to Wales. With Peter's help, Denise's beloved *Dunlin of Wessex* was sold in early 2019.

In 2020, using some of the money from a Lottery Heritage Grant awarded on the occasion of the Pinnacle Club's centenary year, an oral history was undertaken. It was also the first year of Covid. Denise was 89 years of age, not in the best of health, but still keen to go ahead with her interview by Adele Long. Adele wrote, 'I got an inkling then of the strength and resolve that had led to her remarkable achievements. She came across as fiercely determined but always modest – almost self-deprecating, but not quite'. And Adele added, 'Denise has been an inspiration, and will continue to be, particularly to women climbers and sailors. Her advice was always "give it a go". It was a privilege to have met her and on behalf of the Pinnacle Club I can say we are grateful to her for sharing her story.' This interview is available at the British Library and snippets are on the Pinnacle Club's centenary website.

The film that Denise made on the Pinnacle Club Jagdula Expedition in 1962 lay undisturbed in a cupboard in the house in

Capel Curig for nearly sixty years, having only been shown once to a local audience. Denise had considered it to be underexposed. In 2019 she passed the three reels of 16mm colour film to Cathy Woodhead, who had them digitised, producing 50 minutes of silent film which has been edited with commentary from Jo Scarr and Denise, with additional film and stills. This film *Journey to Jagdula* is available to watch on YouTube.

Around this time Denise told Cathy about the publication of her husband's wartime memoir of his years as a newly qualified doctor in Burma. Pen and Sword, the publishers, had wanted the manuscript pared down and chapters about two treks he made into the Himalayas were removed. Eventually Cathy tracked down the full digital version of the book and, together with small sketches from Charles' diaries, she was happy to produce books for Denise to give away and for the Alpine Club to put a digital copy on their website. It is called *Mandalay and Beyond*.

In around 2019 Cathy suggested to Denise that she needed to write her autobiography. Cathy gave her digital copies of her many journal articles from the Pinnacle, Alpine, Ocean Cruising and Royal Cruising Clubs and she soon began writing about her early life in France. Cathy remembers Denise apologising, after a while, that she 'had not left Paris yet'. Robin observed the effort and time his mother put into writing her book. In the end it ran to 222,000 words but it became quite a focus, and her sons were concerned about how she would fill her time after it was finalised. In March 2023 Denise took receipt of *Waypoints to Eternity*. She seemed very happy with the result and was pleased to be able to give copies to her family and to visiting friends. Copies went to the Alpine Club and Pinnacle Club libraries.

Denise died at home in Capel Curig on 25th November 2023, at the age of 92, leaving her two surviving sons, Robin and Peter; four grandchildren, Natasha, Charlie, Freya and Kai; and great-granddaughter Dido.

# Glossary

| | |
|---|---|
| *anemometer* | device that measures wind speed and direction |
| *Bara Hakim* | senior government official in Tibet |
| *bergschrund* | crevasse |
| *bergy bit* | medium to large fragment of ice, generally rising between 3 and 16 feet above sea level, with an area between 1,000 and 3,000 square feet; larger than a *growler* |
| *bonxie* | another name for the great skua, a seabird about the size of a herring gull |
| *boom* | horizontal pole or spar, attached to the main mast, below the sail |
| *BST* | British Summer Time |
| *arak* | millet-based alcohol in Tibet |
| *CAF* | Club Alpin Français |
| *caleta* | cove or bay |
| *careen* | put a ship or boat on its side to clean, caulk or repair the hull |
| *chang* | barley or rice beer made in Tibet and Nepal |
| *chorten* | Buddhist religious monument |
| *coaming* | vertical surface on a boat or ship, designed to deflect the entry of water |
| *comber* | long, curling wave |
| *coolie* | (now considered offensive) unskilled labourer or porter |
| *couloir* | gully or vertical fissure on a mountain |
| *cringle* | an eye in the edge of a sail, through which to pass a rope |
| *cross tree* | attachment on the mast used to spread the shroud; also known as spreader |
| *CQR anchor* | Coastal Quick Release anchor, a popular design of plough anchor |
| *dacoit* | bandit |

| | |
|---|---|
| *dodger* | frame-supported structure that partially protects a helmsman from harsh weather and seas; also known as a spray-hood |
| *fender* | inflatable object used to protect the hull of a boat from damage caused by contact with a dock and/or other vessels |
| *forfait* | ski pass |
| *gardien* | warden |
| *gendarme* | rock pinnacle on a mountain |
| *genoa* | large jib that extends past the mast on a boat and so overlaps the main sail when viewed from the side; also known as a *yankee* |
| *glissade* | slide down a snow-slope in a controlled way |
| *gompa* | Tibetan Buddhist meditation room or shrine |
| *goosewing* | sailing directly downwind with the mainsail and foresail extended outwards on opposite sides of the boat, to maximise the area of sail exposed to the wind |
| *GPS* | Global Positioning System |
| *growler* | piece of floating ice (about the size of a truck) that has broken off a glacier and can pose a danger to boats; smaller than an iceberg |
| *gut* | narrow coastal channel or strait, usually subject to strong tidal currents |
| *gybe* | turn the stern of a sailing vessel through the wind, which then exerts its force from the opposite side of the vessel |
| *icefall* | very steep part of a glacier, resembling a frozen waterfall; mass of ice overhanging a precipice |
| *inner lead* | narrow waterway, used as a route to the open sea |
| *kedge anchor* | light, secondary anchor |
| *Khamba* | people who inhabit the Yang-Sang-Chu valley in westernmost Arunachal Pradesh, close to Tibet and Bhutan |
| *kharka* | mountain hut in Nepal |
| *lama* | Tibetan Buddhist spiritual leader |

| | |
|---|---|
| *lingam stone* | egg-shaped quartz stone which represents the male and female creative energy of the god Shiva |
| *névé* | partially compacted granular snow that forms the surface part of the upper end of a glacier |
| *nullah* | narrow stream or watercourse, characteristic of mountainous country where there is little rainfall |
| PAs | rock boots by Pierre Allain |
| *pelorus* | device which allows the operator to take bearings when it would be impractical to do so from a compass |
| *rakshi* | traditional distilled alcohol made in Nepal |
| *rubbing strake* | moulding fitted to the outside of a boat's hull, usually at deck level, to protect the topsides |
| *scend* | push or surge created by a wave |
| *shag* | species of cormorant |
| *schist* | silvery grey, fine-grained metamorphic rock, with shiny layers |
| *schrund* | short for bergschrund (German for 'mountain cleft'); a crevasse that forms where moving glacier ice separates from the stagnant ice above |
| *serac* | ridge of ice on the surface of a glacier |
| *sirdar* | chief sherpa or lead mountain guide |
| *sherpa* | mountain porter or support worker; *Sherpa* (capitalised) refers to an ethnic group of people living at higher altitudes in Nepal |
| *skua* | seabird |
| *stupa* | Tibetan Buddhist shrine |
| *téléphérique* | cable car |
| *thwart* | part of an undecked boat that goes across the hull, providing seats for the crew |
| *trog* | walk, especially aimlessly or heavily |
| *tsampa* | flour made from roasted, ground barley or corn |
| *williwaw* | sudden, violent squall blowing offshore from a mountainous coast |
| *yankee* | see *genoa* |
| *yawl* | two-masted fore-and-aft rigged sailing boat |

# *Further reading*

Barker, Ralph (1959), *The Last Blue Mountain,* Chatto & Windus.

Bridges, Lucas (1987), *The Uttermost Part of the Earth*, Pimlico.

Evans, Charles (1955), *On Climbing*, Woodstock, VT, USA: The Countryman Press.

Evans, Charles (1955), *Eye on Everest: A sketch book from the great Everest expedition*, Dobson Books.

Evans, Charles (1957). *Kangchenjunga: The Untrodden Peak*, New York, NY, USA: E.P. Dutton and Co.

Evans, Charles (1997), *Doctor in the XIVth Army,* published by Pen & Sword Books Ltd.

Evans, Charles (2019), *Mandalay and Beyond: An Army Doctor's Diary*. http//:www.alpine-club.org.uk/documents/ac_library/mandalay_and_beyond.pdf

Franco, Jean (1957), *Makalu*, Trans. Denise Evans. Jonathan Cape.

Kurz, Marcel (1959), *Chronique Himalayenn, l'Age d'Or 1940–1955*, Zurich, Switzerland: Fondation suisse pour explorations alpines.

Martin, Martin (1698), *A Late Voyage to St Kilda* https://quod.lib.umich.edu/e/eebo2/A52112.0001.001

Minney, Penny (2017), *Crab's Odyssey: Malta to Istanbul in an Open Boat*, Taniwha Press.

Morin, Micheline (1955), *Everest, from the First Attempt to the Final Victory*, George Harrap Ltd.

Morin, Nea (1968), *A Woman's Reach*, Eyre & Spottiswoode.

Pigafetta, Antonio (2010), *The First Voyage Round the World by Magellan*, Reissued. Cambridge University Press.

Scarr, Josephine (1966), *Four Miles High*, Victor Gollancz Ltd. Republished by the Pinnacle Club (2021).

Slocum, Captain Joshua (1900), *Sailing Alone Around the World*, Republished as a Penguin Classic (1999).

Tilman, H.W. (2015). *Mischief in Patagonia*, 2nd edition. (Tilman).

## Articles by Denise Evans

*Taterat and Tupilak* (Pinnacle Club Journal, No. 8, 1951-1958)

*The Pirates of the Bustach* (Pinnacle Club Journal, No. 9 1951-1958)

*Spectre* (Pinnacle Club Journal, No. 10, 1961-1962)

*The Jagdula Expedition 1962* (The Alpine Journal, Vol. LXVIII, 1963)

*To St. Kilda* (Pinnacle Club Journal, No. 17, 1977-1980)

*In Tilman's Wake: A Circumnavigation of South America* (Flying Fish 1991/2, Ocean Cruising Club Journal)

*In Tilman's Wake Part II* (Flying Fish 1992/1, Ocean Cruising Club Journal)

*Waypoint to Eternity* (Flying Fish 1995/2 Ocean Cruising Club Journal)

*The Lure of the Hinlopen Strait* (Roving Commissions 42, Royal Cruising Club Journal 2001)

*A Hurried Cruise Round Iceland* (Roving Commissions 43, Royal Cruising Club Journal 2002)

## Weblinks

*The Pinnacle Club Centenary Project* https://www.pc100.org/

*A Journey to Jagdula* https://www.youtube.com/watch?v=d4NeH7s_bqc

*The 1953 British Everest Expedition* https://en.wikipedia.org/wiki/1953_British_Mount_Everest_expedition

*The 1955 British Kangchenjunga Expedition* https://en.wikipedia.org/wiki/1955_British_Kangchenjunga_expedition

*The Alpine Club* http://www.alpine-club.org.uk